Closing 'Em Down

ALSO BY DAVID M. JORDAN
AND FROM MCFARLAND

*Occasional Glory:
The History of the Philadelphia Phillies* (2002)

*The Athletics of Philadelphia:
Connie Mack's White Elephants, 1901–1954* (1999)

Closing 'Em Down

Final Games at Thirteen Classic Ballparks

David M. Jordan

McFarland & Company, Inc., Publishers
Jefferson, North Carolina, and London

LIBRARY OF CONGRESS CATALOGUING-IN-PUBLICATION DATA

Jordan, David M., 1935–
    Closing 'em down : final games at thirteen classic ballparks / David M. Jordan.
        p.   cm.
    Includes bibliographical references and index.

    ISBN 978-0-7864-4968-2
    softcover : 50# alkaline paper ∞

    1. Baseball fields — United States — History. 2. Baseball — United States — History. I. Title.
GV879.5.J67   2010
796.357068 — dc22   2010029498

British Library cataloguing data are available

©2010 David M. Jordan. All rights reserved

No part of this book may be reproduced or transmitted in any form or by any means, electronic or mechanical, including photocopying or recording, or by any information storage and retrieval system, without permission in writing from the publisher.

On the cover: Crosley Field after the final game on June 25, 1970 (Associated Press/Gene Smith)

Manufactured in the United States of America

McFarland & Company, Inc., Publishers
  Box 611, Jefferson, North Carolina 28640
    www.mcfarlandpub.com

For my lovely granddaughter, Grace

Table of Contents

Introduction 1

1. Bad Times on Broad Street 5
2. League Park 17
3. The Other Place in Boston 25
4. Hit Sign, Win Suit 34
5. A Capital Place 48
6. A Fit Place for Polo 60
7. Home of the Browns 72
8. Redland Field aka Crosley Field 91
9. Barney's Playground 107
10. Mister Mack's House 122
11. The South Side of Chicago 140
12. Used to Be Briggs Stadium 154
13. Ballpark in the Bronx 172

A Few Final Words 191
Chapter Notes 195
Bibliography 201
Index 203

Introduction

People love baseball for countless reasons. To many, the game itself strikes them as the best ever invented — nine players to a side, with defense and offense balanced (at least before the ill-considered introduction of the designated hitter), with a pitcher who knows how he's going to throw the ball and fielders who have chances to catch even the hardest-hit shots. For others, the numbers are fascinating, the numbers that make baseball the most statistically sound of all sports (even more so since the advent of Bill Jamesian extensions of the old-time statistics). And for still others, it is the fact that the game has a palpable history, a stretch back into time that somehow connects the Ty Cobbs, Willie Keelers, Walter Johnsons, Honus Wagners and Babe Ruths with the Mickey Mantles, George Bretts, Lou Brocks and Tom Glavines of more recent times. Part of that history has been tied up with the places where the game has been played.

Ever since the game of base ball turned professional, back in the nineteenth century, it has needed spectators. People have always loved to watch baseball, but the professional game needed a way to transfer that love into cash. For the players to be compensated, there had to be money from paid admissions. And to get people to pay to see the players compete, there had to be limitations on who could watch — only those who had paid. Those limitations necessitated gates — gates to admit the paying customers, gates to exclude those who had not paid. It is little wonder that baseball has always called its admission proceeds "gate receipts."

So, baseball put together seating areas for those who had paid to watch the game, together with gates at which to take their money and let them in as well as to keep out those who did not pay. Indeed, getting in without paying became a prime sport for youngsters who hung around the gates. "Ballparks," these areas were called, and they dated back to the earliest days of the professional game. Ballparks were pretty rudimentary in those early years, mostly consisting of wooden grandstands with wooden fences. They caught fire and burned down with some regularity. These fires, of course, interfered with the playing of games and with the production of gate receipts.

As the nineteenth century waned and the twentieth century dawned, owners of big league baseball teams felt that they could take advantage of technological progress and build ballparks that would be far less susceptible to the constant threat of destructive fires. There were new developments in the sciences behind steel and concrete, developments that could be easily transferred to the construction of a baseball park. And so there was a spurt of ballpark building in the early years of the new century which produced what became known as the "classic ballparks."

The first of these new structures was Shibe Park in Philadelphia, which opened in 1909. It was quickly followed that year by Pittsburgh's Forbes Field and Sportsman's Park in St. Louis. Two more venues were opened in 1910, Comiskey and League parks, and the new version of the Polo Grounds in New York the next year. In 1912, new ballparks made the scene in Detroit, Boston (Fenway Park), Cincinnati and Washington. Over the next three years, Ebbets Field, Weeghman Park, and Braves Field were opened, after which the surge of ballpark construction came to an end. Eight years later, though, New York saw the christening of Yankee Stadium in the Bronx. The histories and ultimate closures of these establishments (except for the two still in use) will be the subject of this work.

These new parks seemed sumptuous indeed in comparison with their predecessors, and the fans loved them. They could relax in their new surroundings, sit in upper decks if they wanted a different perspective on the game, enjoy food and beverages, and cheer for their favorites. These were structures pretty much built for baseball; if football, boxing or other activities were conducted within them from time to time, these other activities had to accommodate themselves to the shape of baseball.

These ballparks had personalities; they were different from each other. As a writer for the *New Yorker* put it, "Ballparks weren't the same because the urban places they belonged to weren't the same." Unlike football gridirons, which must be identical to one another, baseball fields, beyond the diamond, do not, "which is part of the reason that even the ugliest ones are loved so fiercely by the fans and become such repositories of civic feeling." These are the ballparks we will be talking about.[1]

The names of these classic ballparks are familiar to baseball historians and to generations of baseball fans. The names changed from time to time over the years, (as did the ballparks, physically, in many cases): Comiskey

Park became White Sox Park, and then went back to Comiskey; Navin Field became Briggs Stadium and then Tiger Stadium; Sportsman's Park became Busch Stadium; and Shibe Park changed to Connie Mack Stadium, for a few examples.

As the century moved on, however, these fine old ballparks started to shut down. There were numerous reasons why owners — and in some cases city administrators — chose to replace or abandon them. Some wore out physically. Some were left empty when their teams moved to a different locale. Some were in deteriorating neighborhoods or had little provision for parking automobiles. Some were simply replaced by facilities that could produce more income. In some cases the old ballparks were replaced with stadiums that could house both baseball and football (usually to the detriment of baseball). In almost all cases, the baseball owners were able to have their host cities build and own the replacement ballparks, thereby reducing substantially the overhead for the ball clubs. Whatever the causes, the classic ballparks, one after another, began to shut their doors.

With the closing of Yankee Stadium in September 2008, there are only two of the classic ballparks still serving as homes to major league teams: Fenway Park in Boston and the Cubs' Wrigley Field in Chicago. As the others closed, pieces of baseball's history, of its magic, disappeared. Some of them closed with fanfare, some with solemnity, some with little note taken of the historic significance of the closing, some with riotous behavior on the part of the customers. In most cases, the closure was an irrevocable end to an era (but the Polo Grounds, closed by the Giants, served five years later as the initial home to the expansion Mets, only to have a second closing after a couple more years of service). In one case, Braves Field, no one knew that he was attending the final game there.

Much of baseball's marvelous history took place over the course of the decades of the twentieth century, a substantial part of it in the ballparks we will be looking at. While this work is primarily about the endings of these facilities, the final games played in them, we'll look as well at the momentous and often less-than-momentous things these parks saw, how they were changed physically over the years, and the baseball teams and players who performed in them.

Of course, most of the replacement ballparks, often called the "cookie-cutter stadiums," have now closed as well — the Vet, RFK, Riverfront, Three Rivers and a few others, worn out or made irrelevant in much shorter periods of time. But they are beyond the purview of this work, and their closings certainly produced few of the emotions and reactions generated by the true classics.

Baker Bowl in Philadelphia is not usually considered a "classic" ballpark; it was a bit ahead of the others, and it spent a good part of the first half of the twentieth century falling apart. But it was highly regarded in its early days, and it was a local institution whose crumbling ruin I used to see when I was on my way to Shibe Park. So it is included, as an author's prerogative.

I have been to baseball games in eight of the parks whose ends are chronicled here, although not for their final games. At Forbes Field, I went to a Carnegie Tech-Lehigh football game as well as several Pirates games, and at Comiskey Park my daughter Diana and I even went to a post-game picnic, after the last game before the All-Star break, with the White Sox players under the center field stands (I remember standing in line for a hot dog and potato salad behind Carlton Fisk). I did attend the last game at Connie Mack Stadium (which I always thought of as Shibe Park) with Diana; my wife Barbara, sitting at home watching the madness on television, could only moan and mutter, "He's down there with our eight-year-old little girl!" I've been able to discuss with friends the last games in *their* parks, which they did attend: Dennis Bingham and Comiskey, Bos Crowther and Ebbets Field, Tim Wiles and Tiger Stadium. My friend Fraser Lewis, a Pittsburgh native, helped me with Forbes Field, although he was not there for that disruptive closing.

Anyone writing about old ballparks should acknowledge the help of Phil Lowry's *Green Cathedrals* and *Lost Ballparks* by Lawrence Ritter. And, of course, the local newspapers have been great sources on what really happened on that last afternoon or evening. The librarians at the Hall of Fame in Cooperstown have been of much assistance to me, particularly Gabe Schechter, Tim Wiles, Pat Kelly and John Horne. Joan Searles at the Philadelphia Athletics Historical Society was very helpful, as was the staff in the Newspaper Reading Room at the Library of Congress and at the Free Library of Philadelphia, as well as the folks at Urban Archives, in Temple University's library. My daughter Diana contributed editorial help.

So here they are: the stories of those fine old ballparks, their histories, and how they saw their last days.

Chapter 1
Bad Times on Broad Street

By the time it closed, it was a wreck, a source of laughter and derision. Sportswriters scoffed that it was as bad as the Phillies teams that played there. From time to time, pieces of the building or parts of the stands collapsed, maiming and sometimes killing customers. But Baker Bowl was once thought of as the very latest thing in ballpark construction, the top of the line in the National League of its day.

The park was located in North Philadelphia in the square block enclosed by Broad Street, Huntingdon Street, North 15th Street, and Lehigh Avenue. The first ballpark on the lot was a wooden structure built in 1887, four years after the Phillies arrived in town from Worcester, Mass., by the club's owners, A.J. Reach (one of baseball's early star players and later a sporting goods entrepreneur) and a Philadelphia lawyer named John Rogers. That first park cost some $80,000 to build and had outside walls made of brick. It seated 12,500 spectators, who had the privilege of watching some fairly good Phillies players—Sliding Billy Hamilton, Sam Thompson, and Ed Delahanty among them. Unfortunately, the whole place burned to the ground on August 6, 1894, relegating the fans to temporary seating for the rest of the season after six games were played at the University of Pennsylvania's field.

To replace the original structure, the club erected on the same lot a state-of-the-art building of steel, brick and concrete called, originally, the Philadelphia Base Ball Park. It held 18,800 customers and had a cantilevered design to eliminate many of the columns which interfered with fans' viewing pleasure. The park had a double-decked grandstand and heavy steel supports. Curiously, there was a slight hump in deep center field, to allow for an underground railroad tunnel, something that was hard to find in most other ballparks. Sometimes outfielders could feel the rumblings of the Reading Railroad trains passing beneath them; the ball-

Baker Bowl, with Broad Street behind the right field wall (Urban Archives, Temple University Libraries, Philadelphia).

park acquired an additional nickname, "the Hump," because of this feature.

The new stadium opened for business on May 2, 1895, and it was the pride of the National League. Disaster struck, however, on August 8, 1903, as the Phillies played the second game of a doubleheader with the Boston Braves before 10,000 fans. Out on 15th Street, down behind the third base stands, two drunken men were being taunted by a couple of 13-year-old girls. One of the men became angry and grabbed the hair of one of the young ladies, later identified as Maggie Barry. When Maggie started screaming, there was a sudden rush of spectators inside the ballpark to a wooden gallery looking out onto the street thirty feet below, to see what was going on.

As the next day's *Inquirer* put it:

> Suddenly, jammed with an immense, vibrating weight, a hundred feet or more of the balcony tore itself loose from the wall, and the crowd was

hurled headlong to the pavement. Those who felt themselves falling grasped those behind and they in turn held onto others. Behind were thousands still pushing up to see what was happening. In the twinkling of an eye the street was piled four deep with bleeding, injured, shrieking humanity struggling amid the piling debris.

The result was what the *Public Ledger* called "one of the most shocking disasters that have ever occurred in this city."[1]

The capacity of the city's ambulance and emergency service was inadequate to the carnage. "Everything on wheels that could be captured was used to send the injured away." The police stopped "the automobiles of the rich on Broad Street" and turned them into ambulances, filling the hospitals in the northern part of the city. Twelve persons died as a result of the collapse, and nearly three hundred were injured. Pickpockets and looters preyed on those lying on the street before they could be removed to hospitals.

It was eventually determined that the wooden supports under the balcony had collapsed, hurling the spectators down to the street. The Phillies owners, headed by James Potter, who had purchased the club in 1902, blamed the prior owners, Reach and Rogers, who of course said Potter and his group were responsible. Both groups blamed the original builder, R.C. Ballinger & Co., which swiftly denied liability. Litigation quickly ensued, with more than eighty lawsuits filed by the estates of the deceased as well as by those injured. All of the suits were dismissed, with the courts holding that the rush of spectators, not faulty timbers, was the cause of the disaster.

The Phillies were forced to move for most of the rest of the season to Columbia Park, the home of Connie Mack's Athletics, while the necessary repairs were made to their damaged ballpark.

With the repairs made, the park was back in business, for many years to come. The Phillies gave their fans some things to cheer about, such as the hitting of outfielder Sherry Magee and, in 1908, the pitching of Harry Coveleski. Coveleski, whose younger brother Stanley later pitched himself into the Hall of Fame, was called up from Lancaster late in the season and found himself in the middle of the red-hot pennant fight between the Cubs and John McGraw's Giants. On September 29, Coveleski beat New York, 7–0, and on October 2, he and the Phillies whipped the Giants again, 6–2. Two days later, with McGraw complaining bitterly that the Phillies had pitched Coveleski out of turn against his team, the young left-hander from upstate Shamokin outpitched Christy Mathewson to beat the Giants once more, 3–2, even escaping unscathed from a second-and-third-with-none-out fix in the ninth inning. Harry Coveleski's heroics helped keep the hated Giants from winning the pennant, and "the Giant Killer" he was called ever after, though his best work after 1908 was for Detroit, not the Phillies.

In 1909, Israel Durham, the boss of the city's Republican machine, bought the club, but he soon died, and the new president later in that year was a former newspaperman named Horace Fogel, put in the position by the new owners, members of the Taft family from Cincinnati and Charles Murphy, president of the Chicago Cubs. (Conflicts of interest were not looked into too carefully in those days.) Fogel announced that the team's name was being changed to the "Live Wires," but when the laughter died down everyone continued to call them the Phillies. Fogel had his players in green-and-white uniforms in 1910, but the next year they were back in their customary red-and-white togs.

Fogel was up against it in Philadelphia, with his team competing against Connie Mack's Athletics, who were winning pennants a few blocks down Lehigh Avenue. Fogel had Sherry Magee (although Sherry missed a chunk of the 1911 season when he was suspended for punching an umpire), and that same year the Phils came up with a magnificent rookie pitcher, a kid out of Nebraska named Grover Cleveland Alexander who posted a 28–13 record for the year. In 1912 the team acquired a slugger named Clifford "Gavvy" Cravath, and he helped arouse interest among the fans.

At the end of the 1912 season, however, most of the Phillies news was about club president Horace Fogel, who publicly accused other league club owners of fixing the pennant race for the Giants to beat out the Cubs (and of course Fogel had the not-very-well-concealed ties to Chicago's Charles Murphy). As a result of these accusations, Fogel was banished from baseball. A couple more changes in ownership put the Phillies in the hands of William F. Baker, although it was little noted that title to the ballpark did not change hands, being retained by the former owner (Murphy of Chicago) as an investment, with the ball club signed to a 99-year lease. Bill Baker was a former New York City police commissioner who was noted for his frugality, though Phillies fans simply called him "cheap." Baker bought the club in 1913 and soon thereafter the park, sometimes labeled "the Huntingdon Street Grounds," was called simply "Baker Bowl."

The park's dimensions were unbalanced, caused of course by the necessity of squeezing it into a specific city block. Down the left field line was 341 feet, and it was 408 feet to center field. The short block between Broad and 15th streets, however, made the distance to the right field fence only 280 feet, with the right center power alley at just 320 feet. The right field fence was high, 40 feet, but still many balls cleared it. In 1929, when the Phils' left-handed slugger Chuck Klein was threatening Babe Ruth's recently-set home run record, Bill Baker quailed at the thought of what he would have to pay a home run king, so he quickly added a 20-foot screen on top of the right field fence. When asked why, he explained with a straight face that he did it to protect the automobiles passing outside on Broad Street.

Klein did win the home run title that season, with help from his pitching staff. Tied with the Giants' Mel Ott for the homer lead heading into the final game, Klein hit one out and then watched as the Phillies pitchers walked Ott five times (once with the bases loaded) to make sure that Master Melvin would not hit one himself.

It was unusual for Phillies pitchers in that era to be able to direct their pitches as well as that. In 1930, under manager Burt Shotton the club had a team batting average for the season of .315. It still finished last with a 52–102 record, because the pitching staff put together an earned run average of 6.71, topping their 1929 mark of 6.13.

Phillies outfielders, as well as those playing for visiting clubs, became adept at playing balls off that short right field wall, often throwing out runners at second and sometimes even at first, with particularly slow-footed hitters. Klein became very good at this aspect of the game and still holds the record for outfield assists in a season with the 44 he piled up in 1930.

Old-timers chuckle at the story of a game in 1934, when Hack Wilson was playing out the string for the Dodgers, alternating ball games with bouts of drinking. His pitcher, the aptly named Walter "Boom Boom" Beck, was being shelled, and right fielder Wilson had chased down quite a few shots off the fence behind him. When manager Casey Stengel walked to the mound to remove Beck, Wilson, perhaps a bit hung over from the night before, closed his eyes for a few moments of rest. Beck, angry at being removed and unhappy that Wilson had not caught any of the hard-hit balls to right, suddenly turned and fired the ball at Wilson. He missed and hit the right field wall instead. Wilson was startled to hear another ball clang off the fence, but he quickly turned, gathered up the loose ball, and threw it on a line to second base.[2]

There was a spacious 60-foot-wide foul ground running down both to left and right field, one of the few features in the park welcomed by sorely-taxed pitchers. In later years the right field fence was adorned by a huge sign reading "The Phillies Use Lifebuoy," but the few fans who came to Baker Bowl muttered, "But they still stink." The clubhouse was built high above center field. No one ever hit a ball over the clubhouse, but Rogers Hornsby once hit a ball through a clubhouse window.

There were occasional boxing matches staged in Baker Bowl over the years, featuring such draws as Benny Leonard, Tommy Loughran, Primo Carnera, Mickey Walker, and Luis Firpo.

In the 1920s, Baker Bowl was the site of Negro League games, and in October 1924 it hosted the first two games of the Colored World Series between the Kansas City Monarchs and the local Hilldales. For three years in the 1930s, the ballpark was the home of the brand-new Philadelphia Eagles, who had just joined the National Football League, succeeding the dormant Frankford Yellowjackets. The Eagles were not very good, compiling a record of 3–11–1 in games played at Baker Bowl in the 1933–35 seasons, but they did have one moment of glory there, on November 12, 1933, when they held the mighty Chicago Bears, featuring Red Grange and Bronko Nagurski, to a 3–3 tie.

The Phillies, too, had a moment of glory early in Baker's tenure, when they won their first National League pennant in 1915. Led by the magnificent pitching of Pete Alexander, who won 31 games, the slugging of Gavvy Cravath, who led the league with 24 home runs, and the inspired infield play of rookie shortstop Dave Bancroft, as well as the major contributions of catcher Bill Killefer, first baseman Fred Luderus, and outfielders Dode Paskert and Possum Whitted, the Phillies under first-year manager Pat Moran won by seven games over the Boston Braves. Unfortunately, after Alexander's 3–1 victory in the World Series opener against the Red Sox at Baker Bowl, the club lost the next four games. (The Phillies would not win another World Series game until rookie Bob Walk won the first game of the 1980 Series.) Game Two, in Baker Bowl, saw the first United States president attend a World Series game, when Woodrow Wilson and his fiancée showed up. His attendance did not help the home team, which lost 2–1, and got only three hits against Boston's Rube Foster.

Baker had turned down an offer by the Athletics to use Shibe Park for the Series; its roughly 30,000 seating capacity would have held about ten thousand more fans than Baker Bowl could. Instead, Baker installed temporary bleachers in right-center field to seat a few more spectators in his park, and the Red Sox hit a couple of balls into this area for the winning runs in Game Five.

In 1923, Charles Murphy, the owner of the ballpark, denied a rumor which had been spreading that the grounds had been sold to Henry Ford. The club secretary, Billy Shettsline, said it was "all a joke."[3]

After 1915, the Phillies' fortunes quickly declined (hastened by Baker's ill-considered trades of future Hall of Famers like Alexander and Bancroft), and they became chronic second-division dwellers, most often in last place. Alexander averaged more than 27 wins a year in his seven Phillies seasons, with three earned run titles, five strikeout crowns, and five years leading in shutouts, but on December 11, 1917, Baker, fearing that Alexander would be going into the service, traded him and catcher Bill Killefer to the Cubs for Mike Prendergast, Pickles Dillhoefer and $55,000 cash. Bancroft went to the Giants for two mediocre players and cash a couple of years later. But the Phillies fans still had Baker, and he still had the Phillies. Baker hung onto them until his death in 1930, after which control passed to his former business manager, Gerald P. Nugent.[4]

There was another major disaster in Baker Bowl, on May 14, 1927. Rain chased fans from uncovered bleacher areas to a drier section under the stands, until the stands down the right field line suddenly collapsed from the additional weight and the celebration of an unexpected eight-

The right field stands at Baker Bowl, after the collapse of May 14, 1927, showing where the spectators were sucked down (National Baseball Hall of Fame Library, Cooperstown).

run inning on the part of the Phillies. The collapse was inward, which had the effect of creating a funnel down which spectators were sucked. One man died, another fifty or so were badly hurt, and a couple hundred more were pulled down into the break. Management patched things back together and considered itself fortunate that it had not been worse.

Although the Phillies in their Baker Bowl years were not much of an attraction, they did showcase one bright star, Chuck Klein. The Hoosier outfielder led the league in home runs four times, twice in runs batted in, three times in runs scored, three times in slugging average, twice in hits and doubles, and in 1932 even garnered the title for stolen bases. His greatest season was 1933, when his league-leading .368 batting average combined with his home run and RBI championships to give him the Triple Crown, topping even his Most Valuable Player award production of the year before. It was a symptom of the Phillies' problems that on November 21, 1933, Nugent traded his Triple Crown winner to the Cubs for three undistinguished players and a much-needed $65,000 in cash, because the club's attendance for the year had dwindled to 156,421.

Nugent was a relatively astute baseball operator. His problem was that the club had very little money with which to operate — almost none to spruce up its ballpark — and he had to develop players that he could sell to other teams for cash. As a result, Gerry Nugent's Phillies teams were bad, very bad, they attracted very few paying customers, and they made no money. The club was definitely second rate compared to Mack's Athletics in the eyes of baseball followers in Philadelphia and eastern Pennsylvania. Baseball fans considering a trip to Baker Bowl had to figure into their costs not only the price of a ticket but also dry-cleaning for their clothes from the frowzy, dusty surroundings in the park. And the seven other National League teams considered a visit to Philadelphia as a financial loss, since they very seldom cleared enough revenue to match their expenses, even though they could be pretty sure of tacking a few more victories onto their won-loss records.

As the thirties moved by, it became clearer and clearer that the Phillies would have to abandon decrepit Baker Bowl. It was musty and dirty, misshapen, and falling apart. At that time the place was owned by the Charles W. Murphy estate (in Chicago), Murphy himself having passed away in October 1931, and Gerry Nugent and his ball club were tied up with a long-term 99-year lease. Talks were held with the management of the Athletics off and on over several seasons, but nothing much seemed to come from them. One of the major impediments to the Phillies becoming tenants at Shibe Park was the disposition of concession revenues, since Connie

Mack and his Athletics controlled the food, drink, cushion and scorecard business at their park, rather than letting out a contract for these operations to an outsider.[5]

Finally, in 1938, matters started moving. Phillies fans were upset when first baseman Dolph Camilli was traded to Brooklyn before the season. When pitcher Bucky Walters, the club's other recognizable player, was sent to Cincinnati on June 13, for $43,000 and two players, fans talked about a boycott of the team. "Those few who pay the freight at Baker Bowl were chagrined when Dolph Camilli was sold to Brooklyn and swore that if Walters left they wouldn't back the club."[6]

Nugent recognized that something had to be done. Red Smith reported in an article in the *Record* on June 25 that "after more than forty years in the fusty, cobwebby House of Horrors known as Baker Bowl, the Phillies are preparing to pull up stakes." He noted that written agreements with the A's were being drawn up for the Phillies to move, "possibly before the end of this season," which, he went on, "so far has bordered on the disastrous, both in the box office and on the diamond." Of Baker Bowl, Smith said that "nothing was alive but the ivy on the clubhouse wall," and in the years since the 1915 pennant, "the only genuine, spontaneous excitement in Baker Bowl has been inspired by the occasional collapse of a section of stands."[7]

What Smith did not know when he wrote his column on June 25 was that Baker Bowl's use by the Phillies was now measured in days. Other writers tried to do a bit of nostalgia for the old park but it was difficult to find much good to say about the place. Dave Walsh wrote in the *Record* "once I thought it was grand" but now it was a "shabby-genteel property ... something of a slum," and Bill Dooly recalled going to Baker Bowl as a boy, and "even then ... it was old and beaten ... but, you know — home."[8]

Columnist Robert Sensenderfer wrote in the *Bulletin* of all the good things that had taken place in the old park over the years (that didn't take up too much space) and then concluded, "Antiquated and cramped as the old ball field has become, its passing cannot come without regret by the older generation of fans."[9]

On June 29, the Phillies attracted 7,000 viewers to a doubleheader with the New York Giants; the Phillies lost both games. The next day, lawyers for the Murphy Estate in Chicago announced that "a friendly agreement" had been reached, permitting the Phillies to abandon the old park. Jimmy Wilson, the Phils' manager, instructed his players to remove all personal belongings from the Broad and Huntingdon grounds.[10]

That day, June 30, 1938, only 1500 showed up for what was the very

Final game at Baker Bowl for the pitiful Phillies, June 30, 1938, with a lackluster crowd in attendance (Urban Archives, Temple University Libraries, Philadelphia).

last game the downtrodden Phillies would play there. Dooly wrote the next day that "Baker Bowl passed out of existence as the home of the Phillies yesterday afternoon. Equal to the occasion, the Phillies almost passed out with it by providing one of their inimitable travesties," a pasting by the score of 14–1. The Giants, he noted, deserved some credit for their hitting, "but it must be remembered that it was the Phillies who were out there doing the pitching. They were also doing a little catching, mostly on the chin, as was quite fitting unto the day." All in all, Dooly concluded, "The Phils lent the occasion the artistic touch that only they can provide."[11]

Claude Passeau started for the Phillies against the Giants' Slick Castleman. Phil Weintraub, recently purchased from Baltimore in the International League to firm up first base for Nugent's squad, booted a ball in the second which led to three New York runs, and then the Giants scored nine more in the third, including a home run by Hank Leiber, the last circuit clout in the musty old park and a healthy one, deep into the center field bleachers. The visitors got nine hits in that inning, six of them in a row after two were out. At that point the fans started leaving, never to return, few of them to look back at the place with any sense of nostalgia. Sam Leslie, the Giants' first baseman, had five hits in that final game, Mel Ott scored the last run, Weintraub had the last hit, and Stan Stoviak had the distinction of being the last batter struck out in the place (Stoviak had ten at-bats in 1938, his only time in the majors, and got no hits). Jimmy Wilson was said to be the last to leave the park. Baker Bowl's days as a baseball park were over.

Although the club was not technically released from its 99-year lease, the next day Nugent and the Macks signed the lease of Shibe Park at the Phillies' office in the Packard Building downtown. Gerry Nugent smiled as he told the press, "We are definitely through with Baker Bowl. Our contract with the Murphy Estate is now in a suspended state for the next five years. Under our agreement the park will not be used for sports events again except for a few football games for which we already have contracted."

Connie Mack was gracious about it all. "I think the change will benefit both clubs and will make for better baseball in Philadelphia. I am sure the Phils will play better at Shibe Park and I look for a real spurt once they know the field." Unfortunately the Phillies over the next few seasons were just about as bad in Shibe Park as they had been in Baker Bowl, but at least their surroundings were nicer.[12]

At about the same time, the Phillies put Chuck Klein on the waiver list; the club considered him too slow to cover the much larger right-field territory he would find in Shibe Park. No other team claimed Klein, so he stayed with the Phillies until the following season.

When the Phils returned home to their new ballpark on July 4, they were greeted by 12,000 fans, a throng to which they were totally unaccustomed. They gave the first game of the holiday twin-bill to the Boston Bees, Hugh Mulcahy losing 10–5, but they actually won the nightcap, 10–2, behind Passeau.

And what of the wreck of a ballpark they left behind at Broad and Huntingdon? It stood for a few more years, the scene of small-time events like midget auto races, high school football games, ice skating shows, and the like, as it became more and more decrepit. In the 1940s, the center-field clubhouse housed an establishment called the Alpine Musical Bar, facing out to the corner of Broad and Lehigh, and a part of the field served as a used-car lot. When a portion of the brick wall along the third-base line fell apart in 1950, blocking 15th Street, the time had come. The rest of the place was torn down, and Baker Bowl came to its final ending. Very few noticed.

Chapter 2
League Park

Back in the late '70s, a young freelance writer in Cleveland named Peter Jedick sat down to write what turned out to be a 4500-word pamphlet called "League Park." He had a thousand copies printed, sold those in the city's book stores at $1.95 each, and had another thousand made up. Eventually, with a revised edition in 1992, the easy-reading pamphlet sold more than 10,000 copies. In early 2009, a copy was listed for sale on Amazon.com for $134.71. For many people, however, hearing of all this, the question arises, "What is League Park? Why a book about it? What was it?"[1]

Old-timers in the Forest City, of course, knew the answers. League Park was a ballpark located at East 66th Street, Linwood Avenue and Lexington Avenue in Cleveland, about three miles east of downtown, and it was here that big league baseball was played in Cleveland from 1891 through the end of the 1946 season. A commercial neighborhood grew up around the ballpark, on East 66th Street, with a drug store, blacksmith shop, barber shop, and a bowling alley and billiard parlor among the available facilities. When people started coming to games in automobiles, homeowners in the neighborhood charged them 25 cents to park in their yards.

The first version of League Park, a single-deck wooden grandstand with a covered pavilion behind first base and a tiny section of bleachers, was opened on May 1, 1891. Nine thousand spectators showed up to watch the big game, taking advantage of the streetcar lines which conveniently stopped right at the ballpark's entrance. (Frank Robison, who owned the ball club, called the Spiders, also happened to own the trolleys.) There was much hoopla, featuring a parade complete with circus animals, and then Denton "Cy" Young pitched for the hometown team and had no trouble beating the Cincinnati Redlegs by a score of 12–3.

The Spiders fell on hard times later in the decade, particularly when Robison bought the St. Louis franchise and took most of the better players

League Park, Cleveland, also known for some years as Dunn Field (Philadelphia Athletics Historical Society).

from the Cleveland club with him. In 1899, the Spiders had a dismal record of 20–134, their attendance slumped off to a pitiful 3,179 for the season, and they were dropped by the National League.

For 1900, the Grand Rapids franchise of Ban Johnson's Western League was transferred to Cleveland, named the Blues, and made to feel welcome at League Park. Charles Somers, a coal magnate, and Jack Kilfoyl, who had a popular men's furnishings store in Cleveland, owned this minor league club, and they were ready when, the next year, Johnson changed his league's name to the American League. He challenged the reigning National League magnates and, over much opposition, established his circuit as a competitive major league. Somers was the money man behind the American League team set up in Cleveland, and he also helped Johnson finance new teams in other cities, including St. Louis, Chicago, and Philadelphia. In fact, Somers was the principal owner of the Boston club until he sold it in 1903.

The struggle between the two leagues became ever more heated, and in 1902 Cleveland benefited greatly from it. Connie Mack and his Philadelphia Athletics had signed several star players from the cross-town Phillies, the Phillies had gone to court over it, and in the spring of 1902 the Pennsylvania Supreme Court issued an opinion in favor of the National League club. Rather than returning his players, Mack and Ban Johnson arranged for two of the best of them, second baseman Napoleon Lajoie and outfielder Elmer Flick, to be transferred to Cleveland, beyond the jurisdiction of the Pennsylvania courts.[2]

Lajoie (who had hit .422 for the 1901 Athletics) soon became a superstar in League Park, leading the American League in batting in 1903 and 1904, and was named the team's manager in 1905. The club's nickname was changed from the Blues to the Naps in honor of their leader, and attendance increased through the decade. In 1908, the Naps were nosed out for the pennant by Detroit, by half a game, despite the pitching of the great Addie Joss, with a 24–11 record, earned run average of 1.16, and a perfect game on October 2, as the fight for the flag came down to the finish.

With prosperity, the club owners decided to rebuild League Park as a more permanent structure, with double the seating capacity, and this work commenced after the 1909 season. The new League Park, rebuilt in concrete and steel, was ready for the following season, opening on April 21, 1910, with a capacity of 21,000, and quite a place it was. Double-decked and roofed from right field almost to the left-field foul pole, it had a large section of single-decked grandstand in left field and a smaller bleacher section running from left-center to center field. The distance down the left-field line was 385 feet, and it was 505 feet to deep center field. There was a problem with right field: because of the location of Lexington Avenue, the right-field fence was built just 290 feet from home plate.

The right-field wall was 20 feet of concrete, with an additional 20 feet of chicken wire on top of that, to prevent cheap home runs. There were steel beams imbedded in the concrete to hold up the chicken wire; oddly enough, the beams rose above the top of the wire fence, and a batted ball hitting a beam and bouncing back onto the field was still in play. At times, such bouncing balls found their way across the outfield to where the left fielder had to play them.

Charles Somers owned not only the Cleveland club but several minor league teams as well: in Toledo, Ironton (Ohio), Waterbury (Connecticut), Portland (Oregon), and New Orleans. When the newly-birthed Federal League became a threat to the established major leagues, Somers in 1914 moved his Toledo Mud Hens to League Park, to share it with the hometown team and keep the Federals out of a city where a ball game was scheduled for just about every day of the season.

In 1915, with Lajoie gone, the club needed a new nickname. Somers, the owner, had the local newspapers conduct a survey, and the name they came up with was "Indians," apparently a sort of tribute to the recent success of the Boston Braves. There were some later who said the name was in memory of Louis Sockalexis, a Native American who had played for the Spiders in the '90s, but that was not so.

The following year, Somers, who had earlier bought out his partner Kilfoyl, fell on hard times; the outlaw Federals had forced salaries up, attendance at League Park had fallen way off with a couple of losing seasons, and some personal investments had failed. Somers went broke, and his creditors forced him to sell the franchise for $500,000 to a syndicate headed by a railroad man from Chicago named James C. Dunn, who promptly changed the name of the ballpark to Dunn Field.[3]

The place saw its only World Series in 1920, when the Indians, led by player-manager Tris Speaker, edged the White Sox for the pennant, days after Chicago suspended the suspected participants in the 1919 World Series fix. In mid–August, the Indians had suffered their own tragedy, when shortstop Ray Chapman was beaned in New York by Yankee pitcher Carl Mays and died as a result. A 21-year-old rookie, Joe Sewell, filled in for Chapman and hit .329 in his 22 games.[4]

The Series, between the Indians and the Brooklyn Robins, was tied at two games each, as the teams faced off in Dunn Field on October 10. In the first inning, Elmer Smith of the Indians hit the first grand slam home run in World Series history, and three innings later Jim Bagby of the Tribe hit the first-ever Series home run by a pitcher. These feats were soon overshadowed in the fifth inning when Bill Wambsganss, the Cleveland second baseman, caught a line drive headed into center field, stepped on second to double off a runner there who was well on his way to third, and then tagged out the astonished runner coming from first base. It was the only unassisted triple play in World Series history and one of the very few in big-league annals. Thus inspired, the Indians whipped Brooklyn, five games to two, with pitching ace Stan Coveleski winning three of them.

Unfortunately for Clevelanders, 1920 was the high point in the ballpark's history. Over the years, there were a few changes in the park: the outfield walls in left and left-center came in a bit with some new seats, but there was nothing that could be done about the 290 feet to right field, a boon to left-handed pull hitters. Sunny Jim Dunn died in 1922, and when his widow sold the club in 1926, the ballpark's name reverted to League Park.

Some notable games were played there over the years. On July 7,

Grounds crew working on the field at League Park (National Baseball Hall of Fame Library, Cooperstown).

1923, the Indians beat the Red Sox, 27–3, with Boston's starting pitcher, Lefty O'Doul, giving up sixteen runs, eleven hits, and eight walks in three innings. O'Doul soon gave up pitching altogether and made it back to the majors as a hard-hitting outfielder five years later. Babe Ruth hit his 500th home run in League Park in 1929, and on July 10, 1932, the A's defeated the Indians, 18–17, in a wild game in which Philadelphia's Jimmy Foxx had two singles, a double, and three home runs into the left field stands.

The Tribe played a last game in League Park on July 30, 1932, and then moved the next day to the newly-built Municipal Stadium for the rest of the 1932 season and all of 1933. The large facility down by Lake Erie had been built by the city in an unsuccessful effort to attract the Olympic Games to Cleveland. The Indians' first game in the new park brought out a record crowd of 80,284, breaking the previous mark set by the Yankees in New York in 1928. Despite such a start, attendance actually declined in the new facility, even though its capacity was far larger than League Park's (the Great Depression may have had something to do with the drop), so for 1934 the club moved back home, to East 66th and Lexington.

Off and on over the next few years, the Indians had two homes.

League Park was theoretically the home ball grounds, except when a larger crowd was expected — or hoped for. In addition, there was much more automobile parking at the new facility; League Park's location by the trolley lines became much less of a favorable factor as the years went by. On August 2, 1936, the Tribe played the Yankees at Municipal Stadium, and in 1937 they played there for all Sunday and holiday games between Memorial Day and Labor Day. After April 1938, the club played all of its Sunday, holiday, and selected other games at Municipal Stadium, and when lights were added to the big park by the lake all night games were played there.

There *was* one night game played at League Park, on July 27, 1931. Using a portable lighting system borrowed from the Kansas City Monarchs, the Homestead Grays took on the bearded warriors representing the House of David.

While the Indians seemed to be phasing themselves out of League Park, the Cleveland entries in the Negro American League — the Bears in 1939-40 and the Buckeyes starting in 1943 — were happy to play there. Indians fans, too, were happy to be in League Park when a rookie right-hander from Iowa named Bob Feller appeared on the scene on August 23, 1936, and went on from there, frustrating American League hitters and setting strikeout records. And they cheered third baseman Ken Keltner on July 17, 1941, when his brilliant fielding robbed Joe DiMaggio of several base hits and helped end the Yankee Clipper's 56-game hitting streak.

Those same fans, though, were stunned when their prospective pennant-winners in 1940, headed by star pitchers Mel Harder and Feller, infielders Keltner, Hal Trosky and Lou Boudreau, and outfielders Ben Chapman and Roy Weatherly, turned on manager Ossie Vitt, attempted to get him fired, and lost the pennant to the Tigers by one game. For this, the 1940 Indians were called and have gone down in history as the "Cry Babies."

In March 1945, the Indians owners signed a contract with the city which was announced by Mayor Thomas A. Burke, a five-year deal in which the club agreed to pay a minimum $500 rental for each day it used Municipal Stadium and it committed to at least 28 days per season. The future of League Park seemed to grow a little dimmer with this agreement.[5]

Finally, in 1946, a group headed by Bill Veeck, who had made a name for himself as an imaginative baseball promoter when he had owned the Milwaukee club in the American Association before the war, purchased the Indians franchise. Veeck's group included comedian Bob Hope, who had grown up in Cleveland. If the promotions Veeck had in mind now that he was on a major league stage came across as he envisioned them, he would need lots of seats to fill with his growing number of fans. "Lots of seats," to Bill Veeck, meant Municipal Stadium, which had many more seats than League Park.

League Park, one Cleveland writer said, "was a place built just for baseball." Another scribe looking back years later wrote, "but League Park was not good enough for Veeck. It just did not figure in his plan of conquest. He liked people and customers and the Stadium held three times as many. So Veeck pulled his team out of the old park, to the dismay of many, many people. Even today [in 1976] some will tell you they never should have left."[6]

But Bill Veeck never looked back. He advised the city that the Indians would henceforth, starting in 1947, play their entire home schedule in Municipal Stadium, and League Park would be abandoned. Veeck's critics sometimes overlook the fact that after World War II the greatest part of the major league schedule was played at night, and League Park never had lights installed.

The last American League game in League Park was played September 21, 1946, a few days after it was the scene of the only inside-the-park home run of Boston's Ted Williams' career. The Tribe was going nowhere, as the team would end up in sixth place, 36 games out. The Detroit Tigers, the opposition for the final game, were in second place, but they had no chance to catch the front-running Red Sox. The day before, the Tigers had whipped the Indians, 15–1, before only 2,737 people, as the visitors pounded out 22 hits, six of them by third baseman George Kell, with the Tribe's starting pitcher, Allie Reynolds, giving up six hits in one and two-third innings.

So the game itself the next day meant little, final game or not, and there seemed to be little incentive to attend. The historical significance of the last game in the old park was seen only in retrospect, when the local papers noted the next day that Veeck had said that from that day on all the Indians' home games would be played at Municipal Stadium. It is interesting to conjecture why Bill Veeck, certainly one of the game's greatest showmen, did not build up the final game as an "event," something not to be missed, but he clearly did not. In 1946, the closing of old ballparks was not yet considered something of special interest. The passing of League Park as the Indians' home was treated as simply a step on the way to the greater glories that would come at the big stadium — next year. As Bob Feller said, League Park was "a nice little ballpark," but he had no particular reaction to the permanent move to the big stadium.[7]

At the game itself, the Tigers beat the Indians, 5–3, in eleven innings, before a pitiful turnout of 2,772 spectators. Paul "Dizzy" Trout went the route for Detroit, winning his fifteenth game. "For eight frames," wrote the local paper, "the Tiger bats had been well checked by a rookie hurler of definite promise," southpaw Bob Kuzava, making his big league debut after a late September call-up. Reliever "Jittery Joe" Berry, filling in after eight innings for Kuzava, took the loss. Singles by Hoot Evers and Dick Wakefield drove in the deciding runs in the 11th, with Kell scoring the last run in the park's history. Many of the fans in attendance left as the game dragged on. League Park's day was done, and the Tribe thereafter played in the big stadium by Lake Erie.[8]

Curiously, as the game ended, the *Plain Dealer*'s reporter was still not totally sure that it was the end for the ballpark: "It was probably the last major league game in League Park inasmuch as the Indians will re-establish permanent headquarters in the stadium next spring. No announcement has been made on the disposal of the old orchard."[9]

As a matter of fact, the Indians and Tigers played a Sunday doubleheader the next day in Municipal Stadium, which may, to be fair, have partially accounted for the low turnout for League Park's finale on Saturday. The first game was highly ballyhooed as a meeting between two 25-game winners, Feller of the Indians and Detroit southpaw Hal Newhouser. With 38,103 showing up for this one, Prince Hal beat Feller, 3–0, with a two-hitter. Regardless, there were no more American League games in League Park, which passed from the sporting consciousness with precious little notice at the time. Cleveland, the team and its fans, was looking ahead eagerly to the excitement Veeck promised them at the bigger stadium.

For several years after that, the old park hosted the Negro League games of the Buckeyes, but in 1951, after the city bought it, it was deemed unsafe and torn down, except for the small building which housed the ticket office and a tiny section of grandstand. The baseball diamond is still laid out, available for kids to play on, and the site is utilized as a community recreation center. In the spring of 2009, a vintage base ball club called the Cleveland Blues began using old League Park for its practices and games, playing under very old rules, without gloves or overhand pitching.

A historical marker was placed on the old grounds in 1979, but it takes a good bit of imagination to summon the shades of Cy Young, Nap Lajoie, Tris Speaker, Lou Boudreau, and Ken Keltner, in their primes at old League Park.

Chapter 3

The Other Place in Boston

From 1903 to 1953, there was no movement whatever of the sixteen major league baseball clubs. It was as if the jostling of leagues and franchises which baseball saw in the latter decades of the prior century had been a period of trial-and-error in finding the best locations, and after the American League had settled teams in New York and St. Louis in 1903 all was well and the optimum places had been found for the sixteen clubs. Oh, there was talk from time to time—maybe the bankrupt Phillies might move to Baltimore, or the Browns to Los Angeles, perhaps some other money-loser might find greener pastures—but it was all talk, no more. The baseball world was a fixed and settled place.

That is why it came as a shock to one and all when Lou Perini, the owner of the Boston Braves, announced in March of 1953, only weeks before Opening Day, that the Braves were leaving Boston, the home of the bean and the cod, and moving to Milwaukee, the home of bratwurst and cold beer, out there somewhere beyond the Great Lakes.

Bostonians "were shocked—no major league franchise had jumped to another city since 1903. But there it was on the television news: film of the 1953 tickets being dumped out the Braves office windows into a truck on Gaffney Street. They were taken to a spot behind a wire fence near the outfield flagpole and burned by the groundskeeper."[1]

With the ball club gone, there was little further use for its home grounds, Braves Field, a baseball park located about three miles west of Boston Common and a mile west of Fenway Park. Braves Field was bounded by Commonwealth Avenue, Gaffney Street, the tracks of the Boston and Albany Railroad, and Babcock Street. Beyond the railroad tracks the Charles River provided a picturesque background flowing past the outfield. And the Braves ownership planted fir trees behind the center field fence to absorb and cover up smoke from the railroad trains passing by.

Braves Field had been the last of the wave of thirteen concrete and steel ballparks which opened between 1909, when Shibe Park and Forbes Field led the way, and 1915, when Braves Field made its debut. It was the biggest of the new parks, seating almost 40,000, and its interior dimensions were large as well. Braves Field was built on the site of what had been the Allston Golf Club. The owner of the Braves who built it, James Gaffney, loved to watch baseball games with triples and even inside-the-park home runs, so there was lots of room in the outfield — 402 feet down each foul line, and a mighty 550 feet out to center field. In addition, the prevailing winds blew in from center field, giving pitchers another advantage. There *were* lots of triples and inside-the-park homers — plenty of excitement for Jim Gaffney and his outfielders — but few of the blasts that fans were coming to appreciate, the home runs that soared out of the park or into the stands. In 1915, for example, only eight home runs were hit in the new park, few of them over the fence, and the following year the number increased only to ten. In 1918, only seven homers were hit in Braves Field (although the

Braves Field, Boston, home of the Braves (Philadelphia Athletics Historical Society).

schedule was shortened because of the war), but by 1920 the total had gone up to just sixteen. Gaffney must have been proud of his work.

When it opened in 1915, Braves Field had a covered single-deck grandstand seating about 18,000, stretching from the left field foul line beyond third base all the way around behind the plate and down the right field line past first. Down the foul lines beyond the covered stands were uncovered stands, each seating 10,000, called pavilions, although they were really just bleachers open to the elements with long backless planks for the fans to sit on. There was also a small bleacher area in right-field fair territory, seating another 2,000, called the "jury box," allegedly so named by a baseball writer who noted one day that there were only 12 spectators seated there.

The Braves opened their new park for business on August 18, 1915, happily moving from the South End Grounds which they had used up to that time. The Braves, defending World Champions following their four-game sweep of Connie Mack's Athletics the previous October, beat the St. Louis Cardinals, 3–1, before a crowd well in excess of the ballpark's capacity of 40,000, a crowd which was at the time the largest ever to watch a baseball game anywhere. The Braves were in the hunt for another pennant in 1915, led by Sherry Magee, Dick Rudolph, Johnny Evers and Rabbit Maranville, and were ultimately disappointed to finish second by seven games behind the Phillies.

In 1914, the neighboring Red Sox had allowed the Braves to play their World Series games in Fenway Park, which was considerably larger than the South End Grounds. In 1915, the Red Sox won the American League pennant (and were to face a team from Philadelphia in the Series, just as the Braves had done the year before), and the Braves graciously allowed their cross-town rivals to use brand-new Braves Field for *their* Series games. When the Sox won again in 1916, they once again used Braves Field for the World Series.

As the years went by, however, it began to look as if the Boston Braves themselves were never to play a World Series in their own ballpark. After a third-place finish in 1916, the club settled into a dismal rut in the National League, seldom finishing last (the Phillies had a near-monopoly on that spot) but rarely exceeding .500 or approaching the first division. The 1933 Braves team, under manager Bill McKechnie, was the only one to finish within ten games of first place (nine games out, in fourth place) until after World War II.

One of the most notable games played in the park took place on May 1, 1920, when pitcher Joe Oeschger of the Braves and Leon Cadore of the Dodgers hooked up in a game that went a record twenty-six innings. Each pitcher went the distance, and the game was eventually called on account of darkness as a 1–1 tie.

Over the years, there were occasional pro football teams which leased the premises from the Braves. The Boston Bulldogs of the first, short-lived American Football League played there in 1926, and the Boston Shamrocks, of a later American Football League, used the park in 1936 and 1937 (the only years of that league's existence). In 1932, a National Football League team called the Boston Braves played, appropriately, in Braves Field; in 1933, that team moved to Fenway with a new name, the Redskins, and later moved again, in 1937, to Washington.

In the meantime, however, there were plenty of physical changes to Braves Field. The fans tired of inside-the-park home runs (in the 1921 season, of the 38 home runs hit in the place, 34 of them were inside-the-park jobs), or no home runs at all (in 1926, nine homers were hit at the Braves' ballpark and in 1927 just fifteen). So, in 1928, the club's owner, Judge Emil Fuchs, built new bleachers in left and center fields, reducing home-run distances considerably. The new dimensions were 320 feet down the line in left, 330 feet to the left-center fence, 387 feet to center field, and 364 feet down the right-field foul line. Seating capacity was increased to 46,000 with the new grandstands, but when home runs started dropping with alarming regularity into the new stands, hit mainly by visiting sluggers, Fuchs figured something had to be done. (For the season, 86 home runs were hit at Braves Field, 62 of them by the opposition.) That something was the gradual removal of the new bleachers, from mid–June to the end of the season.

Judge Fuchs (his judicial title came by way of a three-year stint as a magistrate in New York City) was a rare piece of work. A native of Hamburg, Germany, and at one time lawyer for the New York Giants, he had purchased the Braves franchise in 1923, along with former pitching great Christy Mathewson, but Mathewson died in 1925. The club was in financial straits under Fuchs's ownership, and after the 1928 season, needing cash, he sold manager Rogers Hornsby (who had led the league in hitting at .387) to the Cubs for five journeyman players and $200,000. Judge Fuchs then had the rare idea that he should manage the team himself (saving a salary), so that is what he did in 1929. After a 56–98 record and last-place finish, Fuchs went back to a real manager, Bill McKechnie, in 1930, but the club continued to lose money.

The Braves came up with one of the league's top hitters in 1930 with rookie Wally Berger, a right-handed hitting outfielder, who banged 38 home runs in his first year. Berger fell off a little in the next couple of seasons but hit 27 long balls in 1933, 34 the next year, and 34 again in 1935, when he led the league in both homers and runs batted in. But, aside from scrappy infielder Rabbit Maranville, the Braves had little else to attract fans and their attendance sagged.

Early in 1935, desperate for some sort of drawing card, Fuchs signed the elderly Babe Ruth to a contract as vice-president, assistant manager, and active player, leading the Bambino to believe that he would become manager in 1936. When Ruth realized he was no longer physically able to play on a regular basis, he also learned that his two other titles with the Braves were chimera and that there was little to no chance of his becoming manager. On June 2, 1935, Ruth announced his retirement as a player and, on the same day, Fuchs fired him from the other positions. Fuchs himself, deeply in debt, sold the team late in the season, but not before seeing a paid attendance of 95 people for a game with the Dodgers on July 28.

The "Jury Box" in right field, Braves Field, named by a sportswriter the day he saw just twelve spectators sitting there (National Baseball Hall of Fame Library, Cooperstown).

The only All-Star game played in Braves Field took place on July 7, 1936. Even that was somewhat botched; the local media erroneously reported that the game was sold out, so only 25,556 spectators showed up, leaving some 20,000 empty seats. The Nationals won for the first time, 4–3, with Yankee rookie Joe DiMaggio the goat of the game, leaving numerous runners on base in his five futile at-bats, missing a shoestring catch to set up the victors' first two runs, and fumbling a single by Billy Herman to let in the winning run.

In the meantime, the playing field dimensions of Braves Field changed just about on an annual basis, as fences were moved in and out, stands were put up and taken down, and the ownership tried to find a shape for the ball yard which would encourage home runs, despite a wind which generally blew in from the outfield to home plate. At one point, the plate was moved to the right, and the right field foul line was shifted some 25 feet; this change put some of the right-field pavilion into fair territory and necessitated that a portion of it be removed.

From 1936 to 1940, the new ownership of the franchise, under the leadership of Bob Quinn, tried to stir up interest by changing the team's name to the Bees, so of course the ballpark became the Bee Hive. Attendance went up some, which helped, and the team moved up toward the top of the second division under manager Casey Stengel, but it was still a distant second to the Red Sox in the minds of Boston's baseball fans. Stengel, later to be a consistent winner as manager of the New York Yankees, led the Bees/Braves for six years and his team finished seventh four years in a row. In April 1943, Stengel was struck by a Boston taxi and fractured his leg, causing him to miss a good part of the season; at the end of the year, a Boston columnist nominated the cabdriver for an award as the one who had done the most for Boston sports that year.

Through the war years, the club featured players like right-fielder Tommy Holmes, a favorite of the fans in the "Jury Box," Alva Javery, Jim Tobin, Butch Nieman, Connie Ryan, Carden Gillenwater and Whitey Wietelmann, but they never left the second division and attendance languished at the 200,000 level.

Late in 1945, the Braves franchise was acquired by three men who had made their money in the construction business, Louis Perini, Guido Rugo, and Joe Maney, known collectively to the baseball world as "the Three Steam Shovels." Perini took over team leadership, hired former Cardinal manager Billy Southworth, and spruced up the ballpark. Just before Opening Day in 1946, Perini had the place given a new paint job, including the seats; unfortunately, the paint did not have quite enough time to dry and thousands of fans left Braves Field that day with green horizontal stripes on the back of their clothing. The Braves paid out some $6000 to mollify their customers.

But the baseball team improved, to fourth in 1946, to third in '47 (with third-baseman Bob Elliott voted the league's Most Valuable Player), and to the National League pennant in 1948. Attendance climbed over the million mark for the first time in 1947, and it reached 1,455,439 the next year, the highest in Boston Braves history. Led by the pitching of Warren Spahn and Johnny Sain (as well as Vern Bickford and Bill Voiselle, whose names did not fit into the "Spahn and Sain and two days of rain" mantra), and the hitting of Elliott, Holmes, Eddie Stanky, Alvin Dark, and Jeff Heath, Southworth's team outpaced the St. Louis Cardinals by 6½ games. For a while, it looked as if there might be an all–Boston World Series, when the Red Sox finished the American League season in a tie with Cleveland, but the Indians' victory in a one-game playoff dashed that possibility.

While 1948 saw the third World Series played in Braves Field, it was the first one for the Braves. In the opener, Johnny Sain pitched a four-hit shutout to beat Bob Feller, 1–0, with catcher Phil Masi scoring the game's only run after nearly being picked off second in the eighth inning. The next day, however, Cleveland's Bob Lemon outpitched Spahn for a 4–1 victory to tie the Series. The Indians took two of the three games in Cleveland, and they returned to Braves Field to wrap up the World Series, 4–3, in Game Six behind the relief pitching of Gene Bearden.

No one knew it at the time, but 1948 was a last hurrah for the Boston Braves. For the next three seasons they finished fourth, as their attendance dropped. By 1951, it was down to 487,475. In 1952, however, the team fell to seventh place, 32 games behind the pennant-winning Dodgers, and the number of paying customers slumped to 281,278, lowest in the majors and the smallest for the Braves since the war year of 1944. Lou Perini was made quite aware that Boston no longer looked like a "two-team town."

As the sorry '52 season approached its end, on September 20, Carl Erskine of the Dodgers beat Spahn, 1–0, in ten innings before 6038. The nation was fascinated by the story, just unveiled, of the fund which a bunch of Southern California fat cats had raised to make life easier for their senator Richard Nixon, who was at this time on the Republican ticket for vice-president. (Nixon called the story "a deliberate smear attempt.") Nixon met with the head of the ticket, General Dwight Eisenhower, the next day and several days later delivered what would become famous (or notorious) as his "Checkers speech."

The few fans who showed up for the last home game of the 1952 season, on September 21, put Nixon out of their minds, but they had no idea they were watching history being made, as the Dodgers coasted to an 8–2 victory. Nevertheless, they were indeed attending the last game at Braves Field. Before the game, 35 members of the Martha's Vineyard Little League who were on hand presented striped bass to manager Charlie Grimm and several other Braves, presumably leaving a fishy smell in the home clubhouse. While the game meant nothing for the Braves, it was an important contest for the visitors.

Brooklyn's Joe Black pitched a three-hitter, defeating Jim Wilson, as the Dodgers' victory clinched a tie for the National League pennant. Roy Campanella reached Wilson for a home run in the second, but the Braves came back to take a 2–1 lead in the fourth on a Johnny Logan single, a double by Eddie Mathews, and a bad throw by Dodger rightfielder Carl Furillo which allowed Mathews to come all the way around. Brooklyn tied the game in the sixth on Furillo's double and two groundouts, and the visitors put the game away with six runs in the eighth after two were out. Duke Snider singled, and Robinson walked. After Andy Pafko lined out for the second out, Campanella singled, Gil Hodges got an intentional walk, and Billy Cox walked to force in a run. At this point, Virgil Jester replaced Wilson on the mound. Black singled home two runs and Furillo doubled over Sammy Jethroe's head in center for two more, the last runs to score in Braves Field. A sixth-inning single by shortstop Logan was the last Braves hit in the old ball yard, and Jackie Robinson's single off Sheldon Jones in the ninth was the very last hit there. The game ended on a fly to Pafko in left by catcher Walker Cooper. The *New York Times* noted that 8,822 "turned out for the Braves' final home game and there seemed to be a lot of Dodger rooters among them." It *was* the largest single daytime crowd of the season for the Braves.[2]

In the *Boston Globe*, along side the story of the ball game, was an interview Bob Holbrook conducted with Lou Perini that was a kind of foreshadowing of what was to come. Perini first stated that his club in 1952 suffered the greatest financial loss of any team in major league history: "We are picking up the greatest check in baseball history this season." He went on to say that he intended to keep the club in Boston but qualified this by adding, "but I'm not going to be stubborn about this thing. I don't intend to spend ten years here when people don't want to see the Braves."

When Holbrook asked Perini about the possibility of a third major league, the Braves owner spoke about cities like Houston, Toronto, Montreal, Milwaukee, Los Angeles and San Francisco which could support a major league team. He dwelt on Milwaukee, where the Braves happened to own the territorial rights. "They have a stadium now that can be enlarged to seat 60,000. The Braves can't stand in the way of Milwaukee becoming a major league city." Holbrook finished his story by saying that even after the worst financial season in big league history, "Perini is going to stick with Boston. He hasn't quit and he has no immediate intention of quitting but let another season like this 'nightmare' transpire and this city could be a one-team town."[3]

The next March, though, Lou Perini made his surprise announcement that the club was moving to Milwaukee, on the shores of Lake Michigan, and the Boston Braves were no more. His hand had been forced by Bill Veeck of the St. Louis Browns.

Just days earlier, Perini had refused Veeck's offer to buy the territorial rights to Milwaukee, which belonged to the Braves by virtue of their ownership of the local club in the American Association. Veeck had hoped to move his Browns there, to the city where he had seen great success with his promotions as a minor league clubowner before the war. Soon thereafter, the American League owners voted to deny Veeck's attempt to move the Browns to Baltimore. All of the press generated by Veeck's efforts put considerable pressure on Perini: in Boston, where it alerted the Braves' few remaining fans to the fact that Perini was thinking of moving, and in Milwaukee, where the city had just been denied a major league franchise, which Perini had said a few months earlier he would not do. With the Braves withering away in Boston, it became clear to Perini that the time to move was upon him.

As it turned out, the huge success of the Braves club in Milwaukee opened the eyes of the baseball moguls, who suddenly realized that there were millions of baseball fans in cities across the country who were perfectly able and indeed desperately willing to support major league baseball teams. Baseball's "western movement" over the next decades came as a direct result of the Braves' move to Milwaukee.

In the meantime, what became of old Braves Field? It managed to survive, as the property of Boston University, converted into a football facility called Nickerson Field, where the Terriers played their home games until 1997. It is now used as a soccer field. Most of the Braves Field grandstands, including the Jury Box in right field, were taken down, but the right field pavilion is still part of Nickerson Field, as is the first base ticket office. And late at night, who knows? The shades of Rabbit Maranville, Wally Berger, Tommy Holmes, and Johnny Sain might still roam the grounds of what used to be Braves Field.

Chapter 4
Hit Sign, Win Suit

One of the most celebrated of the departed ballparks was Ebbets Field in Brooklyn, longtime home of the Dodgers. Its fame and notoriety came, not necessarily by reason of any structural anomalies in the building, but because in the '40s and '50s the Dodgers came to seem like "America's team" to many followers of the game, although that phrase had not itself become current yet.

The Brooklyn Dodgers did not win anything between 1920 and 1941— indeed, Giants manager Bill Terry was famous for remarking, to his regret, "Is Brooklyn still in the league?"[1]— but in the 1940s they were winners. Baseball fans were regaled with the feats of Leo Durocher, Peewee Reese, Kirby Higbe, Pete Reiser, and Dixie Walker. From 1947 on, when Jackie Robinson — and after him Don Newcombe and Roy Campanella — broke baseball's color barrier, the Dodgers were hailed as forerunners in the civil rights struggle. And, of course, Brooklyn is in the media capital, New York City, but still a bit separate, a little enclave, a borough of its own. During World War II, it seemed that every movie about American GIs had to have at least one guy in the foxhole from Brooklyn. And he usually bemoaned his enforced absence from Ebbets Field and his Dodgers.

The Dodgers, of course, had not always played in Ebbets Field, and they had not always been the Dodgers. Between 1898 and 1912, the home of the Superbas, as they were then called, was at Washington Park, near the foul-smelling Gowanus Canal in that part of the borough called Red Hook. But owner Charles H. Ebbets, dissatisfied with the old park and eager to take advantage of the new technology available for ballpark construction, built a new stadium in Flatbush, several miles to the west, on the site of the old Pigtown garbage dump, at a cost of $750,000. Ebbets had begun purchasing parcels of land for his new park in 1905, but not until 1912 was he able to gather all the land he needed for construction. Work began on March 14, 1912, and took about a year to complete. When the ballpark was done, Ebbets named it after himself.

Ebbets Field, seating 25,000 with a covered double-deck grandstand that ran from the right field foul pole to a spot down the left field line about forty feet past third base, opened on April 9, 1913, with a 1–0 Dodgers loss to the Phillies. Nasty weather that day kept more than half the seats empty, and it was also discovered that no press box had been provided, a lack which was not remedied until 1929. What the fans saw was a spacious playing area, with nine-foot high fences around the outfield. It was 419 feet down the left field line, 477 feet to center, but only 301 feet down the right field line. Inside the main entrance was a rotunda, "an incredible 80-foot circle enclosed in Italian marble, with a floor tiled with the stitches of a baseball, and a chandelier with 12 baseball bat arms holding 12 baseball-shaped globes." The domed ceiling stood 27 feet high.[2]

Over the years, both football and soccer were played in Ebbets Field. From 1930 to 1943, a National Football League team, called, as might be expected, the "Brooklyn Dodgers," used the ballpark as its home. In 1944, the team changed its name to "Tigers," but after a season of no wins and ten losses, the Tigers were merged with the Boston Yanks and went out of existence. There was an earlier Brooklyn Tigers team, in the second American Football League in 1936, but after half a season in Ebbets Field this aggregation moved to Rochester. In the renewed All-American Football Conference after World War II, the Brooklyn Dodgers again played in Ebbets Field from 1946 through 1948, but were then merged with the New York Yankees across the river for the AAFC's final season. And, on the college level, the Manhattan College Jaspers played there from 1932 to 1937. But football was always secondary, an afterthought, at Ebbets Field.

From 1926 through 1959, a number of important soccer matches took place in the Dodgers' ballyard, featuring American teams competing for national titles, as well as foreign squads from such diverse locales as Scotland, Israel, England, Sweden, Germany, Italy, and Austria, playing American all-star teams or each other.

Along the way, the baseball club's name became the Dodgers, originally the "Trolley Dodgers," after the streetcars which ran all through Brooklyn. There was a stretch, though, after Wilbert Robinson became the manager in 1914, when the team was also called the Robins, in his honor. Robinson's tenure at the team's helm lasted until 1931.

Ebbets Field saw two World Series early in its existence, in 1916 against the Boston Red Sox and in 1920 against Cleveland. Unfortunately, the

Ebbets Field, in the Flatbush section of Brooklyn (Philadelphia Athletics Historical Society).

American Leaguers defeated Robinson's boys each time, so a Brooklyn world's championship had to wait.

Uncovered bleachers were installed behind left field during the '20s, and it was with the park in this configuration that there occurred perhaps the most famous — certainly the weirdest — play in Brooklyn's history. In mid–August 1926, with Brooklyn hosting the Boston Braves, slugging Babe Herman came to the plate with the score tied, one out, and the bases loaded. Herman drove a long fly to right, off the wall, and the man on third scored. Pitcher Dazzy Vance, the runner on second, held up to see whether the ball would be caught, but then took off and rounded third when it hit the wall. As the Braves got the ball quickly back to the infield, though, Vance was trapped in a rundown between third and home. Chick Fewster, who had been on first, kept going and made it to third just as Vance, escaping the rundown, slid back into that bag. Herman, the hitter, made it easily to second, then saw that there was a rundown playing out between third and home. Figuring it was Fewster in the rundown, the

Babe hurried on to third. Suddenly, there were three Dodgers — Vance, Fewster and Herman — on third base, much to the astonishment of the Boston third baseman, who quickly tagged all of them. Vance was called safe, Fewster and Herman were called out, and the Dodgers were retired. So Herman had doubled into a double play. For years afterward, if a Brooklyn fan reported that there were three Dodgers on base, he was answered with, "Which base?"[3]

In the off-season of 1931-32, the covered double-deck grandstand, which had stopped part-way down the left field foul line, was run down to the corner, and a similar grandstand was extended from there to center field. There was still a fence across right field, but the seating capacity of the ballpark grew to 32,000 and Ebbets Field had attained its final configuration, although the fences were brought in a little closer, winding up at 348 feet to left, 297 feet to right, and 389 feet to deepest center field. The power alley to right-center field was about 315 feet, and hitters, particularly lefties, loved batting in Ebbets Field.

On June 15, 1938, the first Ebbets Field night game was played, with the Cincinnati Reds as the guests. The Dodgers were overly hospitable, for that night Johnny Vander Meer of the Reds pitched his second consecutive no-hitter, having thrown his first a few days earlier, at home against the Braves.

The first major league game to be televised was on August 26, 1939, between the Dodgers and the Reds, from Ebbets Field, over an experimental NBC station W2XBS. The Dodgers' radio voice, Red Barber, described the goings-on to an audience concentrated in the New York area. Barber, who would broadcast thousands of games over radio and television in the coming years, mostly for the Dodgers, had a mellifluous Southern voice and a knack for homespun phrases like "sittin' in the catbird's seat" and "tearin' up the pea patch," which made him a great favorite in Brooklyn and around the country. A native of Mississippi, Barber first broadcast ballgames for Cincinnati, from 1934 to 1938. When Reds general manager Larry MacPhail moved to Brooklyn as president in 1938, he got Barber to go with him a year later, and there Red stayed through 1953. Dodger fans were shocked when "the Ole Redhead," as he was known, left in 1954 to become an announcer for the Yankees, of all teams, for whom he worked until he was fired in 1966, after the Yanks' historic tenth-place finish.

MacPhail was one of the strangest characters in baseball history. One biographer calls him "flamboyant, visionary, ego- or monomaniacal, tempestuous, alcoholic, and self-destructive." Leland Stanford MacPhail was born in a small town in Michigan in 1890, attended Beloit College, the University of Michigan and George Washington University, garnered a law degree, and had an unsuccessful career as a lawyer. MacPhail made some news as a World War I soldier when he and some buddies pulled off an unsuccessful attempt to kidnap Kaiser Wilhelm shortly after the war's end. He got into baseball running the Columbus team in the American Association for Branch Rickey in 1930, and he turned the ailing franchise into a moneymaker, using a new stadium with lights, Ladies Days, and a knothole gang. MacPhail and Rickey, though destined to rub up against each other for years, never got along: the abstemious, religious Rickey was about 180 degrees from the flashy, hard-drinking, loud-talking MacPhail. In 1933, MacPhail went to Cincinnati as general manager of the Reds; he boosted attendance, put lights in Crosley Field (where the first major league night game was played on May 24, 1935), and purchased many of the players who went on to win Reds pennants in 1939 and 1940. Along the way, though, MacPhail alienated owner Powel Crosley, Jr., and soon it was "off to Brooklyn," where he could revitalize another franchise in dire financial straits.[4]

MacPhail fired Casey Stengel as manager of the Dodgers and installed the old spitball pitcher, Burleigh Grimes, in the job. After two unsuccessful seasons, 1937-38, Grimes was let go, and MacPhail gave the position to the veteran shortstop he already had on his roster, Leo Durocher. The light-hitting Durocher, a ten-year veteran with the Yankees, Reds, Cards, and Dodgers, was known for his big mouth and brash personality, and Mac-Phail felt this could be transformed into baseball leadership. It was the start of a 24-year managerial run for Leo the Lip which resulted in a posthumous election to the Hall of Fame, which was also Larry MacPhail's destiny.

Durocher (and all of Brooklyn, for that matter) had a tempestuous relationship with George Magerkurth, a National League umpire from 1929 to 1947. Magerkurth, a large man with a short fuse, was constantly in altercations with Durocher and his Dodgers. In the Brooklyn victory parade after the 1941 pennant, a coffin labeled "Magerkurth" was prominently displayed. A couple of years later, a 21-year-old fan named Frank Germano leaped from the Ebbets Field stands at the end of a game and, after throwing Magerkurth violently to the ground, proceeded to pummel him, while the ballpark attendants stood by. After another game at Ebbets Field, as the umpires were leaving the field, a hefty woman screamed, "Magerkurth, if you were my husband I'd give you poison," to which the umpire shouted back, "Lady, if I were your husband, I'd take it!"[5]

Larry MacPhail and Durocher clashed constantly, with MacPhail frequently firing his manager in an alcoholic fury. When he sobered up in the morning, though, MacPhail would rescind the firing. Leo once said, "There is a thin line between genius and insanity, and in Larry's case it was sometimes so thin you could see him drifting back and forth." What MacPhail did give Durocher, of course, was a number of good ballplayers who would go on to win the 1941 pennant, the first in Brooklyn since 1920. Reese, Reiser, Higbe, Walker, Whitlow Wyatt, Dolph Camilli, Billy Herman, Hugh Casey, Curt Davis, Joe Medwick and Mickey Owen formed the backbone of a Brooklyn club that finished 2½ games ahead of the Cardinals, with Camilli winning the league's Most Valuable Player award.

The Dodgers clinched their pennant in Boston, and MacPhail arranged to board the club's victorious train at the 125th Street Station in New York so that he could be with the players when they disembarked before a happy throng of fans at Grand Central. When Durocher learned that some players were going to get off at 125th Street, though, he ordered the train not be stopped, so that the whole team would greet the fans at Grand Central. Unfortunately, that meant the train rushed past MacPhail standing on the train platform. When he finally caught up with the team later, a livid MacPhail fired Durocher on the spot, though he did rehire him shortly thereafter.

The most famous play in the 1941 World Series, which the Dodgers lost to the Yankees in five games, took place at Ebbets Field in Game Four. With the Dodgers set to tie the Series at two games apiece, ahead 4–3 with two outs in the ninth, Casey threw strike three by Tommy Henrich, only to have the ball get by catcher Owen to keep the game alive. The Yankees then scored four runs to win, and a 3–1 gem by Ernie Bonham against Wyatt the next day clinched the Series for the Bronx Bombers.[6]

The 1942 Dodgers won 104 games, four more than the pennant-winners of the year before, but they finished two behind St. Louis. For the next three years of wartime ball, they finished third, seventh, and third, and were never in contention. In 1941 and '42, the club had achieved its first seasons of attendance over a million; there was a substantial falloff in the next two years, but attendance went over a million again in 1945 and stayed there for as long as the Dodgers stayed in Brooklyn. During the war, outfielder Fred "Dixie" Walker, after seven unsuccessful American League seasons, became a favorite as the "Peepul's Cherce" in Brooklyn, where he won a batting title in 1944 and led the league in RBIs the next year. With Walker in the lead, Brooklyn was ready for the return of players from the service and postwar baseball. A Schaefer beer sign was erected on the top of the scoreboard: the "h" in "Schaefer" lit up for a hit, while the second "e" lit up to designate an error.

In 1946, with newcomers Eddie Stanky, Carl Furillo, Bruce Edwards, and Joe Hatten joining veterans like Reese, Walker, Reiser, Cookie Lavagetto, and Augie Galan, the Dodgers waged a battle down to the wire with their rivals, the St. Louis Cardinals. When the season came to an end, the two teams were deadlocked with records of 96–58, the first such pennant tie in major league history. National League rules called for a best-of-three playoff, and Brooklyn's hearts were broken when the Cards quickly ripped off two straight wins to take the pennant. A familiar cry in the borough became "Wait till next year!"

"Next year," of course, was the year in which the Dodgers revolutionized major league baseball, putting on the field the first acknowledged African-American ballplayer since the nineteenth century. Branch Rickey, who was now running the ball club since MacPhail had gone into wartime service, had signed Jackie Robinson from the Kansas City Monarchs in the Negro National League late in 1945, and Robinson had put together a fine season for the Dodgers' top farm club, the Montreal Royals, in 1946. For 1947, Robinson played first base for the Dodgers (because Stanky was a fixture at second, Robinson's natural position). He had a fine season, earning Rookie of the Year honors in the National League, despite a backdrop of bigotry and controversy, much caused by outside forces, much the product of other teams' players and managers, and some caused by Dodger players, most notably Dixie Walker.

During spring training of 1947, Durocher became embroiled with Larry MacPhail, who now headed the cross-town Yankees, over public and ever-noisier charges of associating with gamblers. Just before the start of the season, Commissioner Albert B. "Happy" Chandler, who had attained his position with MacPhail's support, announced Durocher's suspension for the season for "conduct detrimental to baseball." Rickey, suddenly left without a field leader, called in scout Burt Shotton, who had managed the Phillies from 1928 to 1933, to take over. The 62-year-old Shotton, managing in civilian clothes from the dugout, soon had his Dodgers playing fine ball, after Rickey had faced down an incipient anti–Robinson rebellion in the ranks.

Branch Rickey was the first great master of baseball's "farm system," earlier with the St. Louis Cardinals, and later with the Dodgers, and this mastery led to a steady procession of good ballplayers coming up from farm teams like Fort Worth and Montreal to join the big league club. The system paid big-time dividends in the postwar years.

Led by Walker, Furillo, Reese, and Robinson, and with 21 wins from a tall, young righthander named Ralph Branca, who had won only eight games in limited action in three prior seasons, the Dodgers finished five games ahead of the Cardinals for the National League flag. An exciting World Series went down to the wire, the Yankees winning in seven. The two most memorable moments were the great catch Dodger outfielder Al Gionfriddo made of a Joe DiMaggio drive in Game Six and the double slammed by Cookie Lavagetto in Ebbets Field with two out in the ninth of Game Four, a hit which not only deprived Yankee hurler Floyd Bevens of what would have been the first Series no-hitter, but which also scored the game-winning run for Brooklyn. Despite these heroics, of course, the Yankees won, and Dodger fans again moaned, "Wait till next year."

Next year, unfortunately, was a mess for Dem Bums, as the Dodgers were affectionately called by their fans. In mid-season, with both the Dodgers and the Giants a game under .500, Rickey and Giants' owner Horace Stoneham engineered a deal whereby the Giants took Durocher off the Dodgers' hands, let their manager Mel Ott go, and allowed Rickey to bring back Shotton. Both clubs performed a bit better after the change, but the final verdict for the Brooklyn club was third place, behind both the Braves and the Cards. The club was being reshaped, with converted catcher Gil Hodges installed on first base, third baseman Billy Cox and lefty Preacher Roe coming over from Pittsburgh in the deal that sent Walker away, and Robinson moving to second after Stanky was traded. A veteran Negro League catcher named Roy Campanella was installed behind the plate, and the team that became known as "The Boys of Summer," from the title of a book about the club by Roger Kahn, was coming into being.[7]

In 1949, Shotton managed the club the whole season, Jackie Robinson led the league in hitting with a .342 average and won the MVP award, and a large rookie righthander named Don Newcombe won 17 games. Robinson, Hodges and Furillo each drove in more than a hundred runs, and young center fielder Duke Snider was not far behind with 92. With all this, the Dodgers were able to beat out St. Louis by a game for the National League pennant.

Brooklyn faced the Yankees once again in the World Series. In Game One, Newcombe and Allie Reynolds dueled in a scoreless tie until New York's Tommy Henrich led off the ninth with a game-winning home run. The second game saw a reverse of Game One, when Brooklyn's Preacher Roe bested Vic Raschi by an identical 1–0 score. Unfortunately, when the Series moved across the East River to Ebbets Field, the hated Yankees took the next three games to win the championship once again.

The years 1950 and 1951 saw heartbreaking endings for the Dodgers. In 1950, they were one game behind the Phillies going into the last game of the season, at Ebbets Field, with Newcombe facing Robin Roberts, each looking for his 20th win. In the ninth inning, Dodger Cal Abrams, representing the winning run which would have thrown the two teams into a tie, was gunned down at the plate by Phillies center fielder Richie Ashburn, and an inning later Dick Sisler took Newcombe deep for a three-run homer which won Philadelphia the pennant.

The next year, with Chuck Dressen now the manager, the Dodgers saw a mid–August 13½ game lead over Durocher's Giants disappear by the end of the schedule. In the ninth inning of the rubber game of a three-game playoff with the Giants, Ralph Branca came in to serve up a home run to Bobby Thomson that gave the Polo Grounders their first pennant since 1937. Brooklyn fans moaned once again, "Wait till next year."

The next two years, 1952 and 1953, saw Dodger pennants under Dressen, but both seasons ended with Yankee World Series victories. In Game Three in '53 at Ebbets Field, Dodger right-hander Carl Erskine set a new Series record with 14 strikeouts (Mickey Mantle and Joe Collins fanned four times each), but the team lost in six games. Fans around America were becoming very familiar with the classic Dodger lineup, Hodges-Robinson-Reese-Cox around the infield, Snider in center, Furillo in right, Gene Hermanski and then Andy Pafko in left field, Campy behind the plate, and Newcombe, Roe, Erskine, Billy Loes, and Clem Labine the most frequent pitchers. It was quite a team, but somehow it could never get over that final hump.

Dressen was let go after 1953 when he demanded a multi-year contract (the Dodgers liked to sign their managers for one year at a time), and veteran minor league manager Walter Alston took over as skipper for '54, but Durocher's Giants beat out the Dodgers by five games for the National League pennant. In 1955, though, Brooklyn set a searing pace early in the season and, led by Newcombe's 20–5 record, easily won the pennant, finishing 13½ games ahead of the Milwaukee Braves. Second-year man Jim "Junior" Gilliam had won the second base job by this time, so Robinson played third. A young lefty named Johnny Podres, in his third season, put up a record of 9–10 for the year, but great things were in store for him.

The first two games of the 1955 World Series, played in Yankee Stadium, went to the home team, as Newcombe and Loes took the losses. "Here we go again," moaned Brooklyn fans. But Podres took the mound for Game Three in Ebbets Field and pitched a complete-game 8–3 victory for the Dodgers. The next two games went to Brooklyn as well, but when the teams returned to Yankee Stadium, Whitey Ford evened things at three games apiece with a 5–1 four-hitter. That left it up to Podres in Game Seven, against Tommy Byrne. Hodges drove in runs in the fourth and sixth innings, and Podres kept piling up goose eggs. In the sixth inning, with two runners on base, Yogi Berra hit a long fly down the left field line that looked like it would drop for a double. Dodger fans shuddered until left fielder Sandy Amoros made a spectacular running catch which turned into a double play when he got the ball back to the infield. With three more scoreless innings, Johnny Podres had a 2–0 shutout, the Brooklyn Dodgers had their first world championship, and Dodger fans screamed, "THIS is next year!"

The following season, even with Podres in the military, the Dodgers won the pennant once more, nosing out the Braves by a game, with Newcombe's 27–7 won-lost record leading the way. Once again they played the Yankees in the World Series, and the fall classic was just about a mirror image of the year before. The Dodgers won the first two games at Ebbets Field, and then the Yankees won the next three in their own park. (Of course, Game Five was a bit unusual: Yankee pitcher Don Larsen threw a 97-pitch perfect game, the first no-hitter in World Series history.) Game Six at Ebbets Field was a 1–0 classic by Clem Labine to tie the Series, but in Game Seven, the last World Series game ever played in Ebbets Field, New York's Johnny Kucks shut out the Dodgers on three hits, beating Newcombe 9–0. The Dodgers were runners-up again.

It was the end of an era. After the 1956 season, the Dodgers sold Jackie Robinson to the Giants, and Robinson promptly announced his retirement from the game. Podres returned for 1957 and led the league in shutouts and earned run average, but the Dodgers finished third, far behind the pennant-winning Braves. And Dodger fans contemplated the unthinkable: their heroes, their beloved Bums, were going to leave town.

There had been rumblings, of course. Walter O'Malley, now the president and owner of the club after Rickey was forced out, had gotten a good bit of press with his inchoate plans for a new ballpark at the corner of Flatbush and Atlantic avenues in Brooklyn, where he hoped to erect a bigger stadium with lots more parking than the small amount Ebbets Field's surroundings provided. O'Malley looked to the site of the Atlantic Yards, where a market was being demolished, for his new ballpark. These hopes had been foiled by Robert Moses, the uncrowned king of New York City governance, who directly or indirectly controlled twelve city agencies.

O'Malley and Moses had corresponded about and discussed the issue since 1953, but Moses, the Building and Trades Commissioner, would not permit the erection of a baseball park in the location where O'Malley wanted it; he would only permit one in Flushing, in the borough of Queens. Queens, of course, was not Brooklyn, and the Dodgers would not move to Queens. So O'Malley had opened discussions with officials 3,000 miles from Brooklyn, in the untapped Golden West of Los Angeles. These talks had some ups and some downs, but as the 1957 season progressed it looked more and more as if they would bear fruit. Plans were made for both the Dodgers and Giants to move west (the Giants to San Francisco), and the National League club owners gave tentative approval to the two-pronged move. Over their last two seasons in Brooklyn, the Dodgers played several games each year in Roosevelt Stadium, across the river in Jersey City, as part of O'Malley's campaign to force the hands of city officials. Robert Moses and the other appropriate city officials remained obdurate. And the Brooklyn fans despaired.[8]

There was not much they could do about the situation. They still turned out more than a million strong to watch Alston's third place team. But things were now beyond the control of the people of Brooklyn and, indeed, of the officials of New York City. So the fans reminisced about Ebbets Field — about the unique and sometimes wonderful things that had taken place there.

They thought about Gladys Gooding, for 19 years the ballpark organist, and all the great tunes she had performed season after season. They remembered Hilda Chester, a plump, pink-faced lady with a mop of straggly gray hair, famous for cheering for "her Bums" in the center field bleachers, banging a frying pan with an iron ladle, and ringing the cowbell she always had with her. And Jack Pierce, whose idol through the '30s and '40s was third-baseman Cookie Lavagetto. Pierce usually brought a couple of bottles of Scotch and balloons with him to his seat behind third; as he downed his whiskey, he'd pop his balloons and shout "Cookie! Cookie!" They chuckled over Abe Stark, the clothier from 1514 Pitkin Street, whose sign under the centerfield scoreboard, three feet high and thirty feet long, bore Abe's name and the message, "HIT SIGN, WIN SUIT." This sign inspired a famous George Price cartoon in the *New Yorker* showing the clothier with a fielder's mitt defending his sign (in the cartoon the name on the sign was "Abe Feldman") against batted balls. And they remembered the Dodgers Sym-phon-y Band, consisting of five guys dressed to look like bums, playing (not very well) a trombone, a trumpet, cymbals, a snare drum, and a bass drum, based in Section 8 but also roving through the stands to entertain the crowd. All of these things were Ebbets Field to the fans of Brooklyn, and all would be gone if worse came to worst.[9]

What certainly looked like the last game took place between the Dodgers and Pittsburgh Pirates on September 24, 1957, although that morning's newspaper reported the filing of a taxpayer's suit in Los Angeles Superior Court to block the sale of property in Chavez Ravine to the Dodgers. Still, things in Brooklyn looked dim. Roscoe McGowen, in the *Times*, wrote that "everybody, including the 6,702 cash customers, assumed that the Dodgers were playing their final game in the old ball yard that was opened forty-five years ago." Before the game, Gil Hodges, Roy Campanella, and Sandy Koufax each received an inscribed humidor from the National Conference of Christians and Jews. A couple of loyal young lady fans placed a cardboard sign marked "DIED SEPT 1957" on the Ebbets Field cornerstone plaque in the park's rotunda.[10]

Then Bennie Daniels, for Pittsburgh (making his major league debut), and Danny McDevitt for the home team took the mound. Shortly before that, though, Frank Thomas, the Pirates' first baseman, had the distinction of being the last player injured at Ebbets Field, when he was hit in the mouth with a thrown ball during the visitors' batting practice. His wound required several stitches, and Thomas was taken to a nearby hospital for X-rays.

Bosley Crowther, sitting with his father, the film critic of the *Times*, in the first row behind home plate, noted that about forty nubile young ladies, the Gino Cimoli Fan Club, were seated right behind them, cheering as the game progressed for their hero, the young Dodger outfielder. By the fifth inning, though, the girls had fallen silent, and by the beginning of the seventh they were all weeping. An elderly usher came over to them and said in a kindly voice, "Girls, girls, please stop crying. You're young and have your whole lives to live. But I've been turning out the lights in this park for forty years and tonight I'm going to do it for the last time." The girls kept on crying.

The Dodgers scored a run in the first inning on a walk, a wild pick-off throw, and a double off the wall by Elmer Valo. Gladys Gooding played "After You're Gone" and "Am I Blue." When hits by Cimoli and Hodges produced another run in the third, Gladys played "Don't Ask Me Why I'm Leaving" and "If I Had My Way." There was no more scoring, as young lefty McDevitt pitched a five-hit shutout, with Peewee Reese getting two hits for the Dodgers, but the organist became more nostalgic as the game moved along, playing among others "Que Sera Sera," "Thanks for the Memories," "When I Grow Too Old to Dream," "Say It Isn't So," and "How Can You Say We're Through." Sid Gray in the *Herald-Tribune* wrote, "If there was a dry eye in the house at the finish, nobody can say she didn't

The scoreboard shows the final score — and Abe Stark's famous sign, Ebbets Field, September 24, 1957 (National Baseball Hall of Fame Library, Cooperstown).

try." The game took only two hours and three minutes, and then baseball in the old park was over. "[T]he Dodgers stole away and figuratively folded their tents last night," wrote Gray, "in what will probably be the last game ever at Ebbets Field."[11]

When the game ended, veteran P.A. announcer Tex Rickards made his usual announcement: "Please do not go on the playing field at the end of the game. Use any exit that leads to the street." There were suggestions that this directive could be varied to "Use any exit that leads to Chavez Ravine," the site of the prospective stadium in Los Angeles, but Tex never strayed from his script. The crowd dutifully followed his instructions and filed out with no disturbances, while Gladys Gooding played "May the Good Lord Bless and Keep You" and closed with "Auld Lang Syne." Afterwards Gladys said she had never played at a wake before. Benny Weinrig, the hard-boiled press box custodian, broke down after the game. "Fellers," he said, "Miss Gooding's 'Auld Lang Syne' brings tears to my throat. It's so sad." The ground crew came out and went through its usual post-game routine, raking the infield and covering the mound and home plate, but there would be no more games. Campanella tossed a finger-crab party for his teammates in the clubhouse, but that was it. Brooklyn fans were left with reading about O'Malley's negotiations with Los Angeles over the 300 acres in Chavez Ravine that he wanted, and soon they learned that all was signed and sealed. The Brooklyn Dodgers were no more.

Demolition of Ebbets Field began in February 1960, to make way for a high-rise apartment house on the site. Just before the start of the razing of the old ballpark, singer Lucy Monroe sang the National Anthem, as she had many times before the start of Dodger games. The property was soon occupied by the Ebbets Field Apartments, the name of which was later changed to the Jackie Robinson Apartments.

Of all the classic ballparks that closed down, it was perhaps Ebbets Field which was most loudly mourned, perhaps because it had been mentioned from time to time in works of literature, plays, and movies, and perhaps just because it had, with the Dodgers, Wilbert Robinson, Durocher, Jackie Robinson, Peewee Reese and the others, worked its way deep into America's baseball consciousness. In any event, it was gone, and so was the fabled team which had called it home.

Chapter 5

A Capital Place

"First in war, first in peace, last in the American League"— the old vaudeville comedians used to have a lot of fun ridiculing the Washington Senators, who, for most of their existence, were not much of a baseball team. (To set the record straight, the original Senators and their expansion successors played 71 years in Washington and finished last fourteen times; they had plenty of competition for the bottom spot from the likes of the St. Louis Browns, Boston Red Sox and Philadelphia Athletics over the years.[1]) It should also be mentioned that the club was supposed to be called "the Nationals," but the baseball public persisted in calling it "the Senators."

For most of that time, the Senators/Nationals played in Griffith Stadium, a ballpark which stood at Seventh Street and Florida Avenue in the northwest quadrant of the nation's capital. In the 1890s, Washington had a club in the National League and played in a wooden arena called National Park, which could hold between 6000 and 7000 people. Washington was dumped out of the National League in 1900, but when Ban Johnson established his American League in 1901 a Washington club was part of it, owned by Johnson himself and Frederick Postal. The new club played its home games for a couple of years at 14th Street and Bladensburg Road NE, but in 1903 it moved back into National Park, which had had extra stands built and could hold about 10,000. In 1904, a group put together by Thomas Noyes, part-owner and editor of the *Washington Star*, bought the club from Johnson and Postal.

When fire destroyed old National Park on March 17, 1911 (and the lumber yard which adjoined the left field fence), the Fuller Construction Company was hired by Noyes to erect a replacement structure in the same location, but constructed of steel and concrete. Fuller was ready to open an astonishing three weeks later, on April 12, with enough of the new stadium built to be serviceable. (It was "completed" on July 24.) In its first game, the new ballpark (still called National Park) saw the home team whip the Boston Red Sox, 8–5.[2]

The new structure had a seating capacity of 16,200 and a spacious playing area. It was more than 400 feet down the left field line, 421 feet to center, and 320 feet down the right field line, although the sign on the fence there said "328 feet" for many years until it was actually measured in 1955. The right field wall was 31 feet high, another benefit to pitchers, who loved Griffith Stadium, which was the name given to the ballpark in 1920. The Tigers' star lefty Hal Newhouser once said, "Give any pitcher a ball-hawk in center field and he'll win in Washington."[3]

The center field wall jutted in toward the field, around five houses and a huge tree which belonged to an owner who refused to sell to the ball club at the time of the park's construction. As a result there were additional odd corners in center field, the most distant of which was 457 feet from home plate.

Griffith Stadium, Washington, where the original and expansion Senators played (National Baseball Hall of Fame Library, Cooperstown).

There was a double-deck grandstand covered by a roof, which went from just past third, around past home plate, and down to the end of the infield at first base. Single-decked stands then went down each foul line to the foul poles. A long stretch of open bleacher ran behind a five-foot concrete fence from the left field foul line across to center field. In 1920, a covered upper deck was added to the stands running down the foul lines, but the outfield bleachers remained as they were. The seating capacity was increased to 32,000. In the 1950s, a 56-foot high National Bohemian Beer bottle stood on top of the right field scoreboard; if a batted ball hit the bottle, it was in play.

Late in the stadium's life, in 1956, after right-handed sluggers like Al Simmons, Zeke Bonura, and Bob Johnson had come to the Senators and gone away, frustrated by the faraway barrier in left field, the club put up ten rows of bleachers and an interior fence which reduced the distance to 350 feet, for the benefit of such hitters as Roy Sievers, Jim Lemon, and Harmon Killebrew, although the last-named may not have needed the help. (Paul Richards once viewed one of Killebrew's drives and said, "That one's out of any park, including Yellowstone.")

Once before, in 1947, Clark Griffith had reluctantly permitted a temporary fence in left, shortening the distance from 407 to 375 feet. As an old pitcher, Griff saw no reason to aid hitters, and after Opening Day, when both Tommy Henrich — a left-handed hitter — and Allie Reynolds — a pitcher — hit Yankee home runs over the new fence, Griffith had it down the next morning. When Joe DiMaggio hit three balls the next day that were caught at the base of the permanent bleachers, he said, "I was swinging late — twenty-four hours late!"[4]

Griffith, who had posted a pitching record of 237 wins and 146 losses from 1891 to 1906, came to Washington before the 1912 season as manager, after running clubs in Chicago, New York and Cincinnati from 1901 to 1911. Tom Noyes also allowed him to purchase a 10 percent interest in the franchise. Noyes died unexpectedly on August 21, 1912, after which Benjamin Minor, a prominent D.C. attorney and part-shareholder in the club, became team president. In 1919, Minor and his associates sold the controlling interest in the club to Griffith and a Philadelphia grain broker named William Richardson, who was happy to let Griffith run things thereafter. Griffith, whose nickname developed over the years as "the Old Fox," stepped down as manager after the 1920 season, becoming club president and naming the augmented ballpark after himself.

At the start of the ballpark's career, there were two noted pitchers in Washington. One was President William Howard Taft, the 330-pound

Republican from Cincinnati, Ohio, who threw out the first ball on Opening Day in 1910, in the old park, repeated the feat in 1911, in the new park, and established a tradition which saw many chief executives over the years coming to Griffith Stadium for an Opening Day toss. The President's box was reserved for him, next to the first base dugout, and the last one to occupy it was John F. Kennedy, on April 10, 1961.

The other hurler was a right-handed sidearmer, born in Humboldt, Kansas, but signed by a Washington scout out of Idaho, who may have been the best pitcher baseball has ever known. His name was Walter Johnson, and he spent his entire career, from 1907 to 1927, with the Senators. Johnson won 417 games, the most by any pitcher in the twentieth century (and second all-time, behind only Cy Young), threw a record 110 shutouts, and held the strikeout record with 3,509 Ks for fifty-five years, until it was broken by Nolan Ryan in 1983. Johnson, nicknamed "the Big Train," threw a fastball unlike any other in his time. Sam Crawford of Detroit once talked about Johnson:

> Did you ever see those pitching machines they have? That's what Walter always reminded me of, one of those compressed-air pitching machines. They gear them up so that the ball comes in there just like a bullet. It comes in so fast that when it goes by it *swooshes*. You hardly see the ball at all. But you *hear* it. *Swoosh*, and it smacks into the catcher's mitt. Well, that was the kind of ball Walter Johnson pitched. He had such an easy motion it looked like he was just playing catch. That's what threw you off. He threw so nice and easy — and then *swoosh*, and it was by you.[5]

Johnson was a kind-hearted individual, and he worried about hitting batters with his fastball, fearful that he might maim or kill somebody. Ty Cobb was aware of this fear and took advantage of it, standing closer to the plate against Johnson than he did normally. It did him little good, as Johnson won twenty or more games twelve times (ten years in a row), thirty or more twice (36–7 in 1913), led the league in strikeouts twelve times, and had a career ERA of just 2.17. The Big Train indeed!

For most of those years, the teams that Walter Johnson pitched for were not very good. In his 21 seasons, his team finished in the second division ten times, including seven years in seventh or eighth place. Twenty-six times Johnson lost 1–0 games, and in 65 of his lifetime 279 losses his team scored no runs. Obviously, these Senators were much better with Johnson than they would have been without him. He pitched for two pennant winners, in 1924 and 1925, with a combined record of 43–14, at the ages of 36 and 37.

The Senators won the first pennant in their history in 1924, with second baseman Stanley "Bucky" Harris as the manager, the first year in his long managerial career. Led by the hitting of outfielders Sam Rice and Goose Goslin and the pitching of Johnson, who led just about every hurling category in the league that season, the club finished two games ahead of the Yankees.

For the World Series, Griffith added 17 rows of temporary seats in front of the bleachers in left as well as a few more temporaries in the right centerfield corner. Walter Johnson lost the first game of the Series at home to the New York Giants, 4–3, before 35,760, but the Senators won Game Two by the same score before an even larger crowd. The Giants won two of the three games in New York, defeating Johnson again in Game Five, but Tom Zachary won the sixth game, 2–1, back at Griffith, leaving everything up to the final game. Curly Ogden started for the Nats, but after a walk and a strikeout he was relieved. Manager Harris hit a home run in the fourth, giving Washington a 1–0 lead, but the Giants came back with three in the sixth on Washington errors. In the bottom of the eighth, Harris hit a grounder toward third which bounced over the head of Freddie Lindstrom for two tying runs. Johnson came in to pitch in the ninth and shut the visitors out for four innings, fanning five along the way.

In the bottom of the twelfth, with one out, catcher Muddy Ruel hit a popup behind the plate. Giants' catcher Hank Gowdy tripped over his own mask and missed the foul, and the reprieved Ruel then doubled to left. New York shortstop Travis Jackson then booted Johnson's ground ball, and Earl McNeely hit another grounder to third. Once again, the ball apparently hit a pebble, bounced over Lindstrom's head, and rolled into left as Ruel raced home with the Series-winning run. Griffith Stadium was the home of the World Champions! And the city of Washington had itself a major celebration.

In 1925, the Senators again won the American League pennant and faced the Pittsburgh Pirates in the Series. The Big Train was at his best in the opener, winning a 4–1 five-hitter, with ten strikeouts. The Pirates won the next day, but Washington won the next two at home, with Johnson pitching a 4–0 whitewash in Game Four before 38,701, the largest crowd ever at Griffith Stadium. The Pirates won the last game in Washington and Game Six at Forbes Field, once again bringing it down to the final game. Johnson pitched the full game but gave up fifteen hits and five earned runs, as the Pirates won the Series with a 9–7 victory. Nats' shortstop Roger Peckinpaugh, the American League MVP that year, had a bad day in the field with errors in the seventh and eighth innings leading to four unearned runs which decided the contest.

The most famous moment in that Series took place in Game Three, in Griffith Stadium, when Nats outfielder Sam Rice, with his team leading 4–3, chased a long drive by Pirate Earl Smith into right-center field. Rice, elected later to the Hall of Fame for his 19 years with the Senators as a great contact hitter and speedster, with a career batting average of .322 and 351 stolen bases, appeared to catch the ball at the fence of the temporary stands. He then toppled into the stands, disappearing from view. When he climbed out, he had the ball in his glove and Smith was called out. There was great controversy as to whether Rice actually caught the ball and kept it in his possession the whole time. Sam Rice was always coy about whether he really had it, but he'd say, "the umpires said so." He declined offers to write paid articles about the catch, preferring the mystery, but he wrote a letter to be opened after his death. After a description of the play, Rice said, "At no time did I lose possession of the ball."[6]

After 1925, the Senators stayed in or near the first division for three more seasons under Bucky Harris (who would return for two more tenures as Washington manager, 1935–42 and 1950–54, thirteen more seasons in all, but never approach his earlier success) and four under Walter Johnson, but they never got close to another flag in those years. In 1933, though,

Right centerfield, Griffith Stadium, showing the wall built around houses in center field, August 29, 1959 (photograph by the author).

once again with a player-manager in his first year at the helm, this time shortstop Joe Cronin, the Nats broke through to win a third pennant, finishing seven games ahead of the Yankees.

Led by first baseman Joe Kuhel, second sacker Buddy Myer, and outfielders Heinie Manush and Goose Goslin, as well as Cronin the shortstop, the Senators piled up 99 wins, the most in the team's history, before or after. While Jimmy Foxx of the A's captured the Triple Crown that season, Kuhel, Myer, Cronin and Manush all hit over .300, Manush led the league in hits, and right-hander Alvin "General" Crowder tied Lefty Grove for the most wins, with 24.

Unfortunately, the World Series went to the Giants in five games, with the only Washington win coming via a five-hit shutout thrown by southpaw Earl Whitehill in Griffith Stadium in Game Three. When the next two games were won by the Giants there, no one knew it then but these were the last World Series games ever to be played in the nation's capital (at least to this time). No Washington team has won a pennant since 1933.

In the years since, the Senators were blessed with some very fine ballplayers, like Mickey Vernon, a first baseman who won two batting titles for the Griffmen; infielder Cecil Travis; the inimitable and loquacious Bobo Newsom, who had five different stretches with the Senators, from 1935 to 1952; outfielder Ben Chapman; third-baseman Buddy Lewis; catcher Rick Ferrell and his pitching brother Wes; outfielder George Case, who led the league in stolen bases every year from 1939 through 1943; pitchers Sid Hudson and Early Wynn; and the fine knuckleballer Emil "Dutch" Leonard.

Something else the Senators had which no other team could boast was a comedy duo, coaches Nick Altrock and Al Schacht, the "Clown Prince of Baseball." Altrock had a pitching career from 1898 to 1909 and then served as a Senators coach from 1912 to 1953 (with very occasional game appearances from 1912 to 1933, more for comic effect than anything else), the longest coaching tenure with one team in major league history. Schacht had a brief career as a pitcher for the Nats, with a record of 14–10 from 1919 to 1921, and coached for the team from 1924 to 1934. He and Altrock developed a comedy routine both on the field and in vaudeville during the off-season, which delighted fans at the ballparks and viewers in theatres. Ironically, the two men also came to have deep personal animosity toward one another and eventually refused to speak to each other, even while making thousands laugh.

Two media stars covered the Senators for long stretches of their existence. Arch McDonald, a native of Arkansas whose Southern idiom was beloved in Washington, did the Senators' games on the radio — sometimes recreated, sometimes live — from 1934 to 1956, with one year out — 1940, when he took on and failed at the job of broadcasting New York Yankee and Giant home games, though he coined the phrase "the Yankee Clipper" for Joe DiMaggio. Too homespun for Gotham audiences, McDonald returned to the Senators in 1941 and became a local institution. He was called a combination of a hillbilly show and a carnival. His most famous saying, after a Senators win, was, "Well, they cut down the old pine tree."

In the press box at Griffith Stadium was Shirley Povich, who joined the *Washington Post* in 1923, became a sports columnist in 1933, and wrote about the Nats as long as they were in town, keeping up his column until his death in 1998, although technically he "retired" in 1973. Both McDonald and Povich have been honored with inclusion in Cooperstown's Hall of Fame, in the broadcasters' and writers' wings.

When the Senators fell from first to seventh in 1934, Griffith curtailed his spending, even selling Cronin, his manager and by then his son-in-law, to Boston for cash. Griffith, the "Old Fox," was proud of his frugal operations, and he made money — not always a lot — for twenty-one consecutive seasons. Griffith knew from experience over many years that building a loyal fan base in Washington and its environs was difficult because, as the home of the national government, so many of the residents came from somewhere else around the country. When the Cleveland Indians came in, the Senators might draw some displaced Ohioans for the games, but these folks were unlikely to come back to watch the Tigers or the Red Sox.

Griffith hired Joe Cambria, an Italian-born laundryman from Baltimore, named him chief scout, and sent him off to Cuba to find inexpensive ballplayers there. Over the years, Cambria, "Papa Joe" as he was known to his Cuban protégés, signed an estimated 400 Cubans to Washington contracts. Many of them, from Roberto Estalella his first to Tony Oliva his last, made it up to the majors with the Senators or, later, the Twins. Mike Guerra, Rene Monteagudo, Gilberto Torres, Alex Carrasquel, Pedro Ramos, Camilo Pascual and Julio Becquer were among the Cambria signees to make the grade. After Jackie Robinson made the Dodgers in 1947, Cambria was able to expand his scouting outlook to include black players, quite a few of whom he signed.[7]

In 1945, the Senators, managed by this time by their old third-baseman Ossie Bluege, were notorious for presenting a starting pitching staff made up exclusively of knuckleball throwers: Leonard, Roger Wolff, Mickey Haefner, Marino Pieretti, and Johnny Niggeling. Some wags suggested that catcher Ferrell deserved the Congressional Medal of Honor for his work in handling that bunch (others said this duty was what got Ferrell elected to the Hall of Fame, overlooking the eight All-Star teams Rick was named to). Nevertheless, the '45 Senators came closer to another pennant than any other Washington team, although, amazingly, they hit only one home run all season long in their spacious home ballpark — and that one was an inside-the-park job by first baseman Joe Kuhel. Unfortunately, owner Griffith had made arrangements for the football Redskins to take over Griffith Stadium during the last week of the baseball season (the football rent money thus started coming in earlier), so the Senators were forced to sit out that last week, their schedule completed, and watch the Tigers win the pennant on the last day of the season.

In 1946, the first postwar season, the club had its only year of attendance over a million, 1,027,216 to be precise, but the Senators fell back under .500 and never contended again in their remaining 14 years in Washington. Late in the '50s, the club started to gather promising players like slugger Killebrew (nominally a third baseman, but actually a player management tried to hide in the field; the DH would have been perfect for Harmon), first baseman Roy Sievers, outfielders Bob Allison and Jim Lemon, and pitchers Camilo Pascual and Pedro Ramos, but they would ultimately blossom in Minnesota, after the Senators, now run by Calvin Griffith since his adoptive father Clark died in 1955, moved there following the 1960 season and would win a pennant there in 1965.[8]

There were no more World Series games played at Griffith Stadium after 1933, but the All-Star game was played there in 1937. The American League won it, 8–3, with President Franklin Roosevelt in attendance. Earl Averill hit a line drive in that game which caught Cardinal pitcher Dizzy Dean on the foot, breaking his toe. Dean, anxious to get back on the mound, returned to pitching before the break was fully healed and, as a result, favoring his toe, injured his arm, an injury which ultimately cost him his pitching effectiveness and ended his career long before age might otherwise have done so. Another All-Star game took place at Griffith in 1956. Willie Mays, Stan Musial, Ted Williams, and Mickey Mantle each hit a home run as the Nationals won, 7–3, with Cardinal third-baseman Kenny Boyer getting three hits and playing spectacularly in the field.

The All-Star home runs reminded Washington fans of how hard it had been to hit homers in Griffith Stadium for most of its existence, up until the alterations that had taken place that year. Babe Ruth once hit a ball that soared over the center field fence and landed in the trees beyond. The back wall of the left field bleachers was only cleared three times in the

The stands behind first base and down the right field line, Griffith Stadium, August 29, 1959 (photograph by the author).

park's history, twice by Josh Gibson of the Homestead Grays and once by Mickey Mantle. When Mantle hit his shot, against Nats' lefty Chuck Stobbs in 1953, the Yankees' public relations man Red Patterson promptly went to work to measure its distance, and he came up with 565 feet before the ball came to a stop in a backyard on Oakdale Street. But such drives in or out of old Griffith Stadium were few and far between.

The ball park was home to several Negro League teams over its existence, the Washington Potomacs in 1924, the Washington Pilots in 1932, the Washington Elite Giants in 1936-37, the Homestead Grays (who also played out of Pittsburgh) in 1937–48, and the Washington Black Senators in 1938.

As mentioned earlier, Griffith Stadium was the home grounds of the Washington Redskins in the National Football League for 24 years, from the time George Preston Marshall brought them from Boston in 1937 until they moved to the new D.C. Stadium after the 1960 season. The most famous (or notorious, depending on the vantage point) NFL game played there was the 1940 league championship contest, in which the Chicago Bears beat the Redskins by the astounding score of 73–0. Two years later the two teams met in Griffith Stadium in another championship clash.

Marshall's pregame talk to his team consisted of writing "73–0" on the blackboard, after which the Redskins went out behind their great quarterback, Sammy Baugh, and upset the previously-unbeaten Bears, 14–6.

It was in Griffith Stadium on December 7, 1941, during a game between the Redskins and the Philadelphia Eagles, that the P.A. announcer directed all admirals and generals to report to their duty stations, without informing the game's attendees the reason for such a call, the Japanese attack on Pearl Harbor.

There were also college football games staged in Griffith Stadium over the years. Georgetown University used the field from 1925 until giving up football after 1950, the University of Maryland played there in 1948, and George Washington University played games there in the 1930s and '40s.

The final years of the original Senators and the first year of the expansion team saw fewer and fewer fans coming to the old ballpark. One factor was the move of the St. Louis Browns to Baltimore for the 1954 season (about which old Clark Griffith was none too happy) and the resulting cutoff of Baltimoreans coming to Washington for their big league baseball. The smallest "crowd" of all in Griffith Stadium was the 460 folks who showed up for a game on September 7, 1954, with the Philadelphia Athletics, a team that was used to small turnouts by that time and would soon leave for Kansas City because of them.

The final game at Griffith Stadium took place on the afternoon of September 21, 1961, between the expansion Senators and, ironically, the Minnesota Twins, one year gone from the old park themselves. Neither team was going anywhere, and the worst crowd of the season, only 1498 fans, "faithful to the end," as the *Post* put it, showed up for the finale. "The tug of nostalgia had been overrated," declared veteran columnist Shirley Povich. 85-year-old Nick Altrock was there, but few others. Altrock had seen the first game ever played in the park, and now he saw the last. Bob Addie wrote about the contest for the hometown paper, saying, "There were no eulogies, no ceremonies, no tears.... It was a quiet, peaceful end to the old girl." "The gathering, though small," wrote Povich, "had intimacy."[9]

There were no ceremonies to mark the final game, because club president Elwood "Pete" Quesada, still negotiating rental terms for the new stadium, would not concede officially that this was the old ballpark's finale, although everyone knew that it was. Povich pointed out that the six black players in the starting lineups would have startled the ghost of old Clark Griffith, "whose party line for years had been, 'let them stay in their own leagues.'"[10]

Jack Kralick started for the Twins against Bennie Daniels for the Senators. Daniels, it may be noted, was the losing pitcher for Pittsburgh in the Ebbets Field finale. He was getting used to this kind of thing. Washington took a one-run lead in the second, on an error by Zoilo Versalles, but the Twins scored three in the fifth and two more in the sixth. Lenny Green drove in one run for the visitors, Killebrew and Versalles two each. In the seventh, wrote Povich, the ball park struck back:

> If a ballpark could talk back, that is what Griffith Stadium did to Harmon Killebrew in the seventh inning. That was when Killebrew hit a ball that would have been a home run all over the rest of the world, but in the biggest playing field in the majors it wasn't. The best that Griffith Stadium would yield to Killebrew was an off-the-wall triple at its defiant 428-foot sign in dead center field.

Killebrew later scored the final run in the Senators' 6–3 loss. Kralick got the win, though he left in the sixth with a blister, and Daniels the loss. The last batter in Griffith Stadium history was Danny O'Connell, who hit a feeble tap to the infield with two out in the ninth and Don Lee on the mound for Minnesota. Griffith Stadium was history.

With the final out, there was no reason to stay around the ballpark. No ceremony or other memorial was planned or took place. A few of the fans sat in their seats and gazed around the old place, remembering games that had taken place in years past, bringing back to mind old Senators stars — perhaps Mickey Vernon, Joe Judge, Cecil Travis, and Bobo Newsom — and even some lesser lights like Walt Masterson, Moe Berg, or Firpo Marberry. They looked out at the bizarre center field wall built around the houses out there, maybe recalling the aroma of pastry baking at the nearby Wonder Bread factory that told them they were getting close to the ballpark, then they got up and slowly walked out of Griffith Stadium for the last time.

The Senators moved the following spring to the newly-built D.C. Stadium (later Robert F. Kennedy Stadium, now itself gone). Two landmarks in Griffith Stadium, the memorials honoring Clark Griffith and Walter Johnson located at the main entrance to the first base grandstand, were moved, Johnson's to Walter Johnson High School in suburban Bethesda, Griffith's to D.C. Stadium. The old ballpark was demolished in 1965, its site utilized for Howard University's Medical Center and College of Dentistry.

Bucky Harris, Walter Johnson, Sam Rice and Ossie Bluege would have been sad to see it go. The success of the Senators in the old ballpark was limited, but it held a place, along with Clark Griffith himself, in the history of the nation's capital.

Chapter 6
A Fit Place for Polo

Baseball fans do not usually think of New York City as a place for playing polo. Indeed, most baseball fans, it seems safe to say, do not much think about polo at all. But there was a time, back in the 1870s, when the polo players of Gotham, specifically the Westchester and Manhattan Polo Associations, saddled up their ponies, got out their mallets, and got together for games at a field adjoining the northeast corner of Central Park, west of Fifth Avenue, from 110th to 112th Street. A few years later, John Day, the principal owner of the New York Metropolitans baseball club, an independent team, built a grandstand for a ballpark on that field and called it the Polo Grounds, probably so that his fans would know where to find it.

Day's Mets played there through 1882, at which time he and his associates had the opportunity to organize a team called the Gothams, formerly the Troy Trojans, for entry into the National League. This team played in the original Polo Grounds from 1883 to 1888, when they changed the team name to Giants. Day's Metropolitans, now in the American Association, the other major league at the time, also played in this park in 1884 and 1885.

In 1889, Manhattan officials chose to construct 111th Street through the outfield, so the ballpark had to go. Day decided to build a new facility — another Polo Grounds — in Coogan's Hollow, a meadowy area overlooked by Coogan's Bluff to the north and west, hard by the Harlem River. The Giants' park was between 155th and 157th streets in 1889 and 1890. Next door, between 157th and 159th streets, the rebel New York Players League team, also called the Giants, built a park (called Brotherhood Park) to play in during the 1890 season, a development which certainly did not please John Day, whose Giants lost several players to the PL team. The Giants owner, however, had the last laugh when the upstart Players League collapsed after that one season. Day acquired their ballpark and moved his team there, calling it the Polo Grounds after their old park.

This wooden park saw the coming of John McGraw as the Giants manager in 1902 — he would stay on for 30 years — as well as Fred Merkle's famous baserunning blunder on September 23, 1908, which resulted in a tie game and a makeup two weeks later which the Chicago Cubs won to clinch the National League pennant. It was possible for non-paying fans to climb trees behind the home plate grandstands and see into the park and for others to stand up on Coogan's Bluff and watch what was going on. On April 14–15, 1911, the wooden grandstands were consumed by fire, and all was destroyed except the right and center field bleachers, which were separated from the grandstand by a gap that kept the fire from jumping across.

The final manifestation of the Polo Grounds, the fourth or fifth ballpark to bear that name (depending on how you count some of the earlier ones) and the one that lasted until 1963, was the sixth concrete and steel ballpark in the majors. With part of the bleachers unburned, the team was able to open the new park on June 28, 1911, with a capacity of 16,000, although of course it was not completed by that hurried opener. By the time the Giants played the A's in the World Series that October, seating had been increased to 34,000, with a double-deck roofed grandstand reaching from down the left field line around to far down into fair territory in right. The owner of the Giants at that time, John T. Brush, tried to name the new facility Brush Stadium, but no one picked up on that and it was soon called the Polo Grounds once again.

For ten years, from 1913 through 1922, the Yankees also played their home games at the Polo Grounds, until Yankee Stadium was built. These included the early years of Babe Ruth's Yankee heroics, after his acquisition from Boston in 1920, as he introduced baseball to the longball era. In both 1921 and 1922, the entire World Series was played in the Polo Grounds, with the Giants beating Miller Huggins's Yankees both years.

The Giants franchise was sold in 1919 to Charles Stoneham for one million dollars, in a deal arranged by Arnold Rothstein, the gambling kingpin who was apparently behind the fixing of the 1919 World Series. Stoneham, a Tammany politico who was involved in some shady stock dealings, would own the club until his death in 1936, at which point it devolved upon his son Horace Stoneham, an amiable, hard-drinking man who had been raised in the administration of the ball club.

In 1923, the old bleachers were taken down and replaced by a double-deck grandstand which now encircled the entire ballpark, except for new bleachers and a clubhouse which covered a small part of center field.

The seating capacity was increased to 54,555. The Polo Grounds, as it then existed, was one of the most oddly shaped sites in which big league baseball was played, looking distinctly like a giant bathtub.

The distances down the foul lines were 279 feet to left field and 258 feet to right. Mel Ott, one of the premier Giant hitters over the years, perfected a lefthanded swing which propelled the ball right down the line, taking maximum advantage of that fence 258 feet away, and accounting for a great many of his 511 home runs. In addition, there was a 23-foot overhang in left field, and occasionally this would catch a fly ball for a home run that the left fielder otherwise might have shagged. The stands pulled sharply away from the foul lines, however, leaving the right and left centerfield gaps 455 feet from home plate and dead center field 483 feet out. Only four players — Luke Easter in a Negro League game, Joe Adcock in 1953, and Hank Aaron and Lou Brock on consecutive days in 1962 against Mets pitching — ever hit home runs into the center field stands. No one ever hit a ball to the clubhouse wall, let alone over it.

"Because of its odd shape, its short foul lines, its immense center field," wrote baseball historian Robert Creamer, "anything could happen at any time in the Polo Grounds."[1]

Several feet in front of the clubhouse in center was a five-foot-high memorial to Eddie Grant, a former Giant infielder who was the first major leaguer killed in World War I. The Grant memorial was in play and occasionally became a factor in a game, such as the time that lead-footed Giants catcher Harry Danning hit a ball that rolled behind it and scored while center-fielder Vince DiMaggio had trouble getting to the ball.

Another peculiarity of the Polo Grounds was that the outfield was slightly lower than the rest of the field, eight feet below the infield at the wall. Thus, a manager standing in the dugout could see only the top halves of his outfielders.

Strange though the ballpark was in some ways, it saw many great performances and many great performers. Christy Mathewson, of course, was one of the all-time top pitchers, and he spent most of his career with the Giants, playing for McGraw. Babe Ruth hit many of his early home runs in the three seasons he played in the Polo Grounds. Larry Doyle, Rube Marquard, Dave Bancroft, Travis Jackson, Frankie Frisch, George Kelly, Carl Hubbell, Bill Terry, and Mel Ott were among the Giants greats over the years. One of the greatest of all time, Willie Mays, played his first six seasons under Coogan's Bluff.

The Giants won 12 National League pennants between 1911 and 1937, the last three under Bill Terry after McGraw stepped down. They then had a 13-year drought, a period during which, tradition has it, Leo Durocher, managing the Dodgers, pointed across the field to Ott, his counterpart with the Giants at the time, and sneered that "nice guys finish last." (The Giants *did* finish last twice during Master Melvin's tenure at the helm, and he *was* generally considered a "nice guy.")

In mid-season 1948, there was a major upheaval in the city of New York, one which saw Durocher removed as manager in Brooklyn, only to replace Ott as the skipper of the Giants. Whatever one thought of Durocher as opposed to Ott personally, there can be no doubt that the fortunes of the Giants improved mightily. They went from a team of sluggers, waiting for Johnny Mize, Walker Cooper, Willard Marshall, or Bobby Thomson to bang one over the fence, to a squad of hustlers like Bill Rigney, Eddie Stanky, Alvin Dark and Whitey Lockman, scratching out runs where they could find them. Of course, it helped when a Negro League veteran like Monte Irvin came along, and even more when a youngster like Mays showed up, to help the pitching staff headed by Larry Jansen, Sal Maglie and Jim Hearn.

In 1951, the Giants were puttering along in mid-season, 13½ games behind the hated Dodgers, when they suddenly caught fire, winning 37 of their final 44 games. As August fell behind and September moved along, Durocher's men slowly and steadily cut into that Brooklyn lead until the last day of the season, when the two teams wound up in a tie, forcing a three-game playoff.

This led, in Game Three of those playoffs, to the greatest moment in Polo Grounds history. The first game, at Ebbets Field, went to the Giants, 3–1, when outfielder Bobby Thomson hit a home run off of Dodger right-hander Ralph Branca. Game Two, in the Polo Grounds, was won by Brooklyn, as Clem Labine threw a 10–0 shutout. Game Three matched the aces of the two staffs, Don Newcombe of the Dodgers and Maglie of the Giants.

The game was 1–1 until the Dodgers scored three off the tiring Maglie in the eighth inning. In the bottom of the ninth, Newcombe seemed to be losing his stuff, but he valiantly soldiered on. Alvin Dark led off the inning with a single, and Don Mueller singled to right, sending Dark to third. Monte Irvin, who led the National League in RBIs with 121, popped out on the first pitch. Whitey Lockman doubled down the left field line, scoring Dark and sending Mueller to third, where he slid in with an awkward slide, breaking his ankle. While Durocher put Clint Hartung in as a runner for Mueller, Chuck Dressen relieved the spent Newcombe with Ralph Branca, to face the Scottish-born outfielder Thomson. Branca got strike one on a fastball on the inside corner, then tried a fastball up and in. Thomson turned on it and lashed a line drive to left that soared over leftfielder Andy Pafko and into the lower stands just above the 315-foot marker. Suddenly, the Giants had won, 5–4, and had their first pennant since 1937. Thomson's home run has long been known as "the Shot Heard Round the World," as it was broadcast on Armed Forces Radio.

The resulting all-New York World Series in 1951 went to the Yankees, but the Giants were back in the Series in 1954, after taking the National League pennant by five games over the Dodgers. They took on a heavily-favored Cleveland team which had won 111 games and captured the American League flag by eight games over the Yankees.

With Sal Maglie pitching against the Tribe's Bob Lemon in the Polo Grounds, the score in Game One was 2–2 into the eighth. The first two Indians reached base, and lefthander Don Liddle was brought in to face slugger Vic Wertz. Wertz drove a ball deep to center field, where Willie Mays turned and raced back and improbably caught the ball, about 450 or so feet from the plate — perhaps the most famous catch in World Series history. Marv Grissom then relieved Liddle (the probably apocryphal story is that when Grissom came in after the Wertz out, Liddell said to him, "OK, I got my man") and retired Cleveland without a run. Then the Giants won the game in the tenth on a short fly straight down the right field line by pinch-hitter Dusty Rhodes — an out in most ballparks but a home run in the Polo Grounds. The Indians, bitten hard by both of the Polo Grounds' strangest features, the very short distance to right and the incredibly deep center field, went down meekly in the next three games and the New York Giants were world champs.

In 1955, the Giants dropped to third, 18½ games out, and attendance fell well below the million mark, to 824,112. Durocher was fired and replaced as manager by former infielder Bill Rigney but the team placed sixth in each of the next two seasons (spending most of 1956 in last place before surging at the end), with the gate falling to less than 650,000. The NFL Giants switched from the Polo Grounds to Yankee Stadium after the 1955 season, so revenues for owner Horace Stoneham and his baseball team fell off substantially.

The football Giants had played in the Polo Grounds since 1925, so their departure was a noticeable loss. Over the years a number of college football games were played there, by area teams such as Fordham and Army, and several Army-Navy games had taken place on the field. Soccer and Gaelic football were played in the Polo Grounds from time to time, and many important boxing bouts were held there, including the famous fight in 1923 between Jack Dempsey and Luis Firpo.

The ballpark was becoming obsolete and somewhat dilapidated in the late '50s, and maintenance and upkeep were allowed to lag. Soon Horace Stoneham started to look around for alternatives. His first thought was to move the ball club to Minneapolis. He, as well as all of baseball, watched as the downtrodden Boston Braves became the phenomenally-popular Milwaukee Braves. The Giants had the territorial rights to Minneapolis, with their farm club there, and it seemed to make sense that a team in Minnesota could be as successful as one in nearby Wisconsin.

It was not long, however, before another factor arose. As Walter O'Malley's plans for building a new ballpark in Brooklyn were being stymied by Robert Moses, the Dodgers owner started looking farther afield, much farther afield, to California. O'Malley talked to Stoneham and suggested that both clubs move to California — the Dodgers to Los Angeles and the Giants to San Francisco. The league clubowners who had to give permission for moves would presumably be more favorable if two teams moved to the West Coast rather than just one, and the Los Angeles/San Francisco rivalry could maintain, even three thousand miles west, the historic Dodgers/Giants rivalry. O'Malley did the necessary groundwork with San Francisco officials, so that it was practically a "done deal" for Stoneham.

And so it came to pass that on May 28, 1957, the Brooklyn Dodgers and New York Giants were given permission unanimously by the other clubowners to move to California. The approval, given at the National League's mid-season meeting in Chicago, "was predicated on two points: that the Giants and Dodgers request the shifts before Oct. 1, 1957, and that they make the moves together.... If one club wants to move and one wants to stay, the league would have to reconsider." O'Malley and Stoneham issued bland statements about this as merely giving them a chance to explore possibilities, but the fans in New York and Brooklyn knew what it meant.[2]

On September 26, 1957, Mayor Robert Wagner announced that he was creating a committee of businessmen to try to bring another major league club to New York City if the Dodgers left. Curiously, he did not mention the Giants, who were just as surely on their way west as the Dodgers were. Wagner declined to give any other information, such as who was on his committee. On the same day, New York Supreme Court justice Thomas Aurelio denied, with reluctance he said, a petition by Julius November, holder of ten shares of stock in the Giants' operating company, for an injunction against the Giants leaving town.

The next-to-last game of the Giants at the Polo Grounds drew only

2,768 spectators on September 28 to watch the Pirates win, 1–0, on a home run in the ninth by Frank Thomas against the Giants' Ruben Gomez.

That evening Horace Stoneham hosted a farewell dinner for Giants greats of the past — from the 1890s through McGraw's and Bill Terry's years and up to the stars who played for Ott and Durocher. Many great moments and great games of the past were rehashed at that dinner, but just about all of these gentlemen recognized the inevitability of what would be coming to pass. All of them would be present for the final game the next day.

By the time the Giants played their final home game of the 1957 season on September 29, there was no doubt what was happening. The day before, Bob Cooke in the *Herald-Tribune* said:

> They're going to wrap up the Polo Grounds tomorrow afternoon and say thanks for the memory. The Pirates will be on the lot to play a meaningless game with the Giants but there'll be a good crowd on hand to dignify the passing of the poor old ballpark. The ritual of Stoneham's last stand has been on the schedule for some time now. Each visitor walking through the turnstiles will shuffle the pages of his private album of Polo Grounds tintypes....[3]

It was a warm and sunny afternoon, but only 11,606 onlookers showed up for what everyone knew was the Giants' last game in the Polo Grounds. Tommy Holmes wrote in the *Herald-Tribune* that nothing was

> as intriguing as the crowd itself. There were many youngsters, some middle-aged but surprisingly few of the real old timers. You could easily sense that the elder statesmen among Giant fans felt that this farewell would be too tough to take. They stayed glued to their television sets, haunted by memories, stabbed by regret, frustrated because there was little they could have done to stem the tide of events which made Polo Grounds baseball unfashionable.[4]

Eighty-seven-year-old Jack Doyle, who had managed the team back in the 1890s, was on hand for the finale, as were so many old Giants heroes — George Burns, Red Murray, Larry Doyle, Hans Lobert, Blondy Ryan, Mel Ott, Frankie Frisch, Rube Marquard, Carl Hubbell, Hal Schumacher, Billy Jurges, Willard Marshall, Sid Gordon, Buddy Kerr, Sal Maglie, and Monte Irvin, to name a few — and even the widow of John McGraw. The old-timers reminisced about their days with McGraw or with Terry, and the more recent retirees talked about their experiences playing for Ott and Durocher. Manager Bill Rigney presented Mrs. McGraw with a bouquet of American Beauty roses, and she said, "I can't believe I'll never see the Polo Grounds again," as she struggled to keep back tears. "New York can never be the same to me." She said sadly, "It would have broken John's heart."[5]

Eddie Brannick, the Giants' secretary, who had been with the team since 1906, held court for a stream of sad visitors in his office before the game, and he said, "I still can't realize this thing has happened to us." Matty Schwab, the head groundskeeper, had lived with his family in the ballpark for eleven years, in a two-bedroom apartment under the left-field stands. He commented sadly, "We're dispossessed now, I guess. We'll miss being here," adding, "it has been a very happy home." And Eddie Logan, who managed the clubhouse, reminisced about the years since he had helped his father, who ran the clubhouse before him, starting in 1931: "This may not be the fanciest clubhouse in baseball but it has been a place that a lot of great guys — and I — have been proud to call home for a lot of years."[6]

George "Hooks" Wiltse, who pitched for the Giants from 1904 to 1914, was there. He looked around sadly and said, "New York without the Giants. New York without the Polo Grounds. I never thought it would ever happen. It's a sad day for me. But nobody ever beat time."[7]

Bill Rigney tried to put on the field a team resembling the pennant winners of 1951 and 1954, with Lockman, Thomson, Mays, Mueller, Rhodes, and Wes Westrum behind the plate. The Pittsburgh Pirates won the game, 9–1, with the Bucs' star pitcher Bob Friend throwing a six-hitter. Johnny Antonelli was the starting and losing pitcher for Rigney, and Dusty Rhodes drove in the last New York Giant run at the Polo Grounds, on a first-inning sacrifice fly. Frank Thomas and Johnny Powers hit home runs for the visitors, so there was no joy at all for the home team with a lopsided loss.

When Rigney walked out to change pitchers in the sixth inning, "the crowd booed the Giants' manager, and," wrote Red Smith, "this was the first time its voice was loud, though there had been decent applause before the game for Mrs. John McGraw and some of the old players." There had been "a pretty fair cheer" for Bobby Thomson when he came to bat, but mostly, said Smith, "the quiet was that of a wake." The customers were

> reluctant to leave. Most of them sat it out as the Giants dragged wearily to defeat. Pigeons kept circling overhead, as though impatient to move in, and one could fancy Robert Moses, blueprints of a housing project in hand, waiting to pounce.
>
> These Giants played as though they couldn't wait to get to San Francisco. They couldn't hit the ball or catch it, pick it up or hold it, and Rigney kept calling the bullpen for another bull....[8]

In the ninth inning, the public address announcer repeated the usual message about fans remaining in the stands until the players and umps reached their dressing rooms, and "a boo swept the stands like a cold wind in autumn foliage." When the game ended, after Willie Mays grounded out in the ninth and Rhodes followed suit with a grounder to Pirate shortstop Dick Groat, the young fans started leaping over the fences and onto the field even before Groat's throw reached first-baseman Thomas. The ballplayers had to make a mad dash for the center-field clubhouse, almost running for their lives, as the spectators poured onto the field behind them, snatching for caps and gloves. Manager Rigney and Don Mueller were the last to reach the center-field sanctuary.

When the fans got to the locked clubhouse, they sang a little song:

> We want Stoneham;
> We want Stoneham;
> We want Stoneham — with a rope around his neck.

The players flee to the center field clubhouse at the end of the Giants' last game at the Polo Grounds, September 29, 1957 (National Baseball Library, Cooperstown).

With the Giants owner declining to make an appearance, and with Mays not showing when a chant of "We want Willie" followed, the fans then went to work at tearing apart as much of the park as they could. Within a half hour after the game's ending at 4:35 P.M., the crowd had ripped up the regular and warm-up plates, the pitcher's rubber and the wooden base beneath it, two of the bases, the foam rubber sheathing on the outfield walls, and the bullpen sun shelter. They gouged out chunks of the outfield grass, carried away telephones, telephone books, signs and anything else movable or apparently immovable. Three young men even pried the bronze plaque off the Eddie Grant memorial, although this was later retrieved by the police.

After many of the fans had departed, a trio of musicians, two trumpet players and a trombonist, started playing in the visitors' bullpen in left field. They played a tune called the "Giants Victory March," which Stoneham had commissioned in 1946, and some ten or so fans stood by and sang the words, which they had heard over the years after a New York victory:

> We're calling all fans
> All you Giant ball fans
> Come watch the home team
> Going places 'round those bases.

The Giants management declined to play the song after the final game, and a number of fans who were still in the park wished the impromptu trio had not played it either. One 74-year-old housewife from Staten Island said, "This is a sad occasion. Do they want to hurt me more than they already have? I've still got a few tears left." And a taxi-driver from Manhattan looked at the group and said, angrily, "There's no excuse for what they've done. Imagine playing a song like that at this time. 'Come watch the home team going places 'round the bases.' Sure, they're going places, straight to California looking for gold."[9]

With most of the spectators gone, Bobby Thomson returned to the field from the clubhouse with his movie camera to take some shots of various scenes in the old park, particularly those left field stands where his historic home run off Ralph Branca had landed six years before. Then Thomson went home, too.

John McGraw's widow was the last to leave the old park.

So, the end came for the fabled and historic Polo Grounds. The Giants moved to San Francisco, and the tattered old ballpark sat empty. But then something strange happened, and the old park under Coogan's Bluff became the only one of the classic ballparks to have two closings.

Before the 1962 season, the National League expanded to ten teams, creating new teams from scratch in Houston and New York. The New York club, filling the void in the Big Apple that the league had felt since the Dodgers and Giants left after 1957, was called the Metropolitans, recalling the old 19th century team, and of course its name was shortened to the Mets. The Mets would play in the ballpark in Queens that Robert Moses had tried to force upon the Dodgers, but there was no park there in 1962. The Mets wound up playing 1962 and 1963 in the Polo Grounds.

It took some $250,000 to refurbish the old place for big league baseball, and there was considerable doubt that big league baseball was what the Mets staged there, but their attendance in the two years they played at the Polo Grounds was well above the Giants' attendance their last couple of years in New York.

The Mets' final home game of 1962 was supposed to be their last in the Polo Grounds, but the new Shea Stadium was not ready, so the club played another season in the old park. On September 18, 1963, though, the final game was played there, or, as a reporter for the *Times* put it, "it is hoped that no more Mets games will be played at the Polo Grounds — if only to put an end to the string of finales."[10]

Red Smith covered this final game as he had the finale of the Giants six years earlier, writing, "On the last day, the team and the customers and the script were tired," after the supposed final game at the end of the '62 season. "The weather was dismal. Jim Hickman got a home run but the Mets were never in the ball game as the Phillies made it easy, 5 to 1."[11]

Only 1,753 paying customers — the smallest fan turnout in the Mets' short history to that point — showed up for this finale. "The quiet gathering seemed more akin to a crowd at spring training," reported the *Times* correspondent, and "there wasn't too much fuss and bother about the affair yesterday." Southpaw Chris Short pitched the whole game for Philadelphia, giving up little more than the Hickman home run in the Phillies victory, with Craig Anderson of the Mets absorbing his 17th straight defeat. Three of the visitors' runs were unearned after a Ron Hunt error, and then singles by Tony Taylor, Wes Covington and Clay Dalrymple accounted for the final two runs that "ended the history of baseball scoring at the Polo Grounds." The game ended when Ted Schreiber hit into a ninth-inning double play started by Cookie Rojas, with first sacker Roy Sievers making the last putout ever at the Polo Grounds.

And, as the reporter, for the *Times* wrote, "hardly anyone cared."[12]

Red Smith described how, after the last game the year before, the Mets broadcasters, Lindsay Nelson, Bob Murphy and Ralph Kiner had cornered Mets manager Casey Stengel for an on-field interview, with the fans watching and cheering appreciatively. Now, in 1963, "once more, Nelson, Murphy and Kiner held Stengel at the microphone. They played to an audience of cops, grounds keepers, and news photographers.... The playing field was moist, but eyes were dry."[13]

The Polo Grounds Towers, a high-rise public housing building, was erected on the ground where the historic old ballpark stood, with memories of John McGraw, Bill Terry, Mel Ott, Christy Mathewson and so many other greats and near-greats floating in the breeze.

Chapter 7
Home of the Browns

St. Louis has long been regarded as a fine baseball town. The origins of the professional game in the Mound City go way back, to just about the beginning of professional ball anywhere. For most of that time, Sportsman's Park was where the game was played. The first diamond was laid out on the grounds at Grand Boulevard and Dodier Street on the north side of the city in 1866, with the first grandstand being built on the premises in 1871. This was the first of several structures located there for big league baseball. The park was initially called the Grand Avenue Ball Grounds.

In 1874, an entrepreneur named Gus Solari was granted a franchise in the National Association, the first professional baseball league, and the team, the Brown Stockings, played before a grandstand on the same grounds seating 800 persons, called the St. Louis Baseball Park.

The National Association went out of business after 1877, and St. Louis was without a baseball team. In 1881, a saloon-keeper named Chris Von der Ahe and a young sportswriter named Alfred Spink (some years later the founder of *The Sporting News*) organized the Sportsman's Park and Club Association, which acquired and renovated the old Grand Avenue park, which they now called Sportsman's Park. Spink organized a new Brown Stockings team, which booked games with other independent teams, and was so successful that the new American Association, organized as a major league in 1882, granted a franchise to Von der Ahe, for the Brown Stockings, or Browns. St. Louis was back in business.

Von der Ahe is one of the great characters in the early history of the game. An immigrant from Germany, he came to St. Louis, bought a grocery store near the ballpark, and opened a saloon in the back of the store. After baseball games, he noticed, quite a few of those attending stopped in his saloon, so he applied for and won the St. Louis franchise for $1800.

Though the 31-year-old knew nothing about baseball, he soon called himself "der poss president of der Prowns," with his German accent, bushy mustache, and sense of showmanship. He had the good sense to hire a fine first baseman and manager named Charlie Comiskey, and before long the Browns were the class of the American Association, winning four straight pennants from 1885 to 1888. Von der Ahe set his ticket price at 25 cents, so the Browns led the league in attendance and their fans had lots of money to spend on the owner's beer.

Von der Ahe demolished the old grandstand and erected double-decked covered seats behind the plate, with the stands down the line uncovered, presumably so the fans sitting there on a hot summer day would develop a thirst. He also converted a two-story house in the right field corner into a beer garden, and for several years the beer garden was in play, with the right fielder rummaging around for the ball among the customers and picnic tables. In 1888, the rules were changed to provide that a ball hit into the beer garden was a home run. In 1886, the park's capacity was doubled, to 12,000.

Von der Ahe's franchise flourished through the 1880s, but the Players League of 1890 caused it great harm. Most of the best players deserted the team, and the Browns suffered an economic disaster. The year 1891, the last year of the American Association, was little better, and though the Browns were taken into the National League in 1892, Von der Ahe found himself in financial difficulties. He moved the club to another location in St. Louis, at Natural Bridge and Vandeventer Avenues, in a facility first called New Sportsman's Park and later (with the change in ownership) Robison Field. In 1897, Von der Ahe lost his ownership of the baseball team, with the National League club changing its name first to the Perfectos and then to the Cardinals. Sportsman's Park sat vacant.

In 1901, when Ban Johnson organized his American League as a rival to the established Nationals, one of the original franchises was in Milwaukee, known as the Brewers. It was quickly agreed that Milwaukee at the start of the twentieth century was not quite a major league town, and plans were afoot almost from the start of the season to move the club, which finished last with a record of 48–89.

Ban Johnson persuaded a 33-year-old Cincinnati buggy manufacturer named Robert Lee Hedges to put up $35,000 for the Milwaukee club and move it to St. Louis. Hedges was a savvy operator; he sold his carriage business for good money in 1900, in part because he could see the threat the emerging auto industry would pose to his operation's profitability.

Hedges refurbished Sportsman's Park, named his new ball club the

Browns to recall the pennant-winning tradition of the 1880s, and promptly went out and signed almost all of the best players from the cross-town Cardinals. The National League team was unsuccessful when it sought an injunction against Hedges and the Browns, but the raid of the Cardinals talent produced a backlash of support for the senior circuit team, as well as a lasting resentment of Hedges.

Nevertheless, the Browns had a successful season in their first year, leading the American League most of the way, although in September they fell behind the Philadelphia Athletics and finished second. The Browns had money to spend; Hedges said, "We are in a position to pay as much as anyone for those we want."[1]

After the season, "Colonel Bob," as Hedges was known, showed that he meant what he said. He signed the New York Giants' emerging ace pitcher, Christy Mathewson, as well as Mathewson's catcher, Frank Bowerman, to Browns' contracts.[2]

Over the 1902-03 winter, negotiations were held between the American and National League magnates, in an effort to end the interleague war, which was driving down profits. One of the major issues was the disposition of players who had signed contracts with both leagues. As his contribution to the peace settlement, Hedges agreed to return Mathewson and Bowerman to New York. In Colonel Bob's obituary many years later, it was written that "Hedges was the one who held the key to the famous peace treaty of 1903." It is tempting, though, to think of the difference in the Browns' history if they had Christy Mathewson pitching for them over the next dozen or so years.[3]

While the Browns made Sportsman's Park their home during the baseball season, there was another group which made some history there — the football team of St. Louis University (not yet known as the Billikens). Eddie Cochems, the coach of the St. Louis squad, became known as "the Father of the Forward Pass," a play which was legalized in college football by a rules change after the 1905 season. The first legal forward pass was thrown by Cochems' star back Bradbury Robinson in a road game at Carroll College in Waukesha, Wisconsin, early in the 1906 season, but most of the St. Louis passes were thrown at Sportsman's Park. The locals walloped Iowa 39–0, and beat Kansas 34–2 on their way to an undefeated 11–0 season, outscoring their opponents, 407–11. Surprisingly, it was another seven years before Knute Rockne at Notre Dame made the forward pass an integral part of his offense. But they were throwing the ball around at Sportsman's Park for a number of seasons before the boys back east started doing it.

In the baseball season of 1908, the Browns, behind aging pitchers Rube Waddell and Bill Dinneen, were in the pennant race until late September, finally finishing fourth but only six and a half games back, exciting their fans after several years in the second division. The club drew 618,000 customers that year and Hedges made a profit of $165,000. Hedges, who liked to say that "I went into baseball purely as a matter of business," was delighted, and he poured much of that profit into major changes in his ball park for 1909, moving home plate to where the right field corner had been, and building a new steel and concrete grandstand, the second such in the American League, after Shibe Park in Philadelphia. The old wooden grandstand (formerly behind home plate) became the left field bleachers in the new configuration. The new capacity of Sportsman's Park was 18,000 at the start of the 1909 season, and it was up to 24,040 by June.[4]

Unfortunately, the Browns collapsed into seventh place in 1909, their attendance little more than half that of the preceding year, and Jimmy McAleer, the club's manager since it had joined the American League, was let go. Jack O'Connor managed the 1910 team, which lost 107 games and finished in the cellar. Hedges decided to sell the team after the 1910 season, and a local syndicate paid him $30,000 for an option to buy the club, an option on which it was never able to close. Hedges, $30,000 richer, carried on with the Browns but the next three seasons were just as bad. On October 7, 1911, with the Browns stuck in last place, only 66 customers showed up to see a game with Detroit.

Late in the 1913 season, Hedges named as manager a former Browns catcher, who also happened to be a lawyer, a teacher and a man of many ideas, a man named Branch Rickey. Hedges had an idea that the secret to building winning baseball teams was to own several minor league clubs, where promising players could be developed — an idea that Rickey enthusiastically shared. Unfortunately, before Hedges and Rickey could put their plans into action, the other major league owners, who disliked Hedges because they regarded him as cheap, changed the rules to make it illegal for a major league team to own a minor league club. At about the same time, the war with the Federal League erupted, and Hedges was fully occupied in keeping his Browns team intact against Federal raids.

Rickey managed the Browns in 1914 and 1915, finishing in the second division both seasons, with declining attendance, and when the major leagues worked out a peace settlement with the Federals after the 1915 season, Robert Hedges was ready to say "enough." One of the terms of the settlement was that Philip Ball, the owner of the St. Louis Terriers in the outlaw league, was to be allowed to buy a club in the majors. At first it

Sportsman's Park, St. Louis, home of the Browns and later the Cardinals (Philadelphia Athletics Historical Society).

looked as if Ball would buy the Cardinals, but when that fell through Hedges agreed to sell the Browns, including Sportsman's Park, to Ball, for a reported $525,000, representing a tidy profit for Colonel Bob, who was the only owner of the Browns ever to make money from the ball club.[5]

Phil Ball was a hard-drinking former cowhand and construction worker who had made a bundle manufacturing ice machines. Ball's first major mistake was a blow-up with Branch Rickey, over alcohol, of all things. Rickey, a teetotaler, was supporting the push for the national prohibition of alcohol sales, a position which offended Ball, who promptly sent Rickey on his way. Rickey's "way" was across town to the Cardinals, where he would stay for many years — as manager from 1919 to 1925 and as vice president and business manager (later called general manager) to 1942 — and develop the local National League club into a profitable winner.

In 1920, Ball decided to take in the Cardinals as tenants in Sportsman's Park, a move which allowed Sam Breadon, now the Cardinal owner, to sell decrepit Robison Field and invest the proceeds in Rickey's pet project, a farm system, now legalized. The farm system, which allowed the Cardinals to sign unproven talents and groom them at several levels on the way to the major league team, helped make the Cardinals a big-league power.

In 1922, the Browns, led by their great first baseman George Sisler, who batted .420; Ken Williams, whose 39 home runs led the league, four ahead of Babe Ruth; Urban Shocker and Baby Doll Jacobsen, almost won the American League pennant, ultimately losing out by one game to the Yankees. Attendance for the season jumped from 355,978 in 1921 to 712,918, a figure never before approached by the Browns (and never approached again). Ball made a profit that year, which he eventually chose to plow back into his ballpark. After the 1925 season, Ball proceeded with a major reconstruction of Sportsman's Park, putting a covered upper deck on the pavilions that went down to the foul poles, getting rid of the old wooden bleachers in the outfield and replacing them with concrete stands, and roofing over the single-decked right field bleachers. The seating capacity for the stadium was increased to 34,000, and the ballpark had now assumed the form it would retain for the rest of its existence.

Unfortunately for Phil Ball, his Brownies never needed the additional seats, but they came in very handy for the Cardinals when they won the National League pennant and then the World Series in 1926, outdrawing their landlords by 668,000 to 283,000. In the years ahead, Browns attendance was very low, reaching a nadir of 80,922 for the entire 1935 season. The Cardinals, as consistent winners, outdrew the Browns by multiples of two or three to one. From then on, the Cardinals owned St. Louis, and the poor Brownies were mostly just an afterthought. If you wanted to see the mighty Yankees or Athletics, you went to see them play the Browns, but otherwise you stayed home until the Cards were back in town.

Sportsman's Park's dimensions were slightly favorable to left-handed hitters. It was 310 feet down the right-field foul line and 351 feet to left. To dead center was about 422 feet, to left center 379, and to right center it was some 354 feet. The fences were 11.5 feet high. After a while, however, it was determined that the right field line was a bit too easy for southpaw swingers, so a 21.5 foot screen was put up in 1929 from the foul line to right-center field. This screen has been the source of a minor historical controversy, because it was not there in 1927, when Babe Ruth hit his 60 home runs, and it *was* there in 1932, when Jimmy Foxx of the A's hit 58. Of Ruth's 60, he hit only four in Sportsman's Park, although it is logical to suppose that one or two of them may have gone into the unscreened

Fans lined up for the Cardinals' 1926 World Series, Sportsman's Park (National Baseball Hall of Fame Library, Cooperstown).

right field pavilion. It has been claimed that Foxx hit the screen 12 times in 1932, balls that would have been homers in '27 but remained in play in '32. This may be so, although 12 shots to right in at most 11 games seems quite a lot for a right-handed power hitter. It makes for an interesting argument.

In 1927, a tornado blew through the ballpark, sending the pavilion roof off into the street and ripping phone booths loose to end up in the outfield. It was just one more misfortune that bedeviled Phil Ball and the management of the Browns.

Ball died on October 22, 1933, having watched the Cardinals play three more World Series (1928, 1930, 1931) in the Browns' park, while his club struggled with ever-declining attendance, finishing with only 88,113 for 1933, including one game that drew but 34. Ball's estate ran the Browns for several years until a buyer could be found. Branch Rickey, of all people, found the buyers: Bill DeWitt, Sr., the Cardinals' team treasurer, and Donald Barnes, president of American Investment Company, who bought the franchise for $325,000, although Ball's estate retained ownership of the ballpark. Barnes put up $50,000, DeWitt $25,000, and they raised the rest by selling stock to the public at five dollars a share. Barnes took over the operation of the team.

Nothing much changed. The Cardinals, now featuring the famous Gashouse Gang led by manager Frankie Frisch with players Leo Durocher, Dizzy and Paul Dean, Pepper Martin, Joe Medwick, Spud Davis and Ripper Collins, won the World Series in 1934 and, with the help of Martin's Mud-Cat Band, captured the attention of the baseball universe. The Browns finished seventh, eighth, seventh and eighth for their new owners. As the years passed, the Browns vied with the A's, the Senators and sometimes the White Sox to keep out of the cellar, while the Cardinals moved from the Gashouse Gang to Billy Southworth's team of Terry Moore, Enos Slaughter, Mort and Walker Cooper, and — the best of all — Stanley Frank Musial.

The most famous fan in Sportsman's Park history was a woman called Screechin' Screamin' Mary Ott, who sat behind first base and drove the Cardinals' opponents crazy with her eerie pig-sounding yells. The park was noted for its many games in 100-degree heat and for the hard-baked infield, which became harder and harder as the summer rolled on with both teams playing on it day after day. "It was a tough infield," Stan Musial later recalled. "With both teams using it, the field never got a chance to relax. It would get pretty chewed up and bare by August and September."[6]

On July 9, 1940, the All-Star Game was played in Sportsman's Park for the first time, and the National League won it, 4–0. Max West of the Boston Bees belted a three-run home run in the first inning against the Yankees' Red Ruffing, and Reds' manager Bill McKechnie called on his pitchers after that. Paul Derringer, Bucky Walters, Whitlow Wyatt and Larry French each worked two scoreless innings, and Carl Hubbell wrapped it up in the ninth, for the first All-Star shutout. The American Leaguers only managed three hits, two by Luke Appling of the White Sox and one by pitcher Bobo Newsom of Detroit.

In 1941, Donald Barnes had lights installed in Sportsman's Park, and the first night game was played on May 24 of that year, against the Cleveland Indians, before 25,562 spectators, the fourth largest single-game attendance the Browns would ever draw. One writer called "the field the best lighted in the world," with "a lighting strength unparalleled to date in any outdoor field." Don Barnes simply hoped that more fans, spared the blazing afternoon sun, would come to his ball games.[7]

There was in the early forties a nightclub under the stands at Sportsman's Park, featuring strip-tease dancers. Unfortunately, even with the occasional night games and strippers, attendance declined in 1941 to 176,240 for the year, and Barnes had had it with St. Louis. People ridiculed the Browns with a parody of the old tribute to George Washington: "First in shoes, first in booze, and last in the American League." So Donald Barnes decided to move his baseball team to Los Angeles after that season. And once again the Browns' ill fortune held true. The league meeting to give Barnes approval for his move was held in Chicago on December 8, 1941. In view of the attack on Pearl Harbor the day before, approval was denied.

Wartime ball saw Southworth's Cardinals win National League pennants in 1942, 1943, and 1944. And, to the amazement of all baseball, the Browns won their first and only pennant in 1944.

Manager Luke Sewell had a few stars like shortstop Vern Stephens and first baseman George McQuinn, and some serviceable journeymen like Chet Laabs, Mark Christman, Mike Kreevich, and Don Gutteridge, who had good seasons in 1944. The club battled down to the last day of the season against the Detroit Tigers, led by Hal Newhouser's 29 wins and Dizzy Trout's 27, and going into the final games the two teams were tied. For that last game, 37,518 fans showed up in Sportsman's Park, the largest crowd the Browns ever drew, and they watched Laabs hit two home runs to beat the Yankees, 5–2, behind Sig Jakucki. Meanwhile, the Senators defeated Trout and the Tigers, and the Browns had won the pennant.

And who would they play in the World Series? None other than the Cardinals, easy winners in the National League. So the entire Series was played in Sportsman's Park. The Cards featured an infield of Ray Sanders, Emil Verban, Marty Marion (voted MVP that season), and Whitey Kurowski, with Musial, Johnny Hopp, and Danny Litwhiler in the outfield. Big Walker Cooper caught a fine pitching staff led by his brother Mort, with Max Lanier, Ted Wilks, and Harry Brecheen. The Browns' strength was in their pitching, with Nelson Potter, Jack Kramer, Bob Muncrief, Sig Jakucki, and Denny Galehouse.

In Game One, the Browns collected just two hits off Mort Cooper, but one of them was McQuinn's two-run homer in the fourth inning, giving Galehouse just enough for a 2–1 victory. Game Two went to the Cards, 3–2 in eleven innings, behind the pitching of Lanier and reliever Blix Donnelly, who threw four brilliant relief innings. The Browns won the third game, 6–2 behind Kramer, but that was it for the American Leaguers. In Game Four, Musial's hitting and Brecheen's pitching gave the Cards a 5–1 win, and the next day Cooper outpitched Galehouse, 2–0, as Sanders and Litwhiler hit home runs. Finally, in Game Six, Ted Wilks relieved

Lanier in the sixth with the Cardinals up 3–1 and the Browns threatening. Wilks retired eleven men in a row, the Cards won, 3–1, and the World Series was theirs.

The next year both St. Louis teams faltered. The Cards finished three games behind the Chicago Cubs, while the Brownies came in third, six games behind the Tigers. The Browns got some headlines in 1945 when they brought up outfielder Pete Gray from the Memphis Chicks. Gray, born Peter Wyshner in the Pennsylvania anthracite region, had lost his right arm in an accident at the age of six, but he was determined to play baseball and taught himself to throw and bat with his left arm. He developed a smooth motion after catching a fly ball whereby he flipped the ball in the air, tucked his glove under the stump of his right arm, caught the ball and was ready to throw. Gray had hit well for Memphis, in the Southern Association, and the Browns purchased his contract. He hit only .218 in 77 games in 1945; his greatest hitting problem was not the fastball, for which he got the timing of his one-armed swing down pretty well, but the curve and change-up, which messed all the timing up. Gray was a fan favorite, but many of his teammates felt that his presence on the Browns roster may have cost them a shot at a second pennant. After 1945, Pete Gray returned to the minors, where he continued to play for several more years.[8]

Even with their one-armed attraction, the Browns' attendance fell off in 1945, and Don Barnes chose once again to let go. On August 10, 1945, he sold his majority interest to Richard C. Muckerman, who took over the reins of the ball club from Barnes and ownership of Sportsman's Park from Phil Ball's estate (for about $450,000). Muckerman, however, was not able to do much with the Browns, although he did some $750,000 worth of remodeling of Sportsman's Park, including installing a rooftop press box and penthouse along with an elevator. The year 1946, the first postwar season, saw great increases in attendance all over baseball, but the gate for the Browns went up only slightly. For the Cardinals, now managed by Eddie Dyer, attendance surged to more than a million, as they finished the season in a tie with the Brooklyn Dodgers. After winning the first two games of a best-of-three playoff, the Cards went on to an exciting seven-game victory over the Red Sox in a World Series highlighted by Harry Brecheen's three pitching victories and Enos Slaughter's daring dash from first to home at Sportsman's Park with the winning run in Game Seven.

The Browns won some lower-case headlines in 1947 when the team purchased two former Negro League stars, Henry Thompson and Willard Brown, from the Kansas City Monarchs. Of course the Browns were the third team to recruit black players, behind the Dodgers and the Indians, but it was still a nice gesture for a club which had maintained segregated seating in Sportsman's Park until 1944 (black fans were restricted to the right field pavilion). The addition of black ballplayers, it might be noted, was not given universal acclaim in St. Louis, many of whose denizens still considered their town Southern. Willard Brown was voted into the Hall of Fame in 2006, but it was for his play in Negro ball, where he was a top slugger, not for the .179 average he compiled in 21 games for the Browns. Thompson hit .256 in 27 games before the Browns let him go; he came back to the majors with the Giants in 1949 and put together eight solid seasons in the Polo Grounds.

The All-Star game returned to Sportsman's Park in 1948. Four of the top American League stars — Joe DiMaggio, Hal Newhouser, George Kell, and Ted Williams — were suffering injuries which curtailed their use: DiMaggio and Williams only as pinch-hitters, Newhouser as a pinch-runner, and Kell not at all. Still, despite a two-run home run by Stan Musial, the Americans behind strong pitching from New York's Vic Raschi and the A's Joe Coleman came through with a 5–2 victory.

The Browns were a bad team after the war, and their attendance figures, down around the 300,000 level or lower, were far behind the million-plus gate the Cardinals were drawing each year. They had occasional standouts, like Bob Dillinger, who led the league in stolen bases for three years, Roy Sievers, who was Rookie of the Year in 1949, and Johnny Berardino, a weak-hitting infielder who left baseball to become a big star on television, playing Dr. Steve Hardy on *General Hospital* from 1963 till his death in 1996. But the fans did not come.[9]

In 1948, Muckerman sold the team to Bill and Charlie DeWitt, and the DeWitt brothers (who employed a hypnotist and metaphysician named David Tracy in a futile effort to get their players to think better) sold it to Bill Veeck in July 1951. The Browns, under Veeck, didn't play much better, but they certainly became more interesting. Veeck put up a canvas streamer across the front of Sportsman's Park, reading "OPEN FOR BUSINESS UNDER NEW OWNERSHIP." The fans sat back to see what would happen. For his first Browns game, the new owner gave out 7,596 free bottles of beer.

About a month after he took over, Sportshirt Bill staged a big party at the ballpark to celebrate the fiftieth birthday of the American League and of Falstaff beer, one of the team's sponsors, and an unusual crowd of more than 20,000 showed up at Sportsman's Park. In between games of that evening's doubleheader with Detroit, a huge cake was rolled onto the field and out of it popped a 3-foot 7-inch midget named Eddie Gaedel, wearing a Browns uniform with a number 1/8 on the back (the uniform had belonged to the seven-year-old son of the former owner, Bill DeWitt, who had stayed with the team). All well and good, until the second game got underway and Gaedel suddenly appeared at home plate to pinch-hit for Frank Saucier, the announced leadoff hitter. Red Rolfe, the Tigers manager, ran up to the plate to protest, but when Browns manager Zack Taylor produced an actual signed contract for Gaedel, umpire Ed Hurley said he could bat. Bob Cain, pitching for the Tigers, called catcher Bob Swift to the mound to see how they could pitch to Gaedel. Swift came back and went down on his knees, while Cain threw four pitches, none of which got into Gaedel's one and a half-inch "strike zone." Veeck had told the midget, "Eddie, I'm going to be up on the roof with a high-powered rifle watching every move you make. If you so much as look as if you're going to swing, I'm going to shoot you dead." Little Eddie dutifully took his walk and trotted down to first base, to be replaced by a pinch runner. The Browns still lost the game.[10]

American League officials tried to have Gaedel's statistics stricken from the records of the game, but Veeck then demanded a decision on whether the Yankees' diminutive shortstop Phil Rizzuto was a short player or a tall midget. Gaedel stayed in the record books.

Five days later Veeck staged Grandstand Manager's Day for a game against the Athletics, with Browns manager Zack Taylor sitting in a rocking chair by the dugout while the fans, armed with "YES" and "NO" placards mailed out ahead of time, voted on whether to hit or take, bunt or swing away, and other decisions that had to be made. Ahead of time the Athletics' general manager, Arthur Ehlers, threatened to protest the game on the grounds that the Browns were making a travesty of the contest, but Veeck said Ehlers was just afraid his amateurs would outsmart the A's professionals. In fact, that was what happened: the Browns won, 5–3.[11]

There were some bright spots for the Browns in 1951. Pitcher Ned Garver had a record of 20–12, the first pitcher ever to win twenty games for a team that lost more than a hundred. The ancient Satchel Paige, who had pitched for Veeck in Cleveland, was signed and pitched in 23 games. Catcher Matt Batts hit .302. And second baseman Bobby Young led the league in double plays. That was about it. Attendance was up, but the Browns finished ten games behind seventh-place Washington.

In 1952, Veeck hired as his manager Hall of Famer Rogers Hornsby, a great hitter who had in the past turned the players on every team he managed against him. So it was with the Browns. After fifty games (with a 22–28 record), with the players constantly complaining about the tyrannical manager, Veeck let Hornsby go, and the players presented him with a two-foot silver loving cup, inscribed "To Bill Veeck, For the Greatest Play Since the Emancipation Proclamation." Former Cardinal great Marty Marion took over as manager and guided the Browns to a seventh-place finish.

Veeck, who lived with his family in a ten-room apartment he created in Sportsman's Park, felt that his imaginative doings would help the Browns overtake the Cardinals, led by a stodgy businessman named Fred Saigh, in popular esteem, perhaps even driving them out of town. (The Cards' lease had seven years to run; Veeck could refuse to renew it, if he were still around, and the Cardinals would have to find somewhere else to play.)

"As I saw it," said Veeck, "Saigh didn't have the foggiest notion of what he was doing." When the time came to paint the ballpark, with the Cardinals paying half the cost, Veeck had it painted brown, with not a trace of Cardinal red, much to Fred Saigh's fury.[12]

Unfortunately for the colorful Veeck, Saigh was caught in an income tax violation by the Federal government, and he wound up selling his baseball team before going to prison. When Bill Veeck learned that August Busch, the owner of America's leading brewery, Anheuser-Busch, was the new owner of the Cardinals, he knew there was no chance to overcome the popularity of the now-flush National League team. He started thinking of ways out of town for his Brownies.

Between the 1952 and 1953 seasons, Veeck worked with officials in both Milwaukee and Baltimore to arrange a move of the Browns. Milwaukee's territorial rights were owned by the Boston Braves, and owner Lou Perini refused to sell the rights to Veeck, ultimately moving his team to Milwaukee himself. The move of the Browns to Baltimore looked almost assured. But Bill Veeck, with his iconoclastic and flamboyant ways, was virtually *persona non grata* with the other American League owners, who denied his requested move.

Soon after the rejection of his move, Veeck sold Sportsman's Park to Gussie Busch. In a press release, Veeck's general manager, Rudie Schaffer said, "Purchase of the park by Anheuser-Busch will materially help the Browns' immediate operations and enable the club to clear debts incurred in recent years." The park's maintenance had fallen off, and ownership by the brewery would jump-start necessary rehabilitation efforts. Gussie Busch toured the ballpark he had just purchased and said, "The way it is now, I'd rather play in Forest Park," but the place was his. And, for the first time since 1920, suddenly the Cardinals became the landlord with the Browns as tenants.[13]

Busch changed the name of the park to Budweiser Stadium, until the National League owners advised him that having a stadium named after a beer was forbidden, an exercise in hypocrisy, of course, given the financial reliance clubs have on the beer sold in their parks. In any event, the name was changed to Busch Stadium, and so it would remain, even after the brewery brought out Busch beer in 1955.

The Browns, of course, still had to play out the 1953 season in St. Louis, with everyone knowing they were headed out of town at the first opportunity. Attendance, already low, dwindled; season tickets were cancelled. Veeck's club approached bankruptcy. And then came Bobo Holloman

Veeck had purchased Alva "Bobo" Holloman, a big right-handed pitcher, from Syracuse for $10,000 on a trial basis, with another $25,000 to be paid if Bobo was still a Brownie on June 15. Holloman was hit hard through spring training and in a few early-season relief appearances, and Veeck prepared to ship him back to Syracuse. Holloman pleaded with manager Marty Marion for a chance to start a game, so on May 6, he got a start against the A's. As Veeck later wrote, "everything he threw up was belted. And everywhere the ball went, there was a Brownie there to catch it." When it was over, Bobo Holloman had himself a no-hitter. He was one with the immortals, and naturally the return to Syracuse was out. Unfortunately, the games he threw afterward were bad, and he became, after Veeck finally managed to sell him back to the minors for $7500, the only pitcher in history whose only complete game in his career was a no-hitter.[14]

The last game of the Browns in their historic old park was played on September 27, 1953, before 3,174 die-hard fans who watched their team lose to the White Sox, 2–1, in eleven innings.

After the 1953 season, another American League meeting turned down Bill Veeck's proposed move to Baltimore, then approved the move to the Maryland metropolis when Veeck agreed to sell the franchise to a local group. St. Louis was now a one-team city, although Sportsman's Park still has the distinction of having the longest tenure of any park — 34 years — housing two major league teams.

For the next 12 and a fraction seasons, the story of Sportsman's Park, now officially Busch Stadium (though a great many St. Louisans still called it by its old name), is the story of the Cardinals. Gussie Busch spent more than a million dollars to spruce the old place up (and remove numerous building code violations that had been incurred in the Browns' late years), and his team continued to draw well.

The flagpole in center field, which had always been in play, was moved beyond the fence for the 1954 season. The center-field bleachers were closed, replaced by shrubbery and reducing seating capacity to 30,500. Every seat was repaired or replaced, and new loges were installed. Roomier dugouts and clubhouses were built. A large Anheuser-Busch eagle was installed on top of the left-field scoreboard, to flap its electronic wings after every Cardinal home run. Advertising was removed from the walls, so only Budweiser beer was promoted in the park. In 1955, Cardinal general manager Dick Meyer and manager Eddie Stanky decided to remove the famous screen in front of the right-field pavilion, given the team's predominantly left-handed lineup. After one season which saw more home runs hit in the ballpark than ever before the screen was put back up again, and four feet higher than before.

Stan Musial, who played his whole big league career in Sportsman's Park, liked to talk about it. "In the box seats around there," he said, "you noticed who was at the park because the playing field was so close to the stands. The same people would have those box seats year-round." The crowds, Musial recalled, were usually subdued. "Midwestern fans were like that," he went on. "In those days, it seemed like there were more businessmen around the box seats and the livelier fans usually sat in the bleachers. Those bleacher fans were something."[15]

There were some highlights in those last years of the ballpark. On May 2, 1954, Musial tore the Giants apart single-handedly, with five home runs, a single, and nine runs batted in during that day's doubleheader. In 1957, another All-Star game came to St. Louis. That was the year that enthusiastic Cincinnati fans stuffed the ballot boxes to elect Reds to seven of the eight starting positions; Musial was the only non–Red to win election. Commissioner Ford Frick intervened, removing two Reds, Gus Bell and Wally Post, and adding Hank Aaron and Willie Mays to the starting lineup. The game itself went to the American League, 6–5, with each team scoring three runs in the ninth.

In 1964, the Cardinals won their first pennant since 1946, taking advantage of the Phillies' historic ten-game losing streak in the final two weeks, while the Cards, led by manager Johnny Keane, just kept winning, finally clinching on the last day of the season. After a World Series win over the Yankees, Keane, who had learned of his probable replacement in mid-season, when the club was going nowhere, surprised the baseball world by walking out on the World Champions to take the manager's post with the Yankees (where his teams finished sixth and tenth in his two seasons).

Busch Stadium served as the home park for the St. Louis Cardinals after that National Football League team moved from Chicago in 1960. In their six years in the old park, the football Cardinals had two winning seasons for owner Violet Bidwell and her two sons, Charles and William, who took over after their mother died in January 1962. They featured some exciting players, like John David Crow, Sonny Randle, Charley Johnson, and Larry Wilson, but they were unable to make the playoffs. In 1964, disappointed with the slow pace that construction of a new stadium was taking, the Bidwell boys flirted with officials in Atlanta about a possible move, but nothing came of it, and the team stayed in St. Louis through 1987 before moving to Phoenix.

The area around Busch Stadium was deteriorating, as the ballpark's neighbors gravitated to the suburbs, and crime was increasing as business decreased. At one point a robber held up a ticket booth at the ballpark during a game and actually fired one shot, which flew past third baseman Ken Boyer on the field and wound up spent in the blouse of a 13-year-old girl spectator. There was very little parking around the ballpark, not a big problem in earlier days, when fans came on the trolley, but increasingly so as the automobile came to dominate transportation. The ballpark was aging, and Gussie Busch made a determination to replace it with a new stadium downtown.

Appropriate arrangements were made with the city of St. Louis, aided by a pledge of five million dollars from Anheuser-Busch, and ground was broken for the new park in 1964. The Cardinals had hoped to move into their new digs at the start of the 1966 season, with a big closing fanfare at the end of the '65 season, but the place was not quite ready, and the team continued to play at the old park until early May.

With the final game scheduled for the 8th, the team and the city got ready for a grand celebration. Gussie Busch said the final game would be televised even though there were still some seats available; this, he said, would "allow the greatest number of fans to see once more the place that must revive many memories for all Cardinal fans." (And perhaps even some old Browns fans.) On May 6, the *Post-Dispatch* headlined it: "Final Countdown Starts at Busch," and that evening there was a ceremony honoring Johnny Mize, "Big Jawn," as he was known, as one of the top eleven living Redbird stars. On Saturday the 7th it was Dizzy Dean who got the star treatment. When old Diz came out on the field, grabbed the p.a. system's microphone, and sang "The Wabash Cannonball," the crowd happily joined in. That evening, Station KSD-TV aired a special program, narrated by J. Roy Stockton, the retired sports editor of the *Post-Dispatch*, with film of old-time highlights in Sportsman's Park/Busch Stadium, and featuring interviews with George Sisler, Joe Medwick, and Terry Moore.[16]

On May 8, with the San Francisco Giants in town, the Cardinals got ready for their last game in the historic grounds at Grand Boulevard and Dodier Street. Before the game, there was a ceremony honoring George Sisler of the Browns, 73 years old, and the Cards' Stan Musial, whose career had ended there in 1963. Musial said, "This is a fine occasion, but a sad one.... There are a lot of memories here." Dizzy Dean, most of whose Hall of Fame career had taken place in Sportsman's Park (as well as seven years as a colorful radio broadcaster), showed up again, saying, "I hate to see this stadium go."[17]

Columnist Ed Wilks pointed out that, "oddly, the Old Lady [Sportsman's Park] wasn't dressed in her finery. Those ten pennants were missing, folded away some place, on the Old Lady's final hour."[18]

There were 17,803 for this last game, 15,503 paid, and they saw the Giants defeat the hometown team, 10–5. Former Cardinal Lindy McDaniel got the win for the Giants, and Tito Fuentes had five straight singles for the visitors. Bob Skinner of the Cards hit a home run; "last games" were becoming a sort of specialty for Skinner, who played for the Pirates in the last games at Ebbets Field and the Polo Grounds in 1957. (It was the last home run of Skinner's major league career.) Outfielder Mike Shannon, who had played in the park as a 14-year-old in the Catholic high school playoffs, hit the last Cardinal homer, and the Giants' Willie Mays hit the last home run of them all, in the ninth, off of lefty Hal Woodeshick, who said, "I made the record book." Jim Hart of the Giants had the last hit, a ninth-inning single, and Jerry Buchek, a local boy, was the last Cardinal baserunner, when he walked in the ninth. But then Alex Johnson bounced a ball to shortstop Jim Davenport, who started the double play that ended the game at 3:15 P.M. Ironically, Orlando Cepeda, the Giants first baseman who caught the final out, was traded right after the game to the Cardinals, so he had the odd distinction of playing the last game in the old ballpark for the visitors and the first game in the new park for the home team.

During the bottom of the ninth, with the Cards at bat for the final time, ushers and police moved onto the field to head off any vandalism. Not until after the closing ceremonies and after most of the crowd had left did they move aside to open the field to souvenir hunters.

Before the game, groundskeeper Bill Stocksick, who had laid the original home plate in 1909, said, tearfully, "I kinda think I'll never live it down, never forget this old place, but I guess I will." After the game, Stocksick dug up the current plate, with help from Gussie Busch and Richard

Amberg, the president of the Herbert Hoover Boys Club, to whom Busch then presented a deed to the ballpark. The plate was then helicoptered to the new downtown stadium where it was planted later that day by Musial and Joan Nolan, Miss Redbird of 1966. The band played "Auld Lang Syne" and the brief farewell ceremony came to an end. A few fans ran onto the field, pulling up turf and tearing at the padding on the outfield walls. Vandalism was light. A daughter of Red Schoendienst gathered up some dirt around second base, where most of her father's Hall of Fame career had transpired, and some fans worked at getting pieces of seats and other souvenirs. Some boys ran into the home team dugout, but not much was left there. A bulldozer drove onto the field and started digging up ground in left field, and the remaining fans started to boo; "it was like watching 'em throw dirt on the coffin," wrote Ed Wilks. Then the fans all filed out. "It's the end of a great era," said one officer, as he looked around the emptying old ballpark, "I hate to see it close." Sportsman's Park's era was over.[19]

The city's celebration, however, had barely begun. The closing ceremonies at the old stadium were followed by the Bicentennial Parade, a grand bit of hoopla with a theme of "St. Louis Through the Years," led by members of the Cardinals and featuring 23 floats (depicting such events as the Fourth of July, Charles Lindbergh's transatlantic flight, the Lewis and Clark Expedition, the 1904 World's Fair and the Gateway Arch), marching bands, and pretty girls. The parade started at 4:15 and at 6:00 it passed a reviewing stand on the east side of the new downtown stadium with Governor Warren E. Hearns, Lt. Gov. Thomas F. Eagleton, Mayor Alfonso J. Cervantes, former Mayor Raymond R. Tucker and others. The loudest cheers of the watching crowd were for Stan Musial, wearing his famous uniform No. 6 on the second float; most of the honored guests were well received, with Mayor Cervantes "the only dignitary to get a thorough booing."[20]

After the dedication of the new ballpark at 7:30, there was an entertainment program starting at eight and running for an hour and a half. Unfortunately, the weather took a turn for the worse, with the temperature dropping from 87 degrees at the end of the game to 54 degrees at 9:00, and cold winds that reached 43 miles per hour. Many of the chilled spectators, most of them in summer attire, departed the new stadium long before the program ended with the Cosmopolitan Singers doing "The Battle Hymn of the Republic" and "God Bless America" for a huddled group of holdouts. How much thought was given to old Sportsman's Park through all the tumult is open to question.

The old stadium would be demolished within six months by the Aalco

Wrecking Co., after season ticketholders were allowed to go in and remove their seats as souvenirs. Then the wrecking company held what was called a "giant garage sale" of whatever else was salvageable and desirable. Musial got four seats, Schoendienst and Ken Boyer had seats sent to their hometowns, and the Anheuser-Busch eagle wound up overlooking Interstate 40–64, near the Vandeventer overpass.

When the grounds were turned over to the Herbert Hoover Boys Club, there was no trace of a building remaining. There is, however, a diamond laid out for the boys to play on, exactly where it was for Stan Musial, Red Schoendienst, Lou Brock, Vern Stephens and Bob Dillinger back in the days of old. And buried beneath what used to be right field is a box containing the ashes of an unknown man whose undertaker brought it one day back in the '40s to Sportsman's Park, along with the man's request to be buried as near to where his idol Enos Slaughter played as was possible. The Cards' public relations director, Jim Toomey, Bill Stocksick and the undertaker went out to right field, long before anyone else was in the park, and buried the box.

Chapter 8
Redland Field aka Crosley Field

Cincinnati, the town on the Ohio River once known as "Porkopolis," later the "Queen City," prides itself on being the home of professional baseball, with the famous Red Stockings in 1869. Its old ballpark does not go back quite that far, but it was pretty old.

The Reds (at various times over the years called the Redlegs) were in the National League when it opened in 1876, and they played in various places — the Avenue Grounds, the Bank Street Grounds, and League Park — until 1894, when they moved into a new park, also called League Park, located at the intersection of Findlay and Western avenues in the West End of the city. In 1902 the name of this park was changed to the Palace of the Fans, and the Reds played there through the 1911 season, when the place burned.

A new ballpark was built on the same site, using modern steel-and-concrete construction technology, and it opened on April 11, 1912, with the Reds beating the Cubs, 10–6, before 23,500 fans. Johnny Evers (of "Tinker to Evers to Chance" fame) was the first hitter. The new structure was called Redland Field, and it was here that the Cincinnati Reds played until the park's closing in 1970. But a lot happened in and to the place along the way.

There was a lower deck grandstand behind home plate and extending down the foul lines all the way to the foul poles in right and left, with an upper deck running about 30 feet past both the first and third base dugouts. Bleachers behind right field, called the "Sun Deck," extended to right center and seated about 4500. Local newspapers called the new ballpark an architectural wonder to rival the pyramids! The distances down the foul lines were a healthy 360 feet to left, 360 feet to right (later pushed back to 400 feet) and 420 feet to center field. The first over-the-fence home run in a regular game at Redland Field was not hit until Pat Duncan of the Reds did it in 1921.

Curiously, there was a terrace in left and left center field, an incline starting twenty feet from the outfield fence and increasing about four feet until it reached the wall. Thus, the fence was fourteen feet high, but it was actually eighteen feet above the level of home plate. Visiting leftfielders over the years cursed the "terrace," particularly when they tried to back-pedal up it in pursuit of a long fly ball. A few days before the end of his career in 1935, Babe Ruth, playing left for the Boston Braves, tripped going up the hill after a fly, fell on his face, and marched off the field in a huff. The Cincinnati leftfielders had enough practice on the terrace that they were usually able to handle it without too much difficulty.

Redland Field was home to its first World Series in 1919, and there were some changes made to the ballpark for the occasion. The street behind left field was blocked off, temporary stands were put up, and portable seats were installed in front of the lower deck. With these changes, the hometown Cincinnati fans were happy to cheer for a winner, as their Reds beat the White Sox in eight games, five games to three. The team, managed by Pat Moran, was led by Edd Roush, Heinie Groh, Hod Eller, Slim Sallee, and Greasy Neale, who would become more famous as a championship coach with the Philadelphia Eagles in the National Football League. The fans' joy was tempered somewhat over the next year or so as the facts came out about the Black Sox taking bribes to throw the Series, and eight of the Chicago players were banned for life by the new commissioner, Kenesaw Mountain Landis.

The Reds players, though, believed that they had won the World Series on their own, no matter what their opponents were doing or not doing. Heinie Groh said, "Well, maybe the White Sox did throw it. I don't know. Maybe they did and maybe they didn't. It's hard to say. I didn't see anything that looked suspicious. But I think we'd have beaten them either way; that's what I thought then and what I think today." And Edd Roush said, "We beat them fair and square. I'll believe that to my dying day."[1]

The notorious 1919 Series had one other result affecting the Cincinnati franchise. From 1903 until the selection of Landis in 1920, baseball had been governed by a three-member body known as the National Commission. The three members were the presidents of the National and American leagues and August A. "Garry" Herrmann, the president of the Reds. With the ascension of Landis, the National Commission went out of existence.

Crosley Field, Cincinnati (Philadelphia Athletics Historical Society).

Garry Herrmann had become a prominent Cincinnati politician through his service as lieutenant to George B. Cox, the "Easy Boss of Cincinnati," one of the most powerful machine bosses in the country. In 1902, Cox, city mayor Julius Fleischmann, and Herrmann purchased the Reds franchise from John T. Brush, and Herrmann ran the team from then until he retired due to ill health in 1927. Cox sold his one-third interest to another friend of Herrmann's, Thomas J. Logan, in 1907, but Herrmann always ran the baseball part of their business.[2]

Herrmann was highly respected in baseball circles, venerated for his services in settling the National-American league war in 1903 and implicitly trusted as the third member of the Commission. He was regarded as the father of the World Series, since he had the inter-league playoff made a fixture in 1905, after John McGraw had refused to have his Giants participate in 1904. Ironic it was, then, that the fixed 1919 Series should serve as the event that ended Herrmann's tenure on the game's governing body.

The Reds went into a long period of decline after the 1919 championship, although they were contenders for most of Pat Moran's five-year tenure. Then, other than a second-place finish in 1926, came the drought. From 1929 through 1934, the team was last or next-to-last, and attendance dropped, as lack of interest combined with the Depression to keep people home.

Between the 1926 and 1927 seasons, a major step was taken to reduce the distance to the outfield fences, which prevented many home runs at a time when the four-bagger was becoming one of the attractions of the game. Home plate was moved forward twenty feet, and the field was turned a bit, bringing the foul line numbers to 339 to left field and a still-distant 383 to right.

One feature of the park that helped to get the fans involved was the location of the home and visitors' clubhouses behind the left-field stands. To get to their dugouts before the game (and to return from the field afterwards), players had to walk through an open area that was often full of spectators, who usually had things to say to or about them..

After Garry Herrmann retired, he sold the club to C.J. McDiarmid, who owned it from 1927 to 1929, when he sold it to Sidney Weil, who soon ran out of money after the stock market crashed. In 1933, operation of the club was taken over by a Cincinnati bank, which brought in the mercurial and imaginative (and sometimes alcoholic) Larry MacPhail to run the team as general manager, after his great success with the Columbus team of the minor league American Association.

In 1934, MacPhail persuaded a local industrialist named Powel Crosley, Jr., to buy the franchise from Sidney Weil and the bank for $450,000. Crosley had started by making auto parts, branched out into the manufacture of the cars themselves, then radios, refrigerators, and household appliances. In 1922, Crosley initiated a Cincinnati radio station, with call letters WLW, and when he outfitted his station with a 500,000-watt transmitter, the most powerful in the country, it was soon being called "the Nation's station." At least with Crosley in command, the Reds were not short of cash, although he was known as a very sharp businessman.

The new owner, of course, inherited MacPhail, and at first the connection prospered. MacPhail convinced him to change the name of the ballpark to Crosley Field, the name which it retained to the end of its existence. With the Crosley money in hand, MacPhail was able to obtain better players for the Reds, whose fortunes started to improve. MacPhail had lights installed in the park, and on May 24, 1935, the first night game in major league baseball took place before 20,422 fans watching history being made. President Franklin D. Roosevelt, sitting in the White House in Washington, threw a switch and the lights went on in Crosley Field. It was the start, slow at first because many owners were resistant to playing at night, of a new era in baseball.

MacPhail staged a night game never to be forgotten a couple of months later, on July 31, against the Cardinals. MacPhail had held a special sale of reserved seats to thousands of fans in neighboring states — West Virginia, Kentucky, and Indiana — for a festive night. The special trains bringing these fans to Crosley Field were late, so hordes of general admission customers poured down into the empty seats. Of course, the trains did at last arrive, and the out-of-state seatholders wanted their seats. Arguments and fights broke out all through the stands, as it became clear that Larry MacPhail had sold many more tickets than there were seats in the ballpark. So, many fans found themselves standing behind ropes along the foul lines or across the outfield. But the fun was not over. In the eighth inning, a local stripper named Kitty Burke ran onto the field, up to home plate, and grabbed the bat out of the hands of a startled Babe Herman. She dared St. Louis pitcher Paul Dean to throw to her, and when he did, underhanded, Kitty swung and hit a ground ball back to him. Dean threw her out at first base, but Kitty Burke, later awarded a Reds uniform by MacPhail, subsequently billed herself in her burlesque act as "the only girl who ever batted in the big leagues."[3]

Before long, Mother Nature, perhaps perturbed at the effrontery of the Redlegs in playing the quintessential afternoon game of baseball at night, made herself felt. Behind Crosley Field's center field ran a stream called Mill Creek, which flowed 26 miles through central Hamilton County and the heart of Cincinnati before emptying into the Ohio River just west of downtown. On occasion, however, the Ohio flowed up into Mill Creek, and one of these occasions occurred in late January, 1937. From January 13 to 24, record rainfalls were recorded along the Ohio, and there was flooding from Pittsburgh to the river's joinder with the Mississippi at Cairo, Illinois. On January 26, water levels in Cincinnati reached the highest mark in the city's history, 80 feet.

Cincinnati and Louisville were hardest hit by the flood. In Cincinnati, "schools, stores, theatres and factories closed. Authorities rationed electricity, suspended streetcar service, and shut off the water supply, except for four hours daily." In the midst of all this, water from the Ohio backed up into Mill Creek, which overflowed and submerged Crosley Field under 21 feet of water. Lee Grissom, a lefthanded pitcher for the Reds, a country boy from Texas and something of a joker, found a rowboat and, with John McDonald, the Reds' traveling secretary, on board, rowed right over the left-field fence and into the ballpark, making sure their picture was taken as he did so. Needless to say, the flood left a ballpark full of debris which had to be cleaned out.[4]

After the 1937 season, MacPhail left the Reds, prodded to do so by Powel Crosley, who was unhappy with some of the publicity that Larry brought on the team, such as fistfights with policemen. The flamboyant MacPhail was succeeded by a man of totally opposite temperament, Warren C. Giles, who believed that a ball club's publicity should center on its ballplayers rather than the front office. Giles, a native of Tiskilwa, Illinois, had been running baseball clubs in the minors since 1919 and came to the Reds in 1936. A year later, he became general manager of the club, starting a major league career that would take him in 1951 to the presidency of the National League and in 1979, after his death, to the Hall of Fame in Cooperstown.[5]

During the 1937 season, Reds' manager Charlie Dressen, who had led the team out of the cellar his previous two seasons, was let go when it fell back into the basement. He was succeeded on a temporary basis by Bobby Wallace, who could do no better. One of Warren Giles' first moves was to bring in for the '38 season Deacon Bill McKechnie, who had won pennants in Pittsburgh and St. Louis.

Pitcher Lee Grissom (waving) and John McDonald, rowing over a flooded Crosley Field, January 1937 (National Baseball Hall of Fame Library, Cooperstown).

Another move that Giles made between the 1937 and 1938 seasons was to move home plate another 20 feet forward, which left the distances down the lines 328 feet to left and 366 to right, with another 387 feet to center field. These were basically the dimensions of Crosley Field for the rest of its existence, except for two postwar periods, from 1946 to 1950 and from 1953 to 1957, when a screen (creating an area nicknamed "Giles' Chicken Run" in 1946) was erected in front of the right-field bleachers, which cut the distance down the line to 342 feet.

With the adjusted Crosley Field, Bill McKechnie went to work. He put rookie Frank McCormick on first base and watched him lead the league in hits while batting .327. From the Cubs the team bought second-baseman Lonny Frey, who solidified the infield. The former second sacker, Alex Kampouris, was traded to the Giants for slugging outfielder Wally Berger, who hit .307 with 16 home runs. Outfielder Ival Goodman boosted his home run total from 12 in '37 to 30 in 1938. And slow-footed catcher Ernie "Schnozz" Lombardi (so called because of his extra-large nose) batted .342 to lead the league, while belting 19 homers. Lombardi, regarded by many experts as the slowest runner ever to play big league baseball well — he never beat out any infield hits and opposing infielders were able to play him back on the outfield grass — was voted the league's Most Valuable Player for 1938.

Righthander Paul Derringer, who had been 10–14 the year before with a 4.04 ERA, improved to 21–14, with an ERA of 2.93 and a league-leading 307 innings pitched. Bucky Walters, a converted infielder, was traded by the Phillies to Cincinnati in June for two players and $50,000 cash (the Phillies always needed the cash) and put together an 11–6 record over the rest of the season. And a 23-year-old southpaw fastballer named Johnny Vander Meer, only 3–5 the year before, won 15 and lost 10 for the Reds in 1938. Two of Vander Meer's wins came on June 11 and June 15, when he pitched successive no-hit games against the Braves at Crosley Field and the Dodgers at Ebbets. No one in the history of the major leagues has ever duplicated that feat, although another Reds pitcher came close.

With all these changes, McKechnie was able to give the Reds their first winning season since 1928, with a record of 82–68, six games behind the pennant-winning Cubs, and a berth in the first division at fourth place, their highest finish since 1926. Home attendance increased by almost 300,000 fans, to 706,000.

The All-Star game was played in Crosley Field on July 6, 1938, before 27,067, and the Nationals won it, 4–1. Coming a couple of weeks after the double no-hitters, it was only natural that Johnny Vander Meer should be the starting pitcher for the National League, and he did fine, giving up but one hit in three innings

Hopes were high for 1939, and McKechnie and his team did not let their followers down. The Reds won their first flag since 1919, finishing at 97–57, four and a half games ahead of the Cardinals. Attendance jumped to 981,000, and the town of Cincinnati was jubilant. Walters led the league with 27 wins, a 2.29 earned run average, and 319 innings pitched, and won the National League MVP award. Derringer was right behind him at 25–7 with a 2.93 ERA. Whitey Moore and rookie Gene Thompson each won 13 games. Reds' pitchers led the league in complete games, strikeouts, earned run average, and fewest opponents' runs allowed. McCormick hit .332 and led the league in both hits and runs batted in. Third-baseman Bill Werber, picked up from the A's for cash, hit .289 and gave the team solid infielding. Goodman and Lombardi fell off some in their hitting, but the story of the '39 Reds was their pitching.

The World Series pitted Cincinnati against the New York Yankees, and it did not go well for the Redlegs. In the first game, Red Ruffing outpitched Derringer, 2–1, and Monte Pearson beat Walters in Game Two, 4–0. Game Three, at Crosley, went to the Yanks, 7–3. In Game Four, the Reds led, 4–2, going into the ninth, but an error by shortstop Billy Myers set up the tying runs. In the tenth, with the Yanks' Charlie Keller on base, Joe DiMaggio singled and outfielder Goodman misplayed the ball. Keller raced home and crashed into Lombardi at the plate, knocking him cold. While the big catcher was lying flat on his back, DiMaggio came around to score as well, and the Yankees won the game to sweep the Series in four straight. "Lombardi's Big Snooze" was harshly criticized in the baseball press around the country, a great injustice to the catcher who had surely not chosen to be knocked unconscious.

The Reds recovered from their World Series setback to do even better in 1940. They put together a record of 100–53, winning the pennant by 12 games over the Dodgers. Again they were led by their pitchers, Walters, Derringer, and Thompson, as well as a rookie relief pitcher named Joe Beggs, who posted a 12–3 record with a 2.00 ERA. Frank McCormick led the league in hits and doubles, drove in 127 runs, and was voted MVP. The team led the league in fielding, in complete games, in earned run average, and in fewest runs allowed the opposition.

One shocking thing which happened to the Reds in the middle of their 1940 run to the pennant was the death of backup catcher Willard Hershberger, who slit his own throat in the Copley Plaza Hotel in Boston on August 3. Hershberger had suffered from depression since his father's

Reds' catcher Ernie Lombardi at bat, Crosley Field, 1940 (Philadelphia Athletics Historical Society).

suicide ten years earlier and always kept to himself away from the ball field. When Ernie Lombardi was injured and Hershberger took over the club's catching duties, he blamed himself for several Redleg losses in the days before his suicide, though he was hitting .309 at the time of his death. On August 2, manager McKechnie took the young catcher into his office, where Hershberger broke down in tears. "My father killed himself and I'm gonna do it too," he said, though after dinner and a long talk with McKechnie he said, "I'm all right now, Bill." Nevertheless, the next afternoon Hershberger went into his hotel bathroom and cut his jugular vein. Afterwards, McKechnie told his shocked and saddened players that "the thing for us to do now is win the pennant and vote Hershie's mother a full share of the World Series money."[6]

The Reds did win the pennant and went on to play Detroit in the World Series. Ernie Lombardi had injured his ankle late in the season, and, without Hershberger, McKechnie's best option behind the plate was 40-year-old coach Jimmie Wilson, who had caught very little since 1937. Wilson rose to the occasion (or squatted to it, perhaps), catching six games and hitting .353, with six hits. The two teams opened at Crosley Field by splitting the first two games, with Derringer losing to Bobo Newsom before Bucky Walters pitched a three-hit 5–3 victory. Tommy Bridges won Game Three for the Tigers, but Derringer evened matters with a 5–2 five-hitter. Newsom threw a three-hit shutout in Game Five, but Walters returned the favor with a 4–0 gem in the sixth game, back in Cincinnati. For Game Seven, Newsom took the mound again for the Tigers, against Paul Derringer. Detroit took a 1–0 lead in the third, but in the seventh inning doubles by McCormick and Jimmy Ripple and a long fly by Billy Myers gave the Reds two runs, enough for Derringer to win the game and the Series.

McKechnie's team declined to third place in 1941, and through the rest of the forties was an also-ran, finishing in the first division through 1944 and dropping lower the next two years. McKechnie left after a sixth-place finish in 1946, to be replaced by Johnny Neun. In 1944, on June 10, in the ninth inning of a game the Cardinals were winning handily, a young lefthander named Joe Nuxhall, still almost two months shy of his sixteenth birthday, took the mound for the Reds, the youngest player ever to perform in a major league game in the twentieth century. What followed was not pretty: the youngster got two outs but he gave up five runs on two hits, five walks and a wild pitch. It was Nuxhalls's only appearance; he went back to high school with his amateur standing restored, then spent time in the minors, and returned to the Reds in 1952 to start a fine career in which he won 135 games, all but five of them for Cincinnati, over 15 seasons. Later Joe became a beloved broadcaster of Reds' games from 1967 through 2004.

There was excitement in 1947 when a tall, lean, side-arming right-hander named Ewell Blackwell was on the mound for the Reds. Blackwell, nicknamed "The Whip" for his buggy-whip style of delivery, posted a record of 22–8, with an earned run average of 2.47 and a league-leading 193 strikeouts. He won 16 games in a row at one stretch, threw a 6–0 no-hitter against the Braves on June 18 at Crosley Field, and four days later came within two outs of duplicating Johnny Vander Meer's record of two consecutive no-hitters. He took his no-hitter against the Dodgers into the ninth, got the first out, and then watched as Eddie Stanky got a broken-bat single right up the middle. Jackie Robinson got another hit in the inning, but Blackie preserved his 4–0 shutout.

Blackwell was a six-time All-Star for the Reds, but he also led the league in hit batsmen six times. His fastball, which looked like it was coming from third base, was said to be 100 m.p.h., and right-handed batters were terrified of it. "I realized my sidearm delivery was intimidating, and I took advantage of it any way I could," Blackwell said. "I was a mean pitcher."[7]

The rest of the team in that period, though, was not quite so impressive. Led by players like Grady Hatton, Eddie Miller, Frank Baumholtz, Benny Zientara, and Vander Meer, the Reds drew pretty well but fared poorly on the field.

In the stands, the headliner was a fan named Harry Thobe, an elderly stonemason from Oxford, Ohio, who danced constantly while dressed in a white suit with red stripes, one red shoe and one white one, and a straw hat with a red band, waving a red-and-white parasol. He earned national recognition with the Reds' pennant in 1939, when he circled the bases at a trot after the game, sliding into home plate, and mugged for the photographers before the World Series games, flashing his twelve gold teeth.

In 1948, the Reds turned first base over to a rookie named Ted Kluszewski, a husky young man who had been All-Big Ten as a tight end for Indiana University. Big Klu, as he was familiarly called, was one of the strongest men playing the game and he quickly settled into his position on the Reds, which he would hold for nine years until back problems sapped some of his prodigious strength. In 1954, Klu led the league with 49 home runs and 141 runs batted in, and he hit .302 overall for his Cincinnati career, with 251 home runs and 886 runs driven home.

For Reds' fans in the '50s, Ted Kluszewski was the man to watch. Otherwise, there was not too much — four sixth-place finishes, three years in fifth place, a couple in fourth, and 1956 in third place, the first year the team ever broke the million mark in attendance, which it would do three more times in Crosley Field. The managers in this decade were Luke Sewell for 2½ seasons, Rogers Hornsby for 1½, Birdie Tebbetts for 4½, Jimmy Dykes for part of a year, Mayo Smith for another part, and Freddy Hutchinson for the start of a tenure which would run through 1964, up to his fatal illness.

The All-Star game returned to Crosley Field in 1953, and the National League, behind the pitching of Robin Roberts, Warren Spahn, Curt Simmons and Murry Dickson, won the game, 5–1. The 30,846 fans in attendance were delighted to see the ageless Satchel Paige of the Browns pitch the eighth inning, although they may have been surprised to see him give up three hits and two runs.

As the decade went on, the team developed new stars, the middle infield combo of Johnny Temple and Roy McMillan, slugging outfielders Frank Robinson, Wally Post, and Gus Bell, and Ed Bailey behind the plate.

In 1956, when the Reds finished two games behind Brooklyn (and one behind Milwaukee), they hit 221 homers and scored 775 runs, league leaders in both categories. Robinson hit 38 home runs, Post 36, Kluszewski 35, Bell 29, and Bailey 28, but the pitching was not quite up to the same standard. When the slugging tapered off the next year, with Big Klu's backache, the team slipped to fourth.

In 1960, the Superior Towel & Linen Service Building, long visible behind the left-field fence, was torn down. With it went the sign that had for years been atop the building, reading "Hit This Sign and Get a Siebler Suit," advertising a downtown clothing store. Wally Post won 16 suits from Siebler's over the years, with Willie Mays leading the way for visiting sluggers with seven.

Fred Hutchinson was named manager of the Reds in July 1959. A fine pitcher for 11 years with Detroit, Hutch had served two and a half years as the Tigers' manager as well as two years running the Cardinals. When he took over the leadership of the Reds from Mayo Smith, the team was ten games under .500; under Hutchinson, the club was 39–35 for the rest of the season. As a footnote, the '59 Reds were celebrated in relief pitcher Jim Brosnan's book, *The Long Season*. Nineteen-sixty was not too successful — the Reds finished in sixth place once again — but 1961 would be different.[8]

For the first time since 1940, the Reds won the National League pennant. Led by the batting of Frank Robinson, Vada Pinson, Gene Freese, Wally Post and Gordie Coleman, and the outstanding pitching of Joey Jay, Jim O'Toole, and Bob Purkey (and the relief work of author Brosnan, who came out with another book, *Pennant Race*), Hutchinson's crew finished four games ahead of the Dodgers. Unfortunately, they ran up against the Mantle-Maris-Ford Yankees and lost the World Series in five games. Joey Jay won Game Two, 6–2, but the final three games, the last World Series games ever to be played in Crosley Field, all went to the Yanks.[9]

Powel Crosley never saw his team's '61 pennant. He died of a heart attack on March 28, 1961, and after the season, general manager Bill DeWitt (the former owner of the St. Louis Browns) bought the club from Crosley's estate. DeWitt ran the team for five more seasons.

In 1963, an interstate highway called the Mill Creek Expressway was constructed behind center field, and the Reds added nine and a half feet of plywood on top of the concrete wall. The plywood part was out of play — a home run for those who hit it, with a white line painted where the concrete and plywood met. After two years of arguments with umpires about whether a ball had hit above or below the white line, the line was painted over and a ball hitting anywhere on the entire 23-foot fence was still in play.

The next two years saw third and fifth-place finishes, but 1964 promised better things. Sadly, Fred Hutchinson was diagnosed with a severe case of lung cancer before the season started and this knowledge hung over the team. Still, led by Robinson, Pinson, Deron Johnson, and a second-year player named Pete Rose, the Reds played well. Hutch was in and out of the dugout with his cancer, and on August 13 the reins were turned over to coach Dick Sisler. In late September, things looked about over — the Phillies had a 6½ game lead with 12 to play — but Sisler's team put on a winning streak just as the Phils lost ten in a row. After the Phillies' seventh loss, the Reds moved into first place, but they treated the lead like a hot potato, getting shut out twice by the Pirates, losing two at home to Philadelphia over the final weekend, and finishing tied (with the Phillies) for second, a game behind St. Louis. Gene Mauch's Phillies have ever since been scorned for one of the great collapses in baseball history, but the Reds blew the 1964 pennant as surely as the Phils did.

To bring an end to the '64 season, Freddy Hutchinson died three weeks later. The Reds stayed around the middle of the league for the next few years, but they were developing a fine nucleus, with Rose, Tony Perez, Pinson, Tommy Helms, and a young catcher out of Oklahoma named Johnny Bench, who came up to stay in 1968. In 1965, the club drew more than a million spectators, helped by a very popular glass backstop, the first installed in a major league park, but attendance declined after that as the fans of Cincinnati looked forward to a new ballpark. Parking around Crosley was becoming more and more of a problem, as was crime in the neighborhood. An agreement was reached with the city and with Paul Brown, the owner of a new American Football League franchise called the Bengals, to build a new facility near the riverfront.

After the 1965 season, Bill DeWitt made a famously bad trade, sending outfielder and future Hall of Famer Frank Robinson to Baltimore for pitcher Milt Pappas, reliever Jack Baldschun, whose best days were behind him, and a journeyman outfielder, Dick Simpson. DeWitt defended the deal by calling Robinson "an old thirty." Pappas was 30–29 in two and a fraction campaigns with the Reds, while Robinson won the American League MVP honors in 1966 and hit 262 home runs over the remaining eleven years of his great career.

In the post–Hutchinson years, the Reds were managed by Sisler, Don Heffner, and Dave Bristol. During the 1966 season, Bill DeWitt sold the franchise to a group headed by Cincinnati newspaper publisher Francis L.

Dale. For 1970, the Reds named as manager a 36-year-old South Dakotan named George "Sparky" Anderson. Anderson's big-league resume was sparse — a 1959 season as the Phillies' second baseman, hitting .218, a year as a coach with the Padres in 1969 — but his successful five years as a minor league manager convinced Reds' general manager Bob Howsam to hire him to run the team. It was a very savvy move on Howsam's part, as Anderson's plaque in the Hall of Fame at Cooperstown demonstrates.

The 1970 Reds were led by Bench, Rose, Tony Perez, Bobby Tolan, Lee May, shortstop Dave Concepcion, and pitchers Jim Merritt, Gary Nolan, Jim McGlothlin, and Wayne Simpson. It was the start of what would become famous as the Big Red Machine. But it would not score its great successes in Crosley Field.

On June 24, 1970, the Reds said farewell to Crosley Field. The old-timers felt it the most. Edward Leyendecker, a ticket-taker at Crosley since 1937, said, "I hate like the devil to see it go. I'm gonna miss the old place." Another ticket-taker, Eddie Nordman, was not unhappy. "Not a bit," he said. "I'm glad it's going. I'm happy to get rid of the poles — the seats that are obstructed." But Gene Smith, an Associated Press photographer who had taken pictures there since 1938, said, "I hate to see the old park go. Before you know it, it'll be like it never existed." Ninety-eight-year-old Hugh Hanley sat behind third base. "Been coming here since Buck Ewing was the manager in 1897," he said. Warren Giles, who still lived in Cincinnati, sat behind the Reds' dugout and wept when they played the National Anthem. Students hung a sign reading "Univ. of Dayton says good bye Crosley" from the second deck. And a 20-year-old named Teresa Campbell ran out during batting practice and planted a kiss on Johnny Bench's cheek, then had him sign her Reds' cap.[10]

Giles and his successors as general manager, Gabe Paul and Bill DeWitt, dined at the Queen City restaurant beforehand and hoisted a final toast to Crosley Field, the site of a lifetime of memories for each of them. There was a short ceremony before the game, with Si Burick, sports editor of the *Dayton Daily News*, talking about the memories, about Pat Moran and Bill McKechnie, about Edd Roush and Ted Kluszewski, about Ewell Blackwell, Johnny Vander Meer and Bucky Walters and others, as well as the writers and broadcasters who had worked at Crosley. "Rest in peace with your wonderful memories, old friend," Burick said, "rest in peace."

When the game started, the sellout crowd of 28,927 roared with excitement as the Reds took on the San Francisco Giants, who put their very best pitcher, Juan Marichal, on the mound. McGlothlin started for the home team. There was some fun early when Marichal picked Bobby Tolan off first and an exchange of words nearly led to a fight. "It was a close game," Tolan said later, "and the tempers were hot." In the fifth, with the Giants ahead, 4–2, Rose doubled on a ball that caromed off Marichal's leg into right field, then ran through the third-base coach's stop sign on Tolan's single to center and bowled over catcher Dick Dietz to score ahead of the throw from Willie Mays. "That was no stop sign," Rose said afterwards, "just a yellow caution sign."[11]

In the bottom of the eighth, with the Reds still down, 4–3, Lee May spoke to Bench as the catcher walked to the plate. "Just get on base and let me win it," May said. Bench did more than that, knocking Marichal's first pitch over the Mountain Dew sign in left center to tie the game. Three pitches later, May did his thing, sending the ball over the center-field fence to give the Reds a 5–4 lead. Wayne Granger pitched the last two innings for Sparky Anderson, saying afterwards, "I was never so excited in my life." In the ninth inning, Granger fielded Bobby Bonds' two-out grounder to the mound and flipped it to May at first to end the game.

"What a great ending for the last game to be played at Crosley Field," chortled Rose. "We beat the highest-paid pitcher in baseball and we came from behind to do it."[12]

There were 60 Cincinnati policemen there to keep people off the field at the end of the game, but they were hardly needed. The fans stayed where they were, sitting or standing, and watched as four men came onto the field, dug up home plate, and loaded it along with Mayor Gene Ruehlmann onto Station WLW's helicopter for delivery to Riverfront Stadium. Ticket stubs were drawn and three fans were awarded the bases from the game. Francis Dale, the club president, presented framed drawings of the park to the brother and grandson of the late Powel Crosley. Bonnie Lou from WLW sang "Auld Lang Syne" and then the spectators started filing out, still orderly, with almost no vandalism and no one on the field. Ronnie Dale, the park organist, played "God Bless America" and "Good Night Sweetheart" as the fans left, with some women crying. Most of the lights went off, but one man, Frank O'Toole of Western Hills, continued to sit in his seat, finally getting up to leave, the last fan to leave Crosley Field.

Six days later the Reds played their next home game in Riverfront Stadium, and Crosley Field was a memory. On July 14, 1970, the All-Star game returned to Cincinnati, but it was to Riverfront. Sparky Anderson's team was nine games in front in the western division when it left the old park, and it went on to win the National League pennant, the first of four for the Big Red Machine.

Over the years, Crosley Field had hosted more than just the Reds. In 1936 and 1937, a Negro League team called the Cincinnati Tigers played there, and during the war the Cincinnati Clowns called it home. Wendell Willkie staged a rally there during his 1940 campaign, and Roy Rogers put on a rodeo in Crosley Field. On August 21, 1966, the Beatles used Crosley for a concert in their final American tour. But after the Reds left, there was not much going on there. The Reds and the city ultimately went to court to determine how much the old ballpark was worth, and a jury fixed its value at $2,500,000. The city then turned the place into an auto impound lot for a couple of years, with room for 750 cars, after which it was gutted and seats and mementos were sold to fans and collectors. In 1974, the old building was demolished. Seven buildings now occupy the site of old Crosley Field, and a street runs through the area as well.

Strangely enough, however, Crosley Field did not die. The city manager of suburban Blue Ash chose to recreate the old ballpark on the town's sports complex. Memorabilia from the park was hunted for, and fans donated other items. Ushers' uniforms, pennants, signs, ticket booths, a recreated scoreboard (with scores and information from the last game) and a wall with CROSLEY FIELD in red letters give a feel of the old place, along with 400 genuine seats from Crosley. Plaques on a wall feature not-to-be-forgotten Reds stars, and many fans have come to visit, as have some old Reds players.

Garry Herrmann and Powel Crosley and Edd Roush would be happy to see it.

Chapter 9
Barney's Playground

A group of Carnegie Tech students back in 1908 felt that they needed a good space for a football field for their college team. They spotted an area near Schenley Park, in Pittsburgh, and went to work on putting it into a safe and presentable condition for a gridiron, carrying rocks away and leveling the ground. When Swarthmore College cancelled its football game with the University of Pennsylvania, Carnegie Tech saw its opportunity. The football people convinced the Quakers to come out to Pittsburgh, and on October 31, the game took place on the newly-cleared grounds, before fans sitting in makeshift wooden bleachers. Penn won the game, 25–0, as expected, but it grabbed a good bit of attention in Pittsburgh.

Barney Dreyfuss, the owner of the Pittsburgh Pirates in the National League, thought that it looked like a fine spot to put up a new ballpark for his team, even though it was a way out from downtown — a ten-minute trolley ride — in the Oakland area. The Pirates had been playing in a ball yard named Exposition Park, on ground less than fifty yards from the Allegheny River, and when the river overflowed, the ballpark was submerged. Dreyfuss felt Exposition Park was just unsatisfactory, and as a tenant he was not permitted to make repairs to it.

Barney Dreyfuss understood that "in order to properly accommodate the public, a first-class grounds, surrounded by commodious and up-to-date stands, should be provided." He purchased (with the help of his friend Andrew Carnegie, who was a trustee of the estate of Mary Schenley, the land's owner) seven acres of the land where the gridiron had been. Then he visited every athletic plant and pleasure park he could get to and hired a prominent civil and landscape engineer, Charles W. Leavitt, Jr., who had designed the Belmont and Saratoga racetracks. Dreyfuss directed Leavitt to design "the very best layout for the Pittsburg Athletic Club's new grounds which had just been acquired ... comprising a block of land lying directly west of Schenley Park and opposite Carnegie Library and the Schenley Hotel."

A reporter writing this up for a local paper waxed ecstatic:

> This is the most superb location ever purchased for a ball park. The immense grandstands on the western side will ... look out over the diamond, which is framed by a most exquisite view over the rolling hills of Schenley Park. It becomes a question whether the spectators will be able to concentrate their attention on the game when they have such an extensive and beautiful panorama before them.[1]

Dreyfuss spent more than a million dollars putting up a steel-and-concrete ballpark; it would be only the second in existence, behind Shibe Park, which was just coming into existence a few months ahead of the park in Pittsburgh. Work started on New Years Day, 1909, and ground for the structure was broken on March 1. Nicola Building Company had the construction contract, and just four months after the ground-breaking the new facility was ready for baseball. Dreyfuss named it Forbes Field after John Forbes, the British general who had captured Fort Duquesne from the French in 1758.

Dreyfuss himself was a 20-year-old German Jew when he emigrated to America to escape conscription into the army in 1881. He went to work for his cousins, Isaac W. and Bernard Bernheim, in their distillery business in Paducah and later Louisville, Kentucky, where they made I.W. Harper bourbon. Young Barney prospered in the bourbon business and was able to buy the Louisville Colonels baseball team in the American Association. When that league folded in 1892, Dreyfuss moved his team into the National League. In 1900, the league dropped four teams, including Louisville, but Dreyfuss was permitted to buy a major share (later the whole interest) in the Pittsburgh club, and he brought with him from his defunct Louisville team several top-notch players, including Tommy Leach, Fred Clarke, Deacon Phillippe and a shortstop named Honus Wagner. With Clarke as manager and Wagner as the outstanding star, the Pirates won pennants in 1901, 1902, and 1903 and continued in the first division thereafter. In 1908 they tied for second place, just a game behind the Chicago Cubs. The club was ready for the move into Barney Dreyfuss's baseball palace.

Forbes Field had a double-decked grandstand covered with a roof that stretched from behind home plate down the foul lines for about 25 or 30 feet beyond first and third base. There was a small third deck — a single row of covered box seats — on top of the grandstand roof. Bleachers extended down the left-field foul line, and temporary bleachers were sometimes installed down the right-field line when sellouts were expected. The park seated 25,000, and those filling the seats watched games take place on a large ball field. It was 360 feet down the left field line, 376 to right, and 462 feet to center field. The backstop was a distant 110 feet behind home plate (it was 60 feet in most ballparks), although this was shortened in later years, to 84 feet in 1938, and 75 in 1959, which still left room for a lot of foul popups to be caught, if the catcher was fast enough. Curiously, starting in the 1920s, the batting cage was always wheeled away after batting practice, out to left-center field where it remained in play, with the closed end facing the field. And there was never any advertising on the walls.

With these dimensions, Forbes Field saw fewer out-of-the-park home runs than most other places, but inside-the-park homers and triples were commonplace. The season record for triples was set by a Pirate, Owen "Chief" Wilson, who hit 36 three-baggers in 1912, a record that has never been challenged.

The Pirates lost their first game in the new park to the Cubs, 3–2, before a standing-room crowd of 30,338, but they went on to win the National League pennant that season by 6½ games over Chicago. Wagner, the bowlegged shortstop, led the league in hitting at .339 and in RBIs with 100. It was the fourth year in a row that Honus won the batting crown, and he would win a total of eight of them before he was done. Four times he led in RBIs, eight times in doubles, three times in triples, twice in total hits and runs, and five times in stolen bases (with a high of 61 in 1907). In the World Series, Wagner outhit Ty Cobb by 100 points as the Pirates beat the Tigers in seven games, with rookie pitcher Babe Adams winning three complete games, including a shutout in Game Seven.

When Forbes Field opened in 1909, the nearby University of Pittsburgh chose to play its home football games there, staying until 1924, when it opened Pitt Stadium a few blocks away. The Panthers had some great seasons at Forbes Field, including 1910, when they allowed not a point to an opponent all season, and they won national championships under Coach Glenn "Pop" Warner in 1915, 1916, and 1918. Carnegie Tech also played some games in Forbes, including a November game in 1924 against the legendary Four Horsemen of Notre Dame.

From their founding in 1933 until the end of the 1963 season, Art Rooney's Steelers (originally called the Pirates) played in Forbes Field most of the time, although from 1958 on they played some home games in Pitt Stadium, where they moved for good after 1963. The Steelers were losers or also-rans in the National Football League while in Forbes Field, although

Forbes Field, Pittsburgh, in the scenic Schenley Park area (National Baseball Hall of Fame Library, Cooperstown).

they did feature some fine players from time to time, including Bill Dudley, Walt Kiesling, Bobby Layne, Ernie Stautner, and, for just one year, future Supreme Court justice Byron "Whizzer" White.

In October 1911, the National Mine Safety and Health Administration put on a mine rescue and safety demonstration in Forbes Field before 15,000 people, including President William Howard Taft. And boxing matches were held there from time to time, often featuring Harry Greb, known as "the Pittsburgh Windmill," and local favorites Fritzie Zivic and Billy Conn. On July 18, 1951, Forbes Field hosted a fight for the heavyweight championship, when 37-year-old Jersey Joe Walcott knocked out Ezzard Charles to win the title.[2]

Forbes Field, of course, was primarily a baseball park, and the Pirates its principal residents. But from 1922 to 1939, the mighty Homestead Grays of Negro baseball fame played there as well as in Washington, D.C. Cumberland "Cum" Posey, the owner of the Grays, was a good friend of Dreyfuss, and Barney tried to see the Grays in action whenever he could.

Among the great stars who performed for the Grays in Forbes Field were Josh Gibson, Cool Papa Bell, Oscar Charleston, Martin Dihigo, Willie Wells, Smoky Joe Williams, and Jud Wilson.

Pittsburgh had a long stretch after 1909 before its next National League pennant-winner: Bill McKechnie's 1925 club, led by third baseman Pie Traynor, shortstop Glenn Wright, and outfielders Max Carey and Kiki Cuyler.

In 1925, the double-deck grandstand in right was extended down to the corner and a new section built several hundred feet into the outfield in right. The home run distance down the line was reduced to 300 feet, from its old distance of 376 feet. To make sure that a flurry of cheap home runs did not follow, Dreyfuss put up a 28-foot-high screen in front of those new seats, from the foul line to a spot 375 feet from the plate in right center.

The Pirates took on the Washington Senators in the 1925 World Series, and Dreyfuss added temporary seats in the outfield to bring the capacity up to 40,000. The Senators won three of the first four games, two on fine pitching by Walter Johnson, and Game Three with the controversial catch in the temporary seats by Washington outfielder Sam Rice. The Pirates won Game Five behind Vic Aldridge and returned to Pittsburgh for the final two contests. After the home team won Game Six, it boiled down to one game. Before 43,000 rain-soaked fans, the Senators gave Johnson a 4–0 lead in the first inning and 6–3 after four. But the Pirates scratched back in the rain and fog, aided by two errors by Nats' shortstop Roger Peckinpaugh and the weariness of Walter Johnson. McKechnie's team pulled out a 9–7 victory and the World Series, though Senator outfielder Goose Goslin always claimed that Kiki Cuyler's Series-winning double landed foul. "It was foul by two feet," Goslin said. "I know it was foul because the ball hit in the mud and stuck there. The umpires couldn't see it. It was too dark and foggy."[3]

The Buccos (short for Buccaneers) won another pennant two years later, with Donie Bush as manager, but they were blown away in four straight in the World Series by the New York Yankees, whose 1927 squad is generally rated the best of all Yankee teams. Babe Ruth hit the only two home runs of the Series, both in New York, and the American Leaguers outscored the Pirates, 23–10. The Pirates' brother outfielders, Paul and Lloyd Waner, had eleven hits between them, but the rest of the Pittsburghers added little more.

Station KDKA was long involved with the Pirates; on August 5, 1921, the station broadcast the first major league game ever heard on the radio.

In 1936, KDKA hired an aspiring poet named Albert Kennedy Rowswell to broadcast the Pirates' games. Rowswell, always known as "Rosey," became an institution in Pittsburgh, broadcasting the games of his beloved Buccos until his death in 1955, 19 years later. His most famous call came on home runs to left, when he would shout, "Raise the window, Aunt Minnie, here it comes!" and his broadcast partner would drop a tray of nuts and bolts on the floor to simulate the glass breaking.[4]

Babe Ruth added a footnote to Forbes Field's history, when he came in with the Boston Braves on May 25, 1935. Ruth, 40 years old, was playing the last week of his fabled career, when he bombed three home runs off Pirate pitching. The last one, off Guy Bush, was reputed to be the longest blast ever hit in the ballpark, the first home run ever to soar completely over the right-field roof.

Through the next three decades after the '27 pennant, the Pirates struggled but could not win anything. They came close in 1938, when they finished two games back of the Cubs. By now, Pie Traynor was the manager, his 17-year Hall of Fame career having ended a couple of years earlier, with a lifetime batting average of .320. The Bucs were led by the Waner brothers, Paul, known as "Big Poison," and Lloyd, called "Little Poison." Paul won three batting crowns in his 15 years in Pittsburgh. Arky Vaughan played shortstop for 10 years in Pittsburgh and hit .300 or above in every one of them. Both Waners and Vaughan are enshrined in Cooperstown. In '38, when it looked as if the Pirates would win the pennant, Bill Benswanger, the son-in-law of Barney Dreyfuss who took over management of the club when Dreyfuss died in 1932, built a covered third deck on top of the second deck behind home plate, creating room for the increased press expected for the Series. Unfortunately, Gabby Hartnett's famous "homer in the gloamin'" won the pennant for the Cubs and doomed the Pirates' championship dreams. The deck remained.

Lights were installed and night games began in Forbes Field in 1940, and in 1943, during World War II, a large wooden Marine Corps sergeant, 32-feet-high, was placed against the left field wall, standing at parade rest.

Through the war years, the Buccos under manager Frankie Frisch were usually in the first division but not too close to first place. They had a good third-baseman named Bob Elliott, Al Lopez behind the plate, a fine infielder in Frankie Gustine, Elbie Fletcher on first, and in center field, Vince DiMaggio, the eldest of the three brothers. Vince, unfortunately for Pittsburgh, was distinguished mainly for his strikeouts, in which category he led the league in six of his 10 years in the majors, only eight of which were full seasons.

9. Barney's Playground

Another headliner for the Pirates was a righthanded pitcher from Alabama named Truett "Rip" Sewell. Sewell perfected a pitch he called his "eephus" or "blooper ball," which would sail on a 25-foot-high arc toward the plate, coming down right in the strike zone, to the bafflement of the batter. With the help of his blooper, Sewell averaged more than 16 wins a season from 1940 through 1945, picking up 21 wins in both 1943 and 1944. The only home run ever hit off the "eephus" was by Ted Williams in the 1946 All-Star game, when Sewell told him the pitch was coming.

The first All-Star game played in Forbes Field took place in 1944, before a crowd of 29,589. The Nationals won rather easily, 7–1, behind the hitting of Phil Cavaretta, Walker Cooper, Connie Ryan and Whitey Kurowski, and the nearly-perfect three innings of Rip Sewell, which delighted the home crowd.

In 1946, Benswanger sold the Pirate franchise, ending the Dreyfuss ownership of the club after 45 years. The new owners were a syndicate headed by an Indianapolis businessman named Frank E. McKinney. Among the other members of the group were Columbus real estate bigwig John W. Galbreath and the world-famous crooner, Bing Crosby, whose interest amounted to 15 percent of the club. By 1950, Galbreath, whose sporting interests also ran to race-horse breeding — he owned Darby Dan Farm in Kentucky and bred two Kentucky Derby winners, Chateaugay and Proud Clarion, over the years — had replaced McKinney as majority owner. He and his family ran the Pirates until the club was sold after his death in 1988.

For 1947, the Pirates bought slugger Hank Greenberg from the Detroit Tigers for what turned out to be his final season and, in order to take advantage of his right-handed power, moved the bullpens into left field, enclosed by a fence which cut down the home-run distance to 335 from 365 feet. The newly-enclosed area was called "Greenberg Gardens," but when Hank retired after that one season in Pittsburgh, its name was changed to "Kiner's Korner."

Ralph Kiner was a young outfielder who had come out of the Navy Air Force to lead the National League in home runs in his rookie season in 1946, with 23. In 1947, with the advice of Greenberg and the help of "Greenberg Gardens," Kiner hit 51 long ones, to tie him with the Giants' Johnny Mize for the league title. In 1948, with Greenberg gone, Kiner again tied Mize for the home run crown, this time with 40; in the next three years he won the title all by himself, with 54, 47, and 42; and in 1952, his 37 shared the title with Hank Sauer of the Cubs. In June of the '53 season, Kiner was traded to the Cubs, the result of continuous salary squabbles with general manager Branch Rickey, and the next year the fence came down, the bullpens were moved from the outfield, and "Kiner's Korner" was no more.

In 1948, another soon-to-be legendary broadcaster joined Rosey Rowswell in the Forbes Field radio booth, a former swimmer at the University of Pittsburgh named Bob Prince, soon to be known as "The Gunner," a nickname conferred upon him by a broadcasting partner. Prince was noted for his gravel voice, the nicknames he conceived for Pirate players, and his colorful phrases, which were obviously called "Gunnerisms." Prince covered the Pirates for 28 years before a conflict with radio executives brought about his discharge in 1975, after the move to Three Rivers Stadium.

In 1966, Prince introduced Pirate fans to "the Green Weenie," a green plastic rattle in the shape of a hot dog, originated by team trainer Danny Whelan, and popularized by Prince as a source of good luck to the Pirates and a hex on opponents. "Never underestimate the power of the Green Weenie," Prince would say, and thousands of them were sold in Pittsburgh.

There were times when Rosey and the Gunner were about all there was for Pirates fans. From 1950 through 1957, the Bucs finished seventh or eighth every season, including a stretch from 1952 to 1955 when they finished dead last each season, an average of 48 games out of first place. These were the years of Bobby Del Greco, Clem Koshorek, the O'Brien twins, Curt Roberts, Gair Allie, and a first-baseman named Tony Bartirome, who hit .220 in his only big league season, but later became much more valuable to the Pirates as their trainer from 1967 to 1985.

The 1952 Pirates were particularly bad. In Billy Meyer's last year as manager, the team won 42 games and lost 112, finishing 54½ games out of first. It was one of the worst records ever for a non-expansion team. Branch Rickey, in his second year as Pittsburgh GM, felt the best way to improve over the team's last-place finish in 1951 was to bring in rafts of young players, which he did. Some of his youngsters turned into fine players — Dick Groat, Frank Thomas, Gus Bell, and Bob Friend. But the others, combined with the declining veterans still on the roster, made up a very bad team. Murry Dickson, who had won 21 games for the last-place team the year before, wound up with a 14–21 record in 1952. Early in August, Rickey brought up a young pitcher named Ron Necciai, who had famously struck out 27 batters in one minor league game. Necciai not only gave up five runs in his first major league inning, he finished the year with a 1–6 record, a 7.08 ERA, and an injured arm, and he never again pitched in the big leagues. It was that kind of a season. Joe Garagiola, who caught for the '52 Bucs (he caught more games that year than in any other season), often referred to that sad Pirate team in his later career as a broadcaster and humorist, calling it "a team that scored runs in bunches of one, or if the other team made ten or twelve mistakes against us we could beat them."[5]

As the decade rolled on, though, the Pirates picked up a piece here and a piece there for a mosaic of success a few years down the road. By 1954, even as they finished last again under manager Fred Haney, they had a 22-year-old rookie named Bob Skinner playing first base, with Friend and a Mormon deacon named Vernon Law taking spots in the rotation. The next year Groat returned from the military, and the right fielder was a young Puerto Rican named Roberto Clemente, whom the Pirates had drafted out of the Dodgers organization. Brooklyn had tried to hide Clemente, but ex–Dodger GM Rickey knew about him and plucked him for the Buccos. In 1956, with Bobby Bragan now the skipper, Pittsburgh brought up from the minors a slick-fielding second baseman named Bill Mazeroski, and in May traded much-traveled pitcher Dick Littlefield and Bobby Del Greco to the Cards for outfielder Bill Virdon. A small right-hander named Elroy Face, whose "out" pitch was a sharply-breaking forkball, had by now become established in the bullpen and led the league by appearing in 68 games.

The '56 Pirates escaped from the cellar, rising to seventh place, but the next year they slipped back again to a tie for last. Bragan was let go after 103 games, and under their new manager, an old infielder named Danny Murtaugh, the team was 26–25, a good sign for the future. Groat, Skinner, and first-baseman Dee Fondy all hit over .300. In 1958, Murtaugh moved the Pirates all the way to second place with a record of 84–70, as Friend won a league-leading 22 games and Face led in games saved with 20.

The Pirates fell to fourth in 1959, still with a winning record, as they settled in with an infield of slugging Dick Stuart at first, where his fielding was so shaky that he was given the nickname "Dr. Strangeglove," Mazeroski and Groat up the middle, and scrappy Don Hoak at third. The outfield was now composed of Skinner, Virdon, and Clemente, while stocky Smoky Burgess handled most of the catching. Friend slipped in '59 to a record of 8–19, but Law won eighteen and lost nine. Elroy Face had an unbelievable year coming in from the pen, winning eighteen games and losing one.

On May 26, lefty Harvey Haddix (known as "the Kitten," because of his pitching resemblance to the old Cardinal lefty, Harry "the Cat"

Brecheen) cranked up one of the greatest games of all time. Before 19,194 at Milwaukee's County Stadium, against a lineup filled with tough hitters like Hank Aaron, Eddie Mathews, Joe Adcock, and Wes Covington, Haddix had the Braves going three-up-and-three-down inning after inning. At the end of nine innings, not a Brave had reached base against Haddix. Unfortunately for the lefty, his Pirate teammates had not scored against Lew Burdette, so the game went into extra innings. Haddix continued to mow down the Milwaukee hitters through the ninth, tenth, eleventh, and twelfth innings, but the Pirates could not score for him. Felix Mantilla led off the home 13th with a ground ball to third, which Hoak threw away for an error, ending the perfect game. After Mantilla was sacrificed to second, Murtaugh ordered Aaron walked intentionally. Big Joe Adcock then hit a ball into the left field seats for the first Braves hit of the game, giving poor Harvey Haddix the loss. When Aaron wandered away from second because the game was over and Adcock passed him, Adcock was ruled out for passing a runner on the bases, his hit was reduced to a double, and the final score was set at 1–0. Still, Haddix had lost one of the greatest games ever pitched.

Haddix's gem, of course, was on the road, not at Forbes Field. It was a curious fact that in its 61 years hosting baseball games, both National League and Negro leagues, no pitcher ever threw a no-hitter at Forbes Field.

Early in July 1959, the All-Star game returned to Pittsburgh, although baseball's powers had cheapened the extravaganza by making it the first of two All-Star games to be played that season. The National League, before a crowd of 35,277, including Vice-President Richard Nixon, won it, 5–4, on an eighth-inning triple by Willie Mays, despite local hero Roy Face being roughed up for three earned runs in 1⅔ innings.

The next year, 1960, was magical in Pittsburgh. The Pirates won the National League pennant by seven games over the Braves, their first flag after 33 years. Dick Groat led the league in hitting with a .325 average and was voted NL Most Valuable Player. Law was 20–9 and won the Cy Young Award as top pitcher. Bob Clemente hit .314 and led the league in outfield assists. Friend, Face, Haddix, and Vinegar Bend Mizell backed up Law on a solid pitching staff. And a Pittsburgh record 1,705,828 attendees reveled in the glory.

The World Series, against Casey Stengel's Yankees, opened in Forbes Field. The opener went to the Pirates, 6–4, as Law and Face won behind a two-run Mazeroski homer. The second and third games were Yankee blowouts, 16–3 and 10–0, but in Game Four Law and Face combined for a 3–2 win to even the Series. The next day Haddix and Face put together a 5–2 win, but Game Six, back in Forbes Field, went to the Yankees and Whitey Ford, 12–0, Ford's second shutout of the set.

The deciding Game Seven took place before 36,683 anxious Pittsburghers, who were happy to see their guys score two in the first and two in the second for a 4–0 lead. The Yankees came back against Law and Face for seven runs to take a 7–4 lead into the bottom of the eighth behind lefty Bobby Shantz, who had entered the game in the third. Pirate pinch-hitter Gino Cimoli singled to lead off the inning, before Virdon hit what looked like a double-play grounder to short. But the ball took a crazy hop off of Forbes Field's notoriously hard-baked infield and hit shortstop Tony Kubek in the throat, winding up as a single for Virdon. Stengel then relieved Shantz, who was still pitching effectively, with righthander Jim Coates, a disastrous move. After hits by Groat and Clemente gave the Pirates two runs, backup catcher Hal Smith blasted a three-run home run to put them ahead, 9–7.

Bob Friend came in protect the lead in the ninth inning but was ineffective. Bobby Richardson and pinch-hitter Dale Long (a former Pirate) got hits, and Haddix replaced Friend. After Roger Maris fouled out, Mantle singled to score one run and send Long to third. Gil McDougald ran for Long, and Yogi Berra hit a ground ball to Rocky Nelson at first. Nelson stepped on the bag to retire Berra and take away the force at second, and Mantle was able to scramble back to first untagged while McDougald scored the tying run.

Into the bottom of the ninth went the tie game, with Ralph Terry on the mound for New York, having gotten the last out in the eighth. After taking one ball, leadoff hitter Bill Mazeroski inscribed his name forever in Pittsburgh history by blasting the ball far over the left-field wall for the winning run in a 10–9 ball game. The Pirates, despite being outscored 55–27 in the Series, were world champions!

The following year, 1961, was a disaster for the Pirates. Arm problems reduced Vern Law to 11 games and a 3–4 record. Friend lost 19 games. The club's record fell to 75–79 as it slid down to sixth place. Clemente's league-leading .351 batting average and a big home run year for Dick Stuart were among the few bright spots for Buccos fans that season. The next year they climbed back to fourth place (93–68) in an expanded ten-team league, but in 1963 they dropped to eighth, though they featured a rookie outfielder named Wilver Stargell, who promised better days to come. In 1964, Clemente's .339 league-leading average was a highlight, but they still could climb no higher than seventh. Murtaugh stepped down after 1964 and was replaced by Harry Walker, who led the team up to third place in 1965. Roberto Clemente again led National League hitters, and the pitching staff, featuring tall southpaw Bob Veale and a rejuvenated Vern Law, was one of the circuit's best.

In 1966, the Pirates again finished third. Little Matty Alou, obtained over the off-season in a trade with the Giants, led the league in hitting at .342, with 154 of his total 183 hits being singles. Clemente hit .317 with 29 homers and 119 runs batted in and won the league's MVP award, and outfielder Stargell banged out 33 long balls. Sixth place was their fate in 1967, with Murtaugh replacing Walker at the helm in midseason. Clemente again led the league in hitting, with Alou finishing third. The next season, former pitching coach Larry Shepard took the reins but could move the club no higher. Clemente dropped to .291 for the season, but young right-hander Steve Blass won 18 games.

In 1969, with two more teams added and the league divided into East and West divisions, Pittsburgh finished third in the East, led by Clemente's .345 average and Stargell's 29 home runs. By this time, it was clear that old Forbes Field's day was done, and a new ballpark was being built across the Allegheny River, to be called Three Rivers Stadium.

The year 1970 saw Danny Murtaugh back as the skipper in the Pirate dugout, as the string was played out at Forbes Field. There was, as with so many of the classic parks, not enough parking around the stadium as the automobile became the primary means of getting to the park. The interior of the ballpark was cramped, and amenities were few. Not only was the park becoming obsolete, the nearby University of Pittsburgh was looking to expand its facilities and the Forbes Field site was the obvious solution to its quest.

So, on June 28, 1970, the Pirates prepared to play their last games in Forbes Field after 61 years, a doubleheader with their ancient rivals from Chicago, the Cubs. Not everyone was sentimental about the end. Syndicated sportswriter Jimmy Cannon wrote sourly, "The hell with Forbes Field in Pittsburgh. Let it all come down. It is a squalid edifice, somber and brutal in its architecture, as joyless as a prison exercise yard." He called it "a perpendicular coal mine." But Bill James wrote that, "Forbes was regarded for many years ... as the crown jewel in the diamond tiara. It was never the biggest, but it seemed, somehow, the best — the sight lines were the best, it contained and expressed the enthusiasm of the crowd the best; it was just the best place to watch a baseball game."[6]

Back to June 28. The Bucs won the opener of the twinbill, their sixth win in a row and the Cubbies' ninth straight loss, which reduced the lead of the New York Mets in the East to just a game and a half over the Pirates. Before the nightcap, Pirate broadcaster Nelson King, who had pitched in relief for Pittsburgh for parts of four seasons back in the fifties, interviewed the home team's great outfielder, Roberto Clemente, who was due to sit out the second game. When King said, "I know it's a joy to be here to wind up Forbes Field and see this great crowd, isn't it?" Clemente responded, "Oh, this is great, Nellie." He went on, "I've been here sixteen years in this ballpark and this ballpark has been great for me right here, and the fans have been great for me here, too." He compared it to losing a wife after 16 years and then looking forward to a new one. "So now we have to wait and see how the other ballpark gonna be good to me or not like Forbes Field was."[7]

One of those attending the last games was 70-year-old Harold "Pie" Traynor. Traynor, whose entire career was spent with the Pirates, from 1920 to 1937, was considered by many to be the greatest third baseman of all time before Mike Schmidt came along. Old Pie, who left midway through the second game, said, "I feel kind of sad. I'll miss this place. It looks like a ballpark should."[8]

An announced 40,918 spectators (the largest crowd in the park since 1956, and the fifth largest ever for a baseball game there) showed up for the final games. Two 90-year-olds who had attended the opener at Forbes 61 years earlier were there for the last game, and one of them, George Catlin, threw out the first ball. A man named Walt Szala ran a souvenir stand in the ballpark, and by the time the second game started his stand had been so overwhelmed by souvenir hunters that he could hardly count his money. Park officials, fearing a robbery, asked him to close down. One reporter said the throng on that day, which was so jam-packed that it could hardly move, demonstrated very well that Forbes Field's ramps, aisles and restrooms could not handle a large crowd.

As the game got under way, King, Gene Osborn and, of course, Bob Prince, "the Gunner," who spoke of his "tremendous overpowering amount of grief" at the end of Forbes Field, described it for their audience. Milt Pappas started for the Cubs against a Pirate rookie named Jimmy Nelson. Both teams scored a run in the first (the Pirates on a home run by Al Oliver, the last homer ever hit in the park), and it stayed tied until Matty Alou drove in two Pirate runs in the fifth, unearned courtesy of a Jim Hickman error. The Pirates added another run in the sixth, Nelson pitched eight strong innings for the win, and Dave Giusti threw a scoreless ninth for the save as the Buccos won, 4–1. Fittingly, Bill Mazeroski got the last hit for the Pirates, a double in the seventh, and the Cubs' Willie Smith's ninth-inning single was the last hit in the ballpark. The final batter, Don Kessinger, was out on a chopper to — who else? — Mazeroski.

In the sixth inning, Bob Prince had taken a look out at the crowd and said, "I know, of course, that nobody will get out of line because we're just going to have a few things given away. All baseball caps have been autographed, and they'll be awarded. There'll be some fifty prizes. Bricks some of them and bases and what have you."[9]

Now Prince's confidence would be tested. He moved out onto the field after the end of the game to raffle off the prizes. The crowd stood along the foul lines as Prince's voice droned out the names of the lucky winners. The impatient spectators gradually inched out onto the field and then to the back of the diamond behind him. "Please stand back," Prince pleaded, until he was swallowed in the sea of humanity and finally fled the scene. The crowd which was already on the field then turned into a mob, first dismantling the scoreboard, ripping out anything removable, and tear-

After the final out in the last game at Forbes Field, June 28, 1970, before the mob scene that followed (National Baseball Hall of Fame Library, Cooperstown).

ing down the ivy, then moving on to the seats and anything else which could be pried loose.

"It was like watching a wave of termites descend on a Stradivarius, or Attila the Hun loosed on a Sunday School picnic, or locusts munching their way through the North 40," wrote *Press* columnist Phil Musick. "But mostly it was like having a kindly old uncle thrown to the piranhas."[10]

The electrical wiring was torn from the lights and phones were ripped from the phone booths. Within 30 minutes of the assault on the scoreboard, "there wasn't a number left." Even the Barney Dreyfuss statue in centerfield was not safe. The bronze plate on the statue was taken by four youngsters, though two of them later returned it to the Pirate office.[11]

Finally, the police moved in on the marauders with their nightsticks, and the place was cleared out. The city of Pittsburgh got some bad press out of the unexpected riot, but the old ballpark was turned over to the University of Pittsburgh as planned. The Pirates went on to win their division in 1970, though they lost to Cincinnati in the playoffs. On December 24, 1970, a five-alarm fire caused extensive damage to the ballpark, and after another fire the next June, Pitt chancellor Wesley Posvar arranged for its demolition that autumn.

But Forbes Field is not totally gone. An ivy-covered section of the outfield wall still stands, on city property, and is maintained by the city. Sometimes, on October 13, groups of Pirate fans gather there and listen to a tape of Bill Mazeroski's legendary home run soaring overhead. The university, which built the Forbes Quadrangle Building on a portion of the old field, maintains home plate on display in the lobby. It was at first claimed that it was placed in its exact spot from baseball days, but the university finally allowed that it had been moved a few feet; the exact spot where home plate had been in Forbes Field was actually in a nearby ladies room.

Nevertheless, old-time fans in Pittsburgh still feel nostalgic about Forbes Field. They may not have seen Honus Wagner or Pie Traynor play there, but they remember Frankie Gustine or Rip Sewell or Elroy Face, and they think, "That was a ballpark!"

Chapter 10
Mister Mack's House

In 1901, as we have seen, Ban Johnson transformed his Western League into a second major, called it the "American League," and took on the established National League. One of the scenes of that challenge was the city of Philadelphia, home since 1883 of the Phillies. Johnson convinced the manager of his Milwaukee club, an old catcher named Cornelius McGillicuddy, or Connie Mack as he was known in baseball circles, to head a new team in the Quaker City. Mack recruited a sporting goods manufacturer named Benjamin Shibe to come up with the money to support the club, and the Philadelphia Athletics were off and running.

"The Athletics" was an old and familiar name in Philadelphia baseball, dating back almost to Civil War times, most recently with the American Association team which had flourished in the city in the 1880s, so it was a logical name to adopt for the new team. Ben Shibe's partner in the sporting goods business was Al Reach, an old-time star ballplayer, who was co-owner of the Phillies, but Reach (who had a shaky relationship at the time with his colleague on the established team, Colonel John Rogers) gave Shibe his blessing when the new league contracted to have all its baseballs made by Reach. Connie Mack was befriended by a couple of local baseball writers, Butch Jones and Frank Hough, who were able to alert him to which Phillies players were unhappy with their situation there. The Athletics then were able to sign several of them, including the best of them all, Napoleon Lajoie. And the writers also tipped off Mack to a site for his quickly-constructed ballpark, a wooden single-deck affair at 29th and Columbia, in the Brewerytown section of the city, a place they called Columbia Park. As a reward for their help, the two writers, Jones and Hough, were given a 25 percent interest in the ball club.[1]

The A's were a big success in Philadelphia, winning pennants in 1902 and 1905, making a mockery of John McGraw's sneering comment to a

New York reporter that "Ben Shibe has a white elephant on his hands down there in Philadelphia." Shibe and Mack defiantly adopted the white elephant as the team's symbol, and the Athletics have kept it as such over the years.

There was not yet a post-season series between the two league winners in 1902 — indeed the war between the leagues was still on at that point — so the pennant was the most that the club could win. In 1905, however, Mack's club ran into McGraw's Giants in a World Series in which Christy Mathewson hurled three complete-game shutouts for New York. The Giants won four games out of five, with Chief Bender's Game Two shutout the only bright spot for the Athletics.

With the club's success, it quickly became apparent to Shibe and Mack that they needed something bigger than Columbia Park, which held at most 13,600 spectators. Ben Shibe located a city block which looked good to him, between Lehigh Avenue and Somerset Street, and 20th and 21st streets, in a North Philadelphia neighborhood called Swampoodle. Both the Reading and Pennsylvania railroads had stations nearby, and trolleys ran up Broad Street and over Lehigh Avenue, so fans would have access from center city and beyond.

Shibe started very quietly early in 1907 buying up lots and houses in that block, using straw parties to complete the purchases so the neighbors would not catch on to what was happening and jack up their prices. He also learned, through connections in City Hall, that the city was planning to close down the Hospital for Contagious Diseases, located a block away on Lehigh Avenue. The "small-pox hospital," as it was called, would not have been an inviting neighbor for baseball fans.

Once Shibe had gained title to the entire block, at a total cost of $67,500, and had two paper streets running through the block stricken from the city plan, construction on his new ballpark got under way in April 1908. The shiny new ballpark was ready for opening day in 1909. The new facility, named Shibe Park, after its owner, was the first baseball park built completely of concrete and steel, running ahead of Pittsburgh's Forbes Field by some eleven weeks. It was a beauty. The park's façade was done "in an ornate French Renaissance style , complete with arches, vaultings, and Ionic columns. The walls were brick with terra-cotta ornamentation."[2]

At the 21st and Lehigh corner, behind home plate, was an octangular tower topped with a dome. The tower, in its upper levels, housed the Athletics' offices; at ground level, it served as a gracious and elegant main entrance and lobby for the spectators coming into the ballpark.

The park's roofed double-deck grandstand ran from behind first base around to third base, and there were uncovered stands down both the foul lines. The playing field dimensions when Shibe Park opened were 340 feet to right, 378 feet to left and 515 feet to deepest center field. There was a healthy 90-foot distance from the plate to the backstop, and seating capacity was 20,500.

The first game in the park was played on April 12, 1909, against the Boston Red Sox, and it was a grand occasion. A huge crowd of more than 30,000 turned out, not counting the additional hundreds who sat on the roofs of houses on 20th Street, overlooking the low right-field wall. Mayor John E. Reyburn threw out the first ball, and at 3:00 P.M. the game got underway. With their great lefthander "Gettysburg Eddie" Plank on the mound, Connie Mack's team had no trouble beating the Sox, 8–1.

The great joy of the season- and ballpark-opening victory was quickly squelched, however, when the popular A's catcher Michael "Doc" Powers was rushed to the hospital with an intestinal infection after catching the game. Over the next week his condition worsened, and on April 26 he died, to the shock of the city and the baseball world.

Nevertheless, the A's prospered in their new surroundings, increasing their attendance by 180,000 and moving from sixth to second in the standings. In 1910, what was later called "Mr. Mack's First Dynasty" came into being, winning both the pennant and the World Series in 1910, 1911, and 1913, and another pennant in 1914. The Athletics beat the Cubs in 1910, and in both 1911 and 1913 Mack's men gained sweet revenge over John McGraw and his Giants. The pitching staff was led by Plank, Chief Bender, Jack Coombs, and Cy Morgan. On the field the Athletics presented what was called "the $100,000 Infield," which, in 1910 dollars, simply meant "beyond price." The group consisted of Stuffy McInnis at first, Eddie Collins at second, Jack Barry at shortstop, and Frank "Home Run" Baker at third base (Baker picked up his nickname with his exploits against the Giants' Rube Marquard and Mathewson in the 1911 Series). At the time, Collins and Detroit's Ty Cobb were generally considered the best two players in the American League, if not in all of baseball. The A's outfield was none too shabby, with Rube Oldring, Bris Lord, and Amos Strunk, while Jack Lapp, Ira Thomas and Wally Schang shared the catching.

In 1912, Ty Cobb was suspended by American League president Ban Johnson when he went into the stands in New York to attack a heckling spectator. His teammates were outraged at the suspension and, after playing one game without their star, chose to boycott the club's next game — which was May 18 in Shibe Park against the Athletics. Tiger management rounded up a squad of Philadelphia amateurs, college, sandlot, and semipro performers, to play as the Tigers. A seminary student named Aloysius Travers pitched the whole game, and the A's routed the thrown-together group, 24–2. The regular Tigers resumed their roles the next game, after Johnson threatened them all with lifetime suspensions. All of those one-day Tigers, though, have their bios and statistics duly recorded in the *Baseball Encyclopedia*.[3]

Connie Mack, who in 1912 used a loan from Ben Shibe to buy out the interests of Butch Jones and Frank Hough, the two sports writers, to make himself a 50 percent owner of the Athletics, believed that Philadelphia fans gladly supported a team climbing toward the top but lost interest in it once the top was attained. In 1914, as the A's cruised toward their fourth pennant in five years, attendance dropped substantially and the club actually lost money. Indeed, in July, when Mack's friend Jack Dunn, owner of the minor-league Baltimore club, offered to sell to the A's a lefthanded pitcher named George "Babe" Ruth, the cash-strapped Mack had to turn Dunn down and suggest he offer Ruth to Boston.

One problem facing the club in 1914 was the presence of the outlaw Federal League, which was making overtures to some of Mack's star pitchers. After the '14 World Series, in which the Athletics were swept in four straight by the Boston Braves, shocking the baseball world, Mack gave it another surprise by releasing his three great pitchers, Bender, Plank and Coombs. Shortly thereafter, he sold Eddie Collins to the White Sox for cash. Then, unexpectedly, Frank Baker chose to sit out the next season when a pay increase was denied him.

As a result of these player moves, the 1915 Athletics plummeted from first place to last, with attendance dropping to less than a third of that in 1914. The 1916 A's were even worse, possibly the worst team in baseball history, with a record of 36–117. The Athletics finished in last place for seven years in a row before ascending to seventh in 1922. Then, they started a slow climb up the American League ladder, as Mack added a useful player here, another there, a Jimmy Dykes, a Cy Perkins, an Eddie Rommel, a Joe Hauser. In 1924, the club reached fifth place, with a second baseman named Max "Camera Eye" Bishop and a right-handed-hitting outfielder from Milwaukee named Al Simmons. Simmons had a bad habit of "putting his foot in the bucket" when he swung, stepping away toward third base. Everyone knew you couldn't hit that way, but Simmons didn't know it and he hit very well.

Shibe Park had some famous fans in the '20s, one of whom was an anonymous heckler known simply as the "Huckster." "He never seemed to shout," one historian has recorded, "but his deep powerful voice coming from the lower grandstand was relentless against the visiting pitcher." The Huckster also razzed Jimmy Dykes at third base so effectively that Mister Mack tried unsuccessfully to have him silenced. The Kessler brothers, "Bull" and Eddie, were notorious as well. One would sit behind first, the other behind third, and they would carry on a stentorian dialogue with each other across the diamond, commenting on the game and various players.[4]

In 1925, Mack was able to afford another lefthanded pitcher from Baltimore, a fellow named Robert "Lefty" Grove. He added a rookie catcher from Portland in the Pacific Coast League named Mickey Cochrane, who hit .331, and he played another outfielder, Bing Miller, who hit .319. These additions, combined with the .384 hitting that Simmons contributed, boosted the Athletics to second place. Attendance jumped to 870,000. In 1926, the club slipped back to third, although Grove led the league in earned run average. Mack was slowly grooming a hard-hitting young infielder from the Eastern Shore of Maryland, a 19-year-old named Jimmie Foxx, who hit .313 in 26 games. Foxx had been recommended to Mack by his old third baseman, Frank Baker.

In 1927, the A's 91–63 record got them second again, though it was well behind that of the Yankees. Grove won 20, Rube Walberg won 16, and 44-year-old Jack Quinn won 15. Connie Mack picked up some veterans to help his youthful squad: Ty Cobb, Eddie Collins, and Zack Wheat, all of whom hit well over .300. In 1928, the club finished second again, though this time they gave the Yankees a close fight and finished just 2½ games back.

The following season was perhaps Connie Mack's finest. The 1929 A's, considered by many baseball historians to be perhaps the greatest team in baseball history, put together a record of 104–46, finishing 18 games ahead of New York. George Earnshaw, a hard-throwing righthander out of suburban Swarthmore College, led the league with 24 wins; Grove won 20 and led in ERA; Walberg won 18; and Eddie Rommel, pitching mostly in relief, was 12–2. The infield was made up of Foxx at first (.334, 33 home runs, 117 RBIs), Bishop at second, Joe Boley at short, and Sammy Hale and Jimmy Dykes sharing third base. In the outfield were Bing Miller (.335, 93 RBIs), Mule Haas (.313, 82 RBIs), and Simmons (.365, 34 home runs, 157 RBIs), with Cochrane (.331, 95 RBIs) doing most of the catching.

The World Series against the Cubs opened in Chicago, and Connie Mack pulled a real shocker. He had on his staff a 35-year-old sidearming righthander named Howard Ehmke, whose career was about over. Mack decided that Ehmke's sidearm pitches, coming out of the center field background of white shirts in Wrigley Field, were just what was needed against the Cubs' predominantly righthanded lineup. So Ehmke pitched the opener and was brilliant. He struck out 13 Cubs (a World Series record) and won 3–1. Game Two went to the A's, 9–3, as Earnshaw and Grove combined and Foxx hit a home run for the second day in a row.

Moving to Shibe Park for the third game, the Cubs got a bit of life back when Guy Bush beat Earnshaw, 3–1, before a full house of 29,921, and hundreds more on the 20th Street roofs. There had been some legal skirmishing between the ball club and the 20th Street homeowners over the right to watch Series games from the rooftops, a right which remained with the homeowners.

In Game Four, Chicago jumped out to an 8–0 lead, only to see it disappear in the A's 10-run seventh inning, highlighted by a Mule Haas inside-the-park home run on a fly ball that the Cubs' Hack Wilson lost in the sun. Philadelphia won, 10–8, with Grove coming in to pitch the last two scoreless innings in relief. Finally, with President Herbert Hoover in attendance at Shibe Park, Pat Malone of the Cubs took a 2–0 lead into the ninth inning of Game Five before Haas hit a two-run homer onto 20th Street to tie the game, Simmons doubled, and Bing Miller doubled him home for the Athletics' Series-winning victory.

In 1930, the A's won again, finishing eight games ahead of Washington. Lefty Grove led the league in wins (28), ERA, and strikeouts, Earnshaw added 22 victories, and Simmons won the batting crown with a .381 average. Big Al also had 36 homers and 165 RBIs, while Foxx hit .335, with 37 home runs and 156 driven in. The Athletics beat the Cardinals in the World Series, four games to two, as Grove and Earnshaw each won two games, and Simmons, Foxx, and Cochrane led the way at bat.

In 1931, Mister Mack's team won another pennant, by 13½ games, with 107 victories, a franchise record. Attendance fell off, confirming Mack's belief about Philadelphia fans (the nationwide Great Depression may have been a factor as well). Earnshaw and Walberg each won 20 games, but Lefty Grove was unbelievable. His won-loss record was 31–4, coupled with an earned run average of 2.06, and he topped the league in strikeouts, shutouts and complete games. Al Simmons won the batting title again, with a .390 average, and he, Foxx, and Cochrane paced the Athletics batters.

The World Series, once again with St. Louis as the opposition, went down to the seventh game, which Earnshaw lost to Burleigh Grimes, 4–

Shibe Park, before the "spite fence" was erected in right field in 1936 (Philadelphia Athletics Historical Society).

2. It was in this Series that a young Cardinal outfielder named Pepper Martin ran wild, batting .500 (12-for-24) and stealing five bases. Connie Mack's Second Dynasty had come to an end, having produced three pennants and two world championships, together with a near miss of a third.

In 1932, the A's fell to second, behind the Yankees, despite 58 home runs and 169 runs batted in by Jimmie Foxx. Attendance fell again, and Mack worried. The club finished in the red, and he and the Shibes had no great pad of wealth to fall back on. So, after the season ended, Mack sold Simmons, Dykes, and Haas to the White Sox for $100,000. In 1933, the club slipped to third, although Foxx won the league triple crown — batting average, home runs, and runs batted in — and his second consecutive MVP award.

After the 1933 season, Pennsylvania repealed its Sunday blue law which barred professional baseball games on that day, although it still maintained restrictive hours. Even though this promised to put some more dollars in the A's cash register, Mister Mack shortly made several deals that effectively broke up his great club. He sold Grove, Walberg, and Bishop to the Red Sox, Cochrane to Detroit, and Earnshaw to the White Sox, all for much-needed cash. And the Athletics slipped into the second division, where they would reside for the next fourteen years, nine of them in last place. Foxx would go to Boston in 1936 (still the reigning AL home run champ), and the last vestige of the Second Dynasty was gone.

Over the years there had been some changes in the A's ownership picture and in the ballpark itself. Ben Shibe passed away in 1921, and his half of the franchise was inherited by his sons Tom and John, who essentially took care of running the business, as their father had done, leaving Connie Mack to look after the team on the field. Tom Shibe died in 1936 and brother Jack a year later. When Mack bought Jack's share of the franchise from his widow, he held the majority interest in the ball club and Shibe Park for the first time.

As to the ballpark, in 1913, the bleachers running down the foul lines were covered, and a new set of bleachers was built in the outfield, running from the left field corner to center field. Again, in 1925, all of the bleachers, those down the foul lines and that in left and left-center field, were double-decked and roofed over. Shibe Park had now assumed pretty much the form which it would maintain for the rest of its days, with just a couple of slight changes ahead. The ballpark dimensions, after the work in 1925, were 334 feet down the left field line, 468 feet to center (where the batting cage was stored, in play), and 331 feet from the plate to the right field wall.

Two more changes were still to come. A small mezzanine was built in 1929 between the two main decks, from first to third base. This area was filled only when there were large crowds on hand; sitting in the mezzanine, a fan would lose track of any fly ball or popup hit more than thirty or forty feet high. Finally, in 1935, the Athletics added 22 feet of corrugated iron on top of the 12-foot high right field wall, to cut off the view of the non-paying customers on the roofs of the houses on 20th Street. The 20th Street homeowners brought suit against what was soon called "the spite fence," but the Athletics, represented in court by future mayor Richardson Dilworth, prevailed and the fence remained. Unfortunately for Mack and his ball club, by the time the fence went up there were regrettably fewer occasions when the neighbors would want to watch the A's in action. The 20th Street neighbors protested again in 1939, when the Athletics added lights to the ballpark, but to no avail.

The Phillies became Mack's tenants in 1938, abandoning broken-down Baker Bowl in mid-season. Gerry Nugent's Phillies were, if anything, an even worse team than the Athletics, so Shibe Park had the honor of hosting two last-place teams instead of just one. From 1940 to 1958 the Eagles of the National Football League played there, before they moved to Franklin Field, although the largest football crowd at Shibe Park was the 43,000 who turned out in November 1946 to see a battle between West Catholic and Roman Catholic high schools. The Negro League Philadelphia Stars played in Shibe Park occasionally, although open dates during the baseball season were rare with both the A's and Phillies playing there.

Something else started at Shibe Park in 1938. A young Texan named Byrum Saam began broadcasting the games for the Athletics on the radio, and the next season the Phillies took him on as well. As it turned out, for nearly forty years By Saam was the voice of Philadelphia baseball, doing the games of both teams when only home games were broadcast live, then electing to stay with the A's when it was determined to broadcast both home and away games. (Gene Kelly came to town to do the Phillies games, including those of the pennant-winning Whiz Kids of 1950.) For years, kids roaming the streets of Ocean City or Stone Harbor or other Jersey seashore resorts could hear Byrum Saam's voice coming out of one house after another, his voice or that of his sidekick Claude Haring reassuring listeners that it was still Philadelphia baseball. After the A's left town, Saam returned to the Phillies and continued to do their games until 1975. He never had a pennant winner to cover, and By Saam probably covered more losing games than any other announcer. Saam had a smooth and pleasant voice, and it eventually landed him in the broadcaster's wing of the Hall of Fame in Cooperstown.

In the '30s and early '40s, Connie Mack had a few good ballplayers, like Indian Bob Johnson, Wally Moses, Doc Cramer, Pinky Higgins, Dick Siebert, Eddie Mayo, and Russ Christopher, but they were never enough to make winners of the A's. The Phillies, during the same period, had even fewer — Danny Litwhiler, who played the entire '42 season without an outfield error, Pinky Whitney, Morrie Arnovich, Hugh Mulcahy, and several they traded away to become stars elsewhere, like Kirby Higbe, Bobby Bragan and Claude Passeau — but there was not much going on to test Shibe Park's capacity. In 1939, though, Bob Schroeder, who took care of finances for the Athletics, had Café Shibe constructed inside the park, for fans who wanted a real meal with their baseball, and this proved a profitable attraction.

The A's were still the better draw in Philadelphia, although it was often a question of which last place team was more fun to watch than the other. On Memorial Day 1943, an eight-year-old boy was taken to watch the A's and the Tigers play a doubleheader. In the first game, Detroit's Hal Newhouser pitched a two-hit shutout, but in the nightcap the home team came back to gain a split. The eight-year-older became a devoted fan of both Newhouser and Connie Mack's Athletics, Hal Wagner, Irv Hall, Eddie Mayo, Roger Wolff, and all.

The All-Star game came to Shibe Park in 1943, the first time the midsummer classic was played at night. Philadelphia had just one representative on each team, Dick Siebert of the A's and the Phillies' Babe Dahlgren. AL manager Joe McCarthy of the Yankees played the entire game without using one of the six Yankee players on his roster, as if to say the Junior Circuit could win even without its best players, and his club did win, 5–3, on a three-run homer by Boston's Bobby Doerr.

Through the war years, when it might have been assumed that the military draft would level things, the Philadelphia teams still usually brought up the rear. In 1945, the A's drew 462,000 while finishing in last place, 34½ games out, and the Phillies attracted only 285,000 to watch their team finish 52 games behind. The only thing the Athletics really had going for them was that they were always favored locally over the close-to-bankruptcy Phillies. The A's did beat the Phillies in their annual mid-season exhibition game in 1945, proving that of the awful wartime cellar-dwellers, the Phillies were somewhat more awful.

That was about to change, however. In 1943, Commissioner Landis had banned Phillies owner William Cox from the game for betting on baseball (he bet on his Phillies to win, which led local fans to jeer that he had to be booted for his own protection). As a result, the club was sold to Robert R.M. Carpenter, Sr., who was vice-president of the DuPont Chemical company and was married to a DuPont; he promptly turned the club over to his son, Robert R.M. Carpenter, Jr., then 28. Bob Carpenter, Jr., had been Connie Mack's partner in the ownership of the Wilmington club in the Interstate League. It was a great turnaround — after all the years of cash-poor operations, the Phillies had money, a lot of money, while the Athletics still depended on gate receipts to keep the Mack family solvent.

The postwar A's started out poorly, finishing last once again in 1946. For the following season, however, Connie Mack made a couple of key acquisitions from the minors, ex-National League shortstop Eddie Joost and first-baseman Ferris Fain, and these two players combined with some young pitchers, Joe Coleman, Carl Scheib and Bill McCahan, and a couple of Canadian war veterans, Phil Marchildon and Dick Fowler, to start the A's upward in the American League standings. In 1948, the club was actually involved in the pennant race (to the utter amazement of Philadelphia's baseball fans, who expected, and got, year after year, second division teams), holding first place in mid-August when Joost got hurt. With a weak bench, the loss of Eddie Joost pushed the club back to a fourth-place finish. The '48 A's set a club attendance record, with 945,056, the last time they would outdraw the Phillies. The next year the club still had a winning record, though it finished fifth, and, with an infield combo of Joost-to-Suder-to-Fain, set a still-standing record for double plays in a season, with 217.

In the '40s and early '50s, spectators at Shibe Park could listen to another legendary fan, a worthy successor to the earlier Huckster and Kessler brothers, a huge man named Pete Adelis. Known, among other things, as the "Iron Lung of Shibe Park," Adelis boomed out his abuse from the upper deck behind third. In 1948, the *Sporting News* published Pete Adelis's seven "Rules of Scientific Heckling," which included, among others, "no profanity, nothing purely personal, keep pouring it on," and "know your players."[5]

Before the 1949 season, the Macks spent $300,000 for ballpark renovations, adding additional seats, installing water coolers around the park, replacing stairways with ramps, upgrading the restrooms, and installing an electric organ, where Dot Langdon played fans' requests (and sometimes drowned out Pete Adelis).

For 1950, Connie Mack's Golden Jubilee as the team's manager for 50 years, the Athletics put together a package of four players and $100,000 for the star third-baseman of the Browns, Bob Dillinger, to add to the team's core of Fain, Joost, Pete Suder, Sam Chapman, Elmer Valo, and Barney McCosky. Mister Mack still sat in his suit and tie on the bench and waved his scorecard, though insiders noted that his coaches really seemed to be running the club. Hopes were high, and Allen Lewis of the *Inquirer* picked the team to win the American League pennant.

The Athletics' year turned into a disaster. Sore arms and ineffectiveness plagued the pitching staff, Dillinger was a disappointment (and was sold off to Pittsburgh in July for far less than was paid for him), family divisions within the Mack clan brought ownership changes, and the club fell into last place. Connie Mack gave up his manager's job, with Jimmy Dykes taking over at the end of the year. And Mack's two sons from his first marriage, Roy and Earle, bought out the remaining Shibe interests, as well as those of the second Mrs. Mack and her family, although they had to take out a hefty mortgage with Connecticut General Life Insurance Company on the baseball team and the ballpark to swing it.

Not only did Mister Mack's "Golden Jubilee" team collapse into the cellar, but the Macks had to watch the Phillies, of all people, win the pennant in the National League.

Starting in 1946, the Phillies, under General Manager Herb Pennock, gathered the players who would come to be known as the "Whiz Kids." These youngsters would win the club's second pennant ever in 1950, the first since 1915. Outfielders Del Ennis and Richie Ashburn, catchers Andy Seminick and Stan Lopata, infielders Granny Hamner, Ralph "Putsy" Caballero, Mike Goliat and Willie "Puddinhead" Jones, and young pitchers Robin Roberts, Curt Simmons, Bob Miller, and Bubba Church made up the core of the flag-winning team. In 1950, they were aided materially by such veterans as first-baseman Eddie Waitkus, outfielders Dick Sisler and Bill Nicholson, and pitchers Russ Meyer, Ken Heintzelman, and Jim Konstanty, a reliever who won 17 games for the Phils as well as the league's Most Valuable Player award. Under manager Eddie Sawyer, the Phillies celebrated a last-day-of-the-season pennant clinching, against the Dodgers in Brooklyn, on Sisler's tenth-inning home run.

Though the World Series returned to Shibe Park for the first time in 19 years, it didn't stay long. The Whiz Kids lost the 1950 World Series to the Yankees in four straight games (the first two in Shibe Park) and in succeeding years did not live up to the promise they had shown, although the team was now and would continue to be the more favored by Philadelphia's fans. Roberts and Ashburn put together lifetime records which would land them in the Hall of Fame, but their teammates could not match them, though some, like Hamner and Ennis, had noteworthy careers.

The Athletics in 1951 and 1952 rebounded from their horrendous 1950 season—Ferris Fain won two league batting titles, outfielder Gus Zernial won a home run crown, and a small lefty named Bobby Shantz won the 1952 MVP award with a brilliant 24-victory season. The A's made it back to the first division in 1952, finishing fourth, but attendance was down, and the big mortgage was a heavy burden on the club's finances.

Nineteen fifty-two saw the return of the All-Star game to Shibe Park. It rained, unfortunately, as the National League won, 3–2, with the Phils' Curt Simmons pitching three scoreless innings as the starter. In the fifth inning, Bobby Shantz came in to pitch for the Americans. He faced three hitters, Whitey Lockman, Stan Musial, and Jackie Robinson, and struck out each one of them. At that point the rain increased and the game was called, so Shantz never had a chance to match Carl Hubbell's famous record of five straight All-Star game whiffs.

In 1953, Shantz had a sore arm, Fain was traded, the A's fell to seventh, crowds dwindled even more, and future prospects looked bleak. In previous seasons, the Boston Braves and St. Louis Browns had moved, and as 1954 opened it looked very much as if the A's might be next. The '54 club, with Joost now as manager, finished last, 60 games behind Cleveland, and attendance was down to 304,666, in spite of the "Save the A's" campaign mounted by Mayor Joseph S. Clark, a campaign which was not taken very seriously by the Philadelphia businessmen at whom it was aimed. After the season, as the remaining A's fans suffered in pain and disappointment, the Mack brothers agreed to sell the franchise to a Chicago real estate man named Arnold Johnson, who had close ties to the Yankees ownership and moved the team to Kansas City, replacing a Yankee farm team there. Old Connie Mack, now suffering from dementia at age 91, could do no more than sit and watch as his team disappeared.

Johnson sold the ballpark (whose name had been changed a year earlier to Connie Mack Stadium) to Bob Carpenter, the Phillies owner, for more than a million and a half dollars. Carpenter did not particularly want to own the facility, but he had no choice if he wanted a place to play. As soon as he could, Carpenter sold the ballpark, which then changed hands a couple of times, winding up in 1964 in the ownership of real estate developer Jerry Wolman, the owner of the Eagles.

So the A's were gone, and now it was the Phillies' ballpark. For the first time, advertising signs appeared on the outfield walls, and a fence was put up in deep center field, behind which the batting practice cage was then stored. This fence reduced the distance to dead center from 468 feet to 447 feet. In 1956, the Phils replaced the old scoreboard in right-center field with a much larger one that had formerly been at Yankee Stadium. This scoreboard was fifty feet high, and it had a 10-foot high Ballantine beer sign on top of it.

There was never much parking around Shibe Park; a modest-sized lot across 21st Street was about it, except for some spaces in the driveways offered for a buck or two by homeowners plus whatever spots could be found along the streets. Of course, a driver who located a usable space on the street often found himself confronted by a neighborhood urchin who offered "to watch his car" for a price — a quarter in the early days, a dollar later — with a flat tire often the fate of the "non-watched" car.

As the '50s and '60s moved along, the neighborhood around Connie Mack Stadium became more crime-ridden and dangerous, the ballpark itself was dingy and old-fashioned, and it became more and more apparent that its days were numbered. In a not very subtle attempt to get the city's attention, Bob Carpenter put together a bloc of land in Marlton, across the river in New Jersey, although of course he denied that it was for a ballpark. "I didn't buy the land expressly to use as leverage," Carpenter said later, "although I was certainly accused of that." Finally, it was agreed that Philadelphia, whose municipal rulers dreaded the thought that the Phillies might move, even across the Delaware, would build a multi-use stadium in South Philadelphia, one which would be home to both the Phillies and the Eagles.[6]

The Phillies, under their new manager, Gene Mauch, gave the city's baseball fans some interesting times. In 1961, the club set a new record with a 23-game losing streak, but better days were ahead. In 1964, Mauch's Phillies, led by hitters like Johnny Callison, Richie Allen, Tony Gonzalez, and Wes Covington, and pitchers like Jim Bunning (who pitched a perfect game against the Mets in New York on Father's Day), Chris Short, Jack Baldschun, and Art Mahaffey, moved well ahead of the rest of the National League. With only 12 games to play in late September, the Phils had a six and a half game lead; the pennant looked rather secure at that point. What followed, however, was a shocking 10-game losing streak that left them in second place, tied with Cincinnati and a game behind St. Louis.

After the great collapse of 1964, a debacle that marked that Phillies team in history, the rest of the decade was none too happy. At first, the team tried trading for stars who might win the pennant that was lost in 1964 — players like womanizing pitcher Bo Belinsky, weak-fielding slugger Dick Stuart, infielders Bill White and Dick Groat, and past-their-prime hurlers Larry Jackson and Bob Buhl. None of this worked, and a pitcher they disposed of in the Jackson-Buhl trade, Ferguson Jenkins, went on to Hall of Fame stardom for the Cubs. Callison's development into a superstar seemed to halt after '64, and Allen, a bona fide hitting standout, became so hard to handle off the field that two men, Mauch and his successor Bob Skinner, lost their managerial jobs trying to do so.

As the decade of the '60s wore down, work was underway on the new ballpark, to be called Veterans Stadium. There were the inevitable delays, construction problems and union troubles, which meant that the Vet could not be used as planned for the 1970 season. The Phillies, with brand new uniforms for their new digs, found themselves back in Connie Mack Stadium for one more season.

Finally, the last game of that 1970 season came around, on October 1. There were some distinguished guests on hand, like former owner Gerry Nugent; pitcher Claude Passeau, who had won the first game for the Phillies in Shibe Park back in 1938; and Connie Mack, Jr., the son of the Grand Old Man of Baseball, who had a few words of welcome and goodbye to address to the assembled spectators before the game. One old-timer who had been invited, former A's outfielder Amos Strunk, then 81 years old, declined to participate: "I hold no sentimental value about the closing of the property," he wrote, "and it means nothing to me at all."[7]

The Phillies, under a new manager up from their farm system, Frank Lucchesi, were at 72–88, in last place in the east, a half-game behind the team they would play in that final game, the Montreal Expos, managed, ironically, by Gene Mauch. Attendance had been so-so all season, so the club was not prepared for the capacity crowd of nearly 32,000 which showed up for the finale. Before the game, the wooden section signs had been removed all around the ballpark, presumably so they would not be taken for souvenirs, but the result was that thousands of fans were unable to find their seats with any certainty. Another move the Phillies made before the game caused more problems. Bill Giles, the club's vice-president, said, "I had the brilliant idea of giving out wooden seat slats with com-

Before the final game at Connie Mack Stadium, October 1, 1970, Connie Mack, Jr., speaking, with Claude Passeau (left) and Bob Carpenter looking on (Urban Archives, Temple University Libraries, Philadelphia).

memorative decals on them." As Tim McCarver, who caught for the Phillies that night, remarked later, "Bill inadvertently armed the militia."[8]

There were some expressions of nostalgia and regret among the fans who showed up. These included older folks with longtime memories of old Shibe Park and some of the great A's and Phillies players who had performed there — and people who said, "I used to see Stan Musial play here, and Ted Williams, and Jackie Robinson." But most of those in attendance seemed to be there simply because of the historic nature of the occasion, the finality of the ballpark's existence, the closure. They were looking to take something home as a remembrance of the place.

Many fans brought their own tools, and some used the wooden slats the Phillies had given them. It was not long before the ballpark sounded like a construction site, with banging and shaking going on all over. Seats were broken loose, telephone booths were dismantled, anything not nailed down was jarred free. "You could hear the ballpark coming apart," one man who was there said later. Soon fans started parading around the stands, holding their souvenirs aloft in triumph — mostly seats, but a roar went up when five young men appeared bearing a urinal ripped out of a men's room.

A man named Bill Farley said he went to find a men's room around the fourth inning. When he got there, "all the lights had been removed, as well as a few of the urinals. Water was spraying everywhere; at least I hope it was water." One young man remembered going out to get a soda, and when he came back his seat was gone.[9]

Throughout the game, fans ran out onto the field, many of them heading out to second base to shake the hand of their favorite on the home team, Tony Taylor, others sliding into bases, many others just running around without much direction. The game was a close one, of some minor importance, because if the Phillies won they would move up to fifth and the Expos would finish in the cellar. Barry Lersch, the Phils pitcher, had a 1–0 shutout going into the ninth, when a youngster ran into left field and grabbed the arm of left-fielder Ron Stone just as a ball was hit to him. Stone was unable to catch the ball, and it turned into the tying run when the next batter, former longtime Phillie Bobby Wine, hit a double.

The umpires then had the public address announcer state that the next fan intrusion would bring about a forfeit of the game. Gene Mauch exploded out of the visiting dugout to tell the umpires not even to think about a forfeit. Mauch knew his Philadelphia fans only too well, and he feared a possible riot in the event of a forfeit.

The game itself ended happily for the Phillies in the tenth when

McCarver singled, stole second, and came home on Oscar Gamble's hit. Dick Selma was the winning pitcher, Howie Reed the loser. The season was over, but the mayhem was still going on. Thousands of fans raced onto the field. "They poured out even before I crossed the plate," recalled McCarver. "And they were not coming to shake your hand. They wanted a piece of you, of your clothing, of whatever else they could get. It got a little hairy."[10]

The mob began ripping up the turf, ransacking the dugouts for bats, gloves, baseballs, and anything else they could find, tearing up the infield cover, removing fire extinguishers, and generally making a chaos of everything. One man left the park triumphantly bearing a door to the ladies' room. A fellow with a large hunk of sod draped over his shoulder was asked what he was going to do with it. "Plant it in my yard," was the reply. "It's better than my grass."[11]

There were 25 casualties after the game, several of them requiring

Fans on the field after the final out, Connie Mack Stadium, October 1, 1970 (Urban Archives, Temple University Libraries, Philadelphia).

hospitalization. The 200 police on hand were unable to stop the dismantling of the stadium, but they were able to prevent too much physical damage to the fans themselves.

The Phillies had planned to award prizes after the game and to have a helicopter remove home plate and transfer it to Veterans Stadium. The prizes had to be given out the next day, those that hadn't disappeared during the post-game melee, and the helicopter, after hovering for a bit over an infield packed with humanity and spraying everyone with dust, finally buzzed off, its mission frustrated. As Allen Lewis wrote, "By the time the last fan had departed, the park wasn't good for much more than a junk yard."[12]

So, Shibe Park, or Connie Mack Stadium to the younger fans, was done. There were no plans for what to do with it, so it sat there on Lehigh Avenue, dilapidated and abandoned. On August 20, 1971, some kids got inside and started a fire, which did a good bit of damage, destroying the roof, bending many girders, and gutting the stands along the first-base line. There was another fire in 1974, and the field was overgrown with high weeds from one wall to the other, while rats ran over the mound where Lefty Grove, Chief Bender and Robin Roberts had worked. Finally, a city judge ordered the old ballpark's demolition, which was carried out in 1976. After some period of years when the site sat empty, it became, in 1992, the home of the Deliverance Evangelistic Church.

Occasionally, an old baseball fan will drive down Lehigh Avenue, past 20th Street to 21st, and remember Jimmie Foxx, the $100,000 Infield, Richie Ashburn, Ferris Fain, Danny Litwhiler, and all the great ones who made the place memorable. He may recall all of the dreadful last-place teams that played there as well as the five A's world championships. Most of all, he may bring back the truth that, for more than six decades, 21st and Lehigh was the beating heart of baseball in Philadelphia.

Chapter 11

The South Side of Chicago

At the start of the new American League, Charles A. Comiskey, at that time a good friend of Ban Johnson, moved his minor league Western League club from St. Paul to Chicago, posing a threat to the established National League team, the Orphans, soon to be known as the Cubs. Comiskey was a well-known figure in baseball, having been the star player and manager of the St. Louis Browns when that club ruled the American Association in the 1880s. He very shrewdly adopted the nickname "White Stockings," soon changed to "White Sox," for his new team on the South Side, taking over the name which the National League club on the north side of town had used for years and recently abandoned.

Comiskey put up his team in a wooden structure called South Side Park (also, Thirty-Ninth Street Grounds), holding some 5000 spectators, but he quickly realized that a larger facility was a necessity for his White Sox, who won pennants in 1901 and 1906 and usually outdrew the Cubs, whom they defeated in the 1906 World Series. Comiskey several times added new seating to South Side Park, but there was a limit to what he could do with his wooden grandstands. In 1909, he bought a former city dump at 35th Street and Shields Avenue in the south side of Chicago, favored because a streetcar line ran past it, and retained a local architect named Zachary Taylor Davis to design a new ballpark. Ed Walsh, the star White Sox pitcher, was assigned to work with Davis in setting out the playing field dimensions. As might have been expected, these dimensions were very pitcher-friendly: 362 feet to the left- and right-field foul poles and 420 feet to center field.

The massive new park was built in four and a half months, at a cost of nearly a million dollars, and was ready to open on July 1, 1910, although the day before it opened a laborer fell to his death from the top of the grandstand — not a good omen. The park was originally called White Sox

Park but within three years the name was changed to Comiskey. It was the fourth concrete-and-steel stadium in the big leagues, its seating capacity was about 28,000, and it was nicknamed "The Baseball Palace of the World."

When the park opened, the St. Louis Browns dampened the enthusiasm of a greater-than-capacity crowd of about 32,000 which saw hometown hero Ed Walsh lose, 2–0. What they saw of the ballpark itself they liked — a covered double-deck grandstand behind home plate that extended down the foul lines about thirty feet beyond the bases. Beyond that were detached covered single-deck pavilions down to the corners, and uncovered bleachers across left-center and right-center field, to a center-field scoreboard. Seven thousand of the ballpark's seats were bleacher seats priced at 25 cents.

The 1910 White Sox slipped back into the second division, although their attendance improved somewhat with the new ballpark. In 1915, Clarence "Pants" Rowland was named manager, and he, with the help of players such as Eddie Collins, Ray Schalk, Joe Jackson, Buck Weaver and Eddie Cicotte, pushed the Sox higher in the standings until his 1917 squad won the pennant with a record of 100–54, the only White Sox team ever to win one hundred games.

Comiskey Park saw its first World Series in 1917, when Rowland's Pale Hose (as the Sox were sometimes called, though their fans never particularly liked the term) knocked off John McGraw's New York Giants in six games, with Red Faber picking up three wins for Chicago. The White Sox collapsed into seventh place in 1918, and Rowland was fired as manager, but the Series returned again that season, when Charles Comiskey permitted the Cubs, pennant winners in the National League, to play in his park, with its greater seating capacity than their own yard. The Cubs lost in 1918, and the White Sox, under new skipper Kid Gleason, lost the World Series in 1919, five games to three, to Cincinnati. In the latter Series, of course, seven of the Chicago players — the Black Sox — took bribes from gamblers to throw the games and were ultimately banned from baseball by Commissioner Landis.

Over the years there have been many who said the Chicago players were driven to financial desperation by Comiskey's penurious, even stingy, ways. Apologists for Shoeless Joe Jackson, the best of the eight Black Sox players (Buck Weaver was banned by Landis for his knowledge of the plot, even though he did not participate in it), have said that since he was illiterate he did not know what he was getting into. However, Jackson certainly knew what the $5000 in cash was when he accepted it, and he knew enough to ask for more when another payment was not made. And Jackson *did* make a statement confessing to what he had done, even though this confession was later stolen from the prosecuting attorney's files. Although the White Sox won three games in the Series, these were games that were pitched by Dickie Kerr, one of the honest players, or games in which the Black Sox players actually tried to win, angry at the gamblers for failing to make promised payments. In the end, the Reds — and the gamblers — won.

In the years after the Black Sox scandal, it appeared that the Chicago White Sox were paying a never-ending penalty for it. Over the '20s, '30s, and into the '40s, the Sox featured two great players, shortstop Luke Appling and pitcher Ted Lyons, and many nondescript nonentities. Jimmy Dykes managed the club from 1934 to 1946, getting many laughs along the way with his witty repartee and irritating a lot of umpires, but his teams did not win many games.

Before the 1927 season, the park underwent a major renovation, as the bleachers were replaced with concrete and steel sections, and all the single-deck stands, out to center field, were double-decked. The seating capacity of Comiskey Park increased to 52,000, and the place had reached the shape it would retain for the rest of its years. However, with the lackluster White Sox teams, the added seating was not often needed. Between 1927 and 1951, historian Rich Lindberg wrote, the park "was filled to capacity only a dozen times, mostly for Sunday doubleheaders with the Yankees."[1]

When the club obtained slugger Al Simmons from Philadelphia after the 1933 season, Comiskey's heirs, who were running the team since the old man, known as "the Old Roman," had died in 1931, moved home plate 14 feet forward to give Simmons a better shot at the seats. After a couple of seasons, Simmons was sold to Detroit and home plate came back again.

On July 6, 1933, Comiskey Park was the site of the very first All-Star game, the brainchild of Arch Ward, the sports editor of the *Chicago Tribune*, who sold the idea to Judge Landis and the owners as part of the Century of Progress Exposition in Chicago that year. The owners reluctantly agreed, and the baseball public chose most of the players for the contest. Two great managerial icons, Connie Mack and the recently-retired John McGraw, ran the two teams. A fine crowd of 47,595 turned out, and the American League team won, 4–2, with 38-year-old Babe Ruth bashing a two-run home run. Jimmy Dykes of the White Sox, playing third, scored the first run in All-Star history in the second inning, coming in on a single by starting pitcher Lefty Gomez. The contest was a great success, the base-

Comiskey Park, the pride of the south side of Chicago (Philadelphia Athletics Historical Society).

ball establishment enjoyed it, and the All-Star game has been a mid-season tradition ever since.

There were lots of other events, some baseball and some not, which took place in Comiskey Park. From 1933 until 1960 (except 1958), the Negro Leagues' All-Star game was played there, frequently drawing bigger crowds than the major leagues' All-Star game of the same season. The Chicago American Giants played Negro League ball in Comiskey from 1941 to 1952. On September 22, 1937, Joe Louis, the "Brown Bomber," won the heavyweight title there, knocking out Jimmy Braddock in the eighth round. Twice more the heavyweight crown changed hands in Comiskey Park, in 1949 when Ezzard Charles beat Jersey Joe Walcott after Louis retired, and in 1962 when Sonny Liston kayoed Floyd Patterson in the first round, in a fight moved to Chicago because the boxing commission in New York, where it was originally scheduled, would not give Liston a license because of his criminal past.

The National Football League's Chicago Cardinals played in the

White Sox ballyard from 1929 until they moved to St. Louis after the 1958 season. Their most famous victory in Comiskey Park was the NFL championship game on December 28, 1947, when the frozen field caused the home team, led by Charley Trippi and Pat Harder, to change to sneakers for better traction, enabling the Cards to beat the Philadelphia Eagles, 28–21. (The Eagles had the last laugh when they beat the Cardinals in the 1948 championship game in Shibe Park, 7–0, in a blinding snowstorm.)

In August 1965, the Beatles filled the place with 55,000 screaming fans when they stopped in Chicago on their World Tour, and Michael Jackson sang and danced there too. In 1968 and again from 1980 to 1985, Comiskey Park served as the home field for professional soccer teams called the Mustangs and the Sting.

Occasionally, there were reminders of the city dump that had been there before the White Sox. During a game in the '30s, shortstop Luke Appling was smoothing the dirt around his position when he felt something hard hit his foot. "I started digging with my spikes," he said later, "and, lo and behold, I uncovered a blue-and-white teakettle. Quite an antique. The ground crew had to fill in the hole before play could continue."[2]

On Opening Day in 1940, young Bob Feller of Cleveland helped the White Sox open their season at home by holding them without a hit, the only Opening Day no-hitter ever. And in 1949, General Manager Frank Lane raised some eyebrows when he put up a low white fence across the outfield that reduced home run distances by 20 feet, then removed it in the middle of the night before the Yankees came to town. These antics caused a rule to be imposed that fences could be moved only once a year.

White Sox mediocrity continued on the field after World War II, through the end of Dykes's tenure and the managerial terms of Ted Lyons and Jack Onslow. One high point in Comiskey's history came on July 5, 1947, when Larry Doby's appearance at bat for the Indians there marked the end of segregation in the American League.

The All-Star game returned to Comiskey Park, its place of origin, in 1950, when the National League won, 4–3, in 14 innings on Red Schoendienst's home run. Ted Williams banged his elbow against the left-field wall catching a Ralph Kiner drive, sustaining a fracture that kept him out until late in the season. A crowd of 46,127 showed up for the game, but the sole White Sox All-Star representative, pitcher Ray Scarborough, did not get into the contest.

In 1951, with an old catcher named Paul Richards now in charge as manager, the Pale Hose had their first winning season since 1943, climbing to fourth place with an 81–73 record. For the first time ever the club drew more than a million fans, pulling in 1,328,234 to watch an exciting team led by a short, tobacco-chewing second baseman named Nellie Fox and the club's first black player, Orestes "Minnie" Minoso, who socked a home run off the Yankees' Vic Raschi in his first at bat.

The Sox finished in third place from 1952 through 1956, under Richards and then Marty Marion. In 1957, Al Lopez took over the team and led it to second place in that year and the next. On March 10, 1959, a syndicate headed by the irrepressible Bill Veeck bought the club from the Comiskey heirs. The fans knew that Veeck specialized in extravaganzas to fill his ballpark, and in 1959 Veeck gave them the very best kind of extravaganza — a pennant winner — which put a club record 1,423,144 spectators in the seats of Comiskey Park. With Lopez at the helm of a ballclub featuring Fox, Minoso, shortstop Luis Aparicio, catcher Sherm Lollar, southpaw Billy Pierce, and outfielder Jim Landis, the "Go-Go-Sox," as they were called because of their reliance on speed, daring, and defense, won the American League flag by five games over the runner-up Indians. The Sox were last in the league in home runs, but first in triples, stolen bases, fielding, saves, earned run average, and fewest opponent runs allowed. For the first time since the Black Sox in 1919, the World Series returned to Comiskey Park, which Veeck had spruced up considerably, creating a picnic area beyond left field, remodeling the rest rooms, and painting the park's exterior white.

The first game of the World Series, fittingly for its return to the park after so many years, went to the White Sox, as they whipped the Los Angeles Dodgers, 11–0. Two of baseball's big stars, nearing the ends of their illustrious careers, had big days. Early Wynn, who won 22 games for Chicago in the regular season, threw seven innings of the shutout, and slugger Ted Kluszewski, acquired by the Sox late in August, hit two home runs. Unfortunately, that was about the high spot for the Pale Hose. They won one more game, a 1–0 victory in Game Five before a record 92,706 in Los Angeles, with Bob Shaw, Billy Pierce and Dick Donovan combining on the shutout, but the Dodgers closed out the Series with their victory in six games, jumping on Wynn and Donovan early in the 9–3 finale in Comiskey Park. Fox, Kluszewski, and Luis Aparicio hit well for the Sox, but the pitching was up-and-down, the rest of the lineup contributed little, and the Dodgers even stole more bases, five, than the two the White Sox picked up.

The following year, Veeck unveiled his masterpiece, a centerfield scoreboard which exploded with a White Sox home run. Veeck rewired the big scoreboard which had been installed behind the centerfield bleach-

Main entrance to Comiskey Park, 1959, before Bill Veeck painted the ballpark white (photograph by the author).

ers in 1951, equipped it for sound and fireworks, and had it ready for Opening Day. Minoso hit two homers in that first game, setting off the foghorns, bugles, sirens, "William Tell" overture, a whistling "Dixie," flashing lights, and a series of fireworks explosions, getting louder with each one. The fans loved it, and the visiting teams hated it.

On May 30, 1960, the mercurial Jimmy Piersall, playing for the Indians, saw Minoso line a ball over his head, off the wall. Somebody on the White Sox staff mistakenly thought it was a homer and ordered the scoreboard into action, momentarily terrifying Piersall. Later in the game, a frustrated Piersall (who later, ironically, became a broadcaster for the White Sox) fired a baseball at the offending scoreboard, gaining some sort of satisfaction out of the gesture.

It was in 1960 that Andy the Clown began appearing at White Sox games. Andrew Rodzilsky was invited to a game by friends, and he decided to wear the clown costume he wore at family and neighborhood events. The crowd at Comiskey loved his act, and the next year he began performing at all home games. He was easily seen at the park, wearing a bowler hat, black-rimmed glasses, and a polka-dotted costume, with a large red nose that lit up. Andy the Clown became a fixture at the ballpark, known for his costume and for his stretched-out cheer, "Gooooo yooouuu Whiiiite Sooooox!" He was never an employee of the team over the thirty years that he performed, but he was provided with free admission to the park.

Sadly, Bill Veeck fell seriously ill and sold the team in June of 1961, to Arthur C. Allyn, Jr. The White Sox under Allyn's direction continued in the first division through most of the sixties, with Lopez managing through 1965, followed by Eddie Stanky. Attendance stayed over the million mark through 1965 and close thereafter, although late in the decade the Sox played some home games in Milwaukee. In 1968, the club installed artificial turf (called "Sox Sod") in the infield, but the team fell to eighth place that season. The next year the park's name was changed to White Sox Park, but the Comiskey name was restored in 1975; most people still called it by that name anyway.

The Sox struggled early in the '70s. On May 6, 1971, only 511 spectators showed up at Comiskey for a game with the Red Sox. Conversely, however, a "Bat Day" promotion a couple of years later drew a huge crowd of 55,555 for a doubleheader with the Twins. But in 1972, slugger Dick Allen, often hard to handle elsewhere, played for manager Chuck Tanner, both coming from the same small town, Wampum, Pennsylvania, and put together a splendid season, hitting .308, with league leading home run and runs-batted-in totals of 37 and 113, and winning the league's Most Valuable Player award. The team finished second in the west. Allen won another home run crown two years later, with 32, though he left the team with two weeks to go, leading the White Sox reluctantly to trade him to Atlanta. Then, in December 1975, a rejuvenated Bill Veeck reacquired the club.

One of the first things that Veeck did was tear up the artificial turf and replace it with real grass. He fiddled with the team's uniforms, briefly trying shorts instead of the regular trousers, but they did not last. Veeck had beer-case stacking contests and an anti-superstition night. In 1977, in celebration of his team called the "South Side Hit Men" (the White Sox actually finished second in the AL in home runs, paced by Oscar Gamble's 31, Richie Zisk's 30, and Eric Soderholm's 25), Veeck had a small section in the left-field upper deck seats painted in a wild multicolor pattern. When asked why, he would never explain.

And then, on July 12, 1979, came "Disco Demolition Night." A promotion thought up by Mike Veeck, Bill's son, and local rock-and-roll disc jockey Steve Dahl, rock fans were invited to bring their hated disco records to the ballpark (for a discounted admission of 98 cents) to be destroyed between games of a twi-nite doubleheader with the Tigers. More than 50,000 showed up, and it was rumored that many thousands more had crashed the gates. Most of them, unfortunately, were not baseball fans. During the first game, many records and other objects were sailed like Frisbees around the grandstands and onto the field, with players ducking and dodging the flying missiles; outfielder Ron LeFlore was almost hit by a golf ball. Between games, while the record demolition was taking place in center field, several thousand mostly intoxicated spectators stormed the field, a riot ensued, and the second game of the doubleheader was forfeited to Detroit, the field being declared by the umpires as "unplayable." A bad night for Bill Veeck and his White Sox, it was a most infamous night for Comiskey Park.

But Veeck always wanted to make sure his fans were having a good time at the ballpark. He put in a barber's chair and shower in the centerfield bleachers and a cocktail lounge where fans could buy mixed drinks. Kenneth Valdisseri, of the White Sox public relations staff, said, "The place used to be called the largest tavern in Chicago."[3]

Organist Nancy Faust, originally hired in 1970, became a Windy City institution playing "We will, we will, SOX YOU" and, as a farewell to ejected managers and battered visiting pitchers, "Na-na-na-na, Na-na-na-na, Hey-Hey, Kiss Him GOODBYE." Veeck encouraged White Sox broadcaster Harry Caray to conduct or sing "Take Me Out to the Ball Game" for the fans at the seventh-inning stretch. And there was always Andy the Clown. "Under Bill Veeck," wrote Phil Lowry, "this was a real ballpark, with everything happening at once and everyone having a good time."[4]

In 1981, however, Veeck, who never operated with a lot of money, recognized that he was unable to compete in the new era of free agent multi-million-dollar contracts. In January of that year, he sold the team to a couple of wealthy operators, Jerry Reinsdorf and Eddie Einhorn. Reinsdorf, who would run the franchise, was a tax attorney who made a fortune in real estate. The new owners spent $14 million fixing up the park, trying to bring the old place up to current building standards, although $5 million of that was on a new scoreboard. After the 1982 season, they moved the plate out eight feet, shortening the home run distances. They even tried to keep Andy the Clown out or to restrict his appearances, but this effort was repudiated instantly by the fans and the media, and the owners quickly backtracked.

In 1983, the All-Star game returned to Comiskey, to celebrate the fiftieth anniversary of the midsummer classic. Fred Lynn marked the occasion with the first ever All-Star grand slam. A couple of months later, the '83 White Sox, managed by Tony LaRussa, clinched the American League West title, winning their division by twenty games over Kansas City, with a 99–63 record. Leading the White Sox were designated hitter Greg Luzinski, outfielders Ron Kittle and Harold Baines, catcher Carlton Fisk, and two 20-game-winning right-handers, LaMarr Hoyt and Richard Dotson. Unfortunately, there would be no World Series in Chicago, as the Baltimore Orioles stomped the Sox in the league championship series, three games to one, with two of the four being played at Comiskey.

The next year Reinsdorf started seriously considering the replacement of his deteriorating ballpark, and proposals were requested from developers for a new stadium. In December 1985, the club bought a parcel of land in suburban Addison, in DuPage County, which started an elaborate dance during the next couple of years over the eventual home of the White Sox. Reinsdorf, Chicago Mayor Harold Washington (who said, "The Addison White Sox make as much sense as a polar bear in Mexico"), Illinois Governor Jim Thompson, officials in DuPage County, and officials in St. Petersburg, Florida (where a ballpark was built with hopes of luring the White Sox south), all were involved in the moves which eventually resulted in the Illinois state legislature passing a bill at the last possible legal moment (or perhaps a few minutes beyond) to underwrite construction of a new stadium in Chicago, right next door to Comiskey Park.

So the countdown to Comiskey's end had begun. Three times in its final decade (1983, 1984, and 1990) Sox fans turned out more than two million strong to cheer the exploits of Carlton Fisk, Robin Ventura, Ozzie Guillen, and Greg Walker. The Pale Hose gave them some good baseball but no championships. Then, in early 1989, nearby buildings started to go, knocked down to make room for the new stadium. On March 27, McCuddy's Bar, across the street from Comiskey, went. The bar was built in 1910, primarily to serve the construction workers building the ballpark. In the old days, on a hot afternoon, Babe Ruth sometimes wandered over between innings for a cold one, and in later times Bill Veeck spent hours at McCuddy's. Now it was gone.

On July 11, 1990, the park saw "Turn Back the Clock Day," with the White Sox players wearing replica 1917 uniforms. Though they lost the game, Ozzie Guillen said, "I wish we could wear these uniforms all the time. I like them better than our real uniforms."[5]

The season wore on. Donn Pall, a White Sox pitcher and a native Chicagoan who was a lifetime Sox fan, walked around the stands the day before the last game, remembering games he had seen as a boy, remembering where he had sat. He recalled that he had even attended Disco Demolition Night, though he had brought no records.

Through the final season, some fans were able to pry loose bricks from the building and smuggle them out under their clothing. Early in the morning of September 7, police caught two young men who had dug up home plate and thrown it over a wall out to the sidewalk beyond; one of the thieves tried jumping off the wall after it and damaged his ankle when he landed, making apprehension easy. During the last home stand, signs and pictures were removed from the ballpark concourses. A number of fans were arrested during games for trying to dismantle seats for souvenirs.

Then it was down to one last game. On the afternoon of September 30, 1990, the White Sox took on the Seattle Mariners in the final contest at old Comiskey Park. (As the Old Roman would have said, "Seattle??!! Playing us??") Fred Friestedt, son of the general contractor for the park's reconstruction in 1927, was there for the last game. "I was very sad about it," he said, "but I had been through it before the last game and I don't know how it got by the city inspectors."[6]

Certificates were handed out to the spectators as they passed through the gates, proof of their attendance at this final game. There were 42,849 of them who showed up, since the game had been sold out as soon as tickets went on sale on June 9. Someone toted up the number 72,801,381, the total baseball attendance since the ballpark opened in 1910. Mayor Richard M. Daley and Chuck Comiskey, there to represent the shade of his grandfather, were on hand. Andy the Clown was there for the last time. After 30 years, White Sox management had notified him that he would not be permitted to perform in the new stadium. From show business, Goldie Hawn and Kurt Russell were there, as were John Candy, Ron Howard, and George Wendt.

Some of the old White Sox players had their say about Comiskey. Wilbur Wood, the knuckleballer who pitched there for 12 years in the '60s and '70s, said, ""It's a shame they're tearing it down. It was a great park for me to pitch in because I had the big outfield to work with." Walt Dropo, who played first for the Sox in the mid–'50s, said, "You hate to see it happen because it is one of the originals. If you hit a homer, you earned it. Comiskey was the fairest. I loved playing there." Slugger Greg Luzinski offered his opinion: "For me, it was a fun place to play ... with the scoreboard and the fans and everything."[7]

There were other opinions. Ozzie Guillen said, "There's a lot of history here, but the fans don't know this is a real uncomfortable place for us.... A lot of people just don't know how bad it is for the players." Carlton Fisk said he would miss nothing about Comiskey. "The showers aren't good. They're only two stalls in the wash room. You can't hardly turn around in the clubhouse. The wind's always blowing in." Jeff Torborg, the manager in 1990, said, "It's a rotten dugout, the worst dugout I've ever seen. I've given signals behind poles for two years."[8]

The legendary Minnie Minoso came out to present the White Sox lineup card to the umpires and then the game was on. Jack McDowell was on the mound for the home team, with Rich DeLucia going for the Mariners. Seattle scored a run in the top of the sixth to take a 1–0 lead, but the Pale Hose came back in the bottom of the inning. Lance Johnson tripled into the right-field corner but stayed on third as the great Chicago catcher, Fisk, struck out. Rookie first baseman Frank Thomas then singled to center to tie the score and came around to score himself when Ken Griffey, Sr., let Dan Pasqua's liner skip by him for a triple. McDowell threw two more scoreless innings, and then the Sox closer, Bobby Thigpen, came in to save the game with a scoreless ninth.

Longtime White Sox fan Dennis Bingham was there and called it an "emotional but strange experience. Is it really over?" he asked himself. "How am I supposed to feel?" He recalled that "before, during and after the game everybody was thinking about how the fans would react," having in mind the riotous scenes at some closing games of other ballparks and the recent attempts to steal souvenirs from the ballpark. As it turned out the fans were well-behaved and stayed off the field, possibly because of the very visible police security there. "During the game," Bingham said, "fans kept saying such statements as, 'That's probably the last triple,' 'I wonder if that will be the last strikeout,' 'Who will be the last batter?'" The final batter in fact was Harold Reynolds of the Mariners, who pulled a Thigpen fastball to second base, where Scott Fletcher picked it up and threw it to Steve Lyons at first to end the game.

Bingham learned that a fan sitting near him was at the ballpark for the first time, "a Cubs fan who had lived in Chicago his entire life but had never visited Comiskey.... He was taking up space that could have been filled by a Sox fan who would have given anything to be at the last game." That last game, he said, "was strange because of the emotions. Not really a 'celebration' but not really funereal either."

Howard Pizer, the Sox executive vice president, estimated that there may have been 2,000 video recorders in the crowd, as well as a very large number of three-generation family groups. Although there were about forty arrests at the ballpark, there was little vandalism. The deputy police

Harold Reynolds grounds out, Scott Fletcher to Steve Lyons, for the final out in Comiskey Park, September 30, 1990 (National Baseball Hall of Fame Library, Cooperstown).

chief on hand said, "What makes me feel good is we weren't added to the ballparks that went up for grabs on their last day."⁹

Mike Lopresti, a Gannett News Service writer, said, "Somehow, it has been the poor cousin in the family of old ballparks, not so treasured as Fenway Park or as hallowed as Yankee Stadium ... Comiskey Park did not become venerable so much as it became old."¹⁰

But Carlton Fisk was called out for a curtain call by the fans after his last at-bat, the crowd sang "Na-na-na-na, hey, hey, hey, kiss him GOOD-BYE" one final time, and they stood and looked out on the field. Fisk said, "I don't think the fans wanted to go out there. They wanted to stand back and reflect and take in what was happening." The players disappeared into their clubhouse, but then the '90 White Sox came back out onto the field, waving their caps to the fans and throwing baseballs up into the stands.

At 4:32 P.M., Nancy Faust, who said she was "pretty depressed," played "Auld Lang Syne" on the organ. The fans stood and sang along, and some threw white socks onto the outfield grass. The scoreboard fireworks went off one last time. Then the fans filed out. Old Comiskey Park was done—

but not quite. Fisk took a stately walk through the outfield, stopping by the stands in left to sign a banner that a fan had displayed for most of the time he'd played for Chicago: "Pitch at Risk to Fisk." He walked back, blew kisses to his parents and daughter in the stands, hugged Ozzie Guillen, shook hands with Andy the Clown, and disappeared into the dugout for the final time.

Forty-five minutes after the game, usher John Brudnak proposed at home plate to fellow usher Debbie Falahee; she accepted. More than an hour after the game ended, White Sox hitting coach Walt Hriniak walked down an aisle and sat quietly in a second-row seat for a few minutes before leaving to get on the team bus.

A week after the final game, head groundskeeper Roger Bossard (whose father Gene Bossard had been head groundskeeper at Comiskey from 1941 to 1983) began carting eight inches of infield dirt across the street to the new park, a four-inch base and four inches of topsoil. "Why change it?" Bossard asked. "The guys are happy with it."[11]

On April 4, 1991, wreckers started in on the demolition of the old ballpark, a demolition which was carried out in stages throughout that summer, eventually turning the site of old Comiskey Park into a parking lot for the new one. The ghosts of Eddie Collins, Luke Appling, Nellie Fox, and Ted Lyons turned their heads away.

Chapter 12
Used to Be Briggs Stadium

For more than a hundred years, baseball in the city of Detroit was concentrated at the intersection of Michigan Avenue and Trumbull Avenue, long known as "The Corner." Here, in 1896, in a part of the city called Corktown for its nineteenth-century Irish immigrants, was erected a wooden grandstand, seating 8000 spectators, known as Bennett Park. It was named after Charley Bennett, a popular catcher for Detroit's old National League team who lost his leg when he fell under a train in 1894. Bennett Park was located on the former site of a haymarket, with a few inches of dirt spread over the old cobblestones.

The team playing in Bennett Park was in Ban Johnson's Western League. When Johnson turned his circuit into a major league in 1901, the Detroit Tigers went right along with him. In the first decade of the league's existence, the ownership of the franchise went through several changes until 1908, when Frank J. Navin bought the club over which he would preside for a quarter century.

It was quite a club, one that won pennants in 1907, 1908, and 1909, led by players like the inimitable Ty Cobb, Germany Schaefer, and Wahoo Sam Crawford. Navin decided that the team needed a bigger ballpark and, following the example first set in Philadelphia, he built one using the new concrete-and-steel technology, with grandstands running from first to third base and behind the plate. Called Navin Field, it opened on April 20, 1912 (the same day the Boston Red Sox unveiled their new Fenway Park), and it seated 23,000 customers, nearly triple the capacity of Bennett Park. In 1924, Navin added a second deck, which pushed the seating capacity up to 30,000.

The Tigers made runs at the American League pennant in 1915, 1916, and 1919, under manager Hughie Jennings, but could get no closer than second place, two and a half games back, in 1915, even though they won a hundred games. For six years in the '20s, Ty Cobb managed the club, but six games back in 1924 (when the club drew more than a million fans for the first time) was the closest he could get. Cobb, of course, had won twelve batting titles, including nine in a row from 1907 through 1915, and outfielder Harry Heilmann won four batting crowns in the '20s — every other year, oddly, from 1921 through 1927 — but these individual achievements (including another batting title in 1926 for Heinie Manush) did not translate into club pennants. George Moriarty ran the team for a couple of seasons, and Bucky Harris managed it for five years into the '30s, but with little success.

Navin, who had a reputation as a penny-pincher (his annual salary tiffs with Cobb were legendary in Detroit), was nearly ruined by the Depression in the '30s, but Walter O. Briggs, who made a fortune manufacturing auto bodies and who had been a part-owner of the baseball club since 1920, put money into the team to help keep it going.

In 1934, Navin and Briggs came up with $100,000 to acquire the great catcher Mickey Cochrane from Connie Mack's Athletics. Cochrane was named manager, and the Tigers finished in first place, seven games ahead of the Yankees. It was quite a ball club. The infield was manned by slugger Hank Greenberg at first, the great Charlie Gehringer at second, Billy Rogell at short, and Marv Owen at third, with an outfield of Pete Fox, Jojo White, and Goose Goslin. Cochrane himself did most of the catching (and won the MVP award for the American League), and Tommy Bridges and Lynwood "Schoolboy" Rowe each won more than 20 games. Curiously, the runner-up Yanks had triple-crown winners in both Lou Gehrig for hitters and Lefty Gomez for pitchers, but it did them little good.[1]

Cochrane's club took on the Cardinals in the World Series and split the first two games at Navin Field, as Dizzy Dean and Rowe gave dominant performances. The Tigers took two of three in St. Louis, with Eldon Auker and Bridges winning after Paul Dean had won Game Three for the Cards. Back in Detroit, Paul Dean outpitched Rowe in Game Six to tie things up, and in Game Seven brother Dizzy won easily, 11–0, to clinch the Series for St. Louis. After Cardinal leftfielder Joe Medwick slid hard into Owen at third base, he was pelted with fruit and bottles from the Tiger fans in the stands behind him the next half inning, until Commissioner Landis had the Cards, safely ahead by nine runs, remove Medwick from the game for his own protection.

The next season, the Tigers won it all, and Frank Navin (who passed away on November 13, 1935) was able to die a happy man. Greenberg led the league with 36 homers and 170 runs batted in and was the American League's most valuable player. Cochrane, Gehringer, and Fox had fine years at the plate, and pitchers Bridges, Rowe and Auker were outstanding. The Tigers whipped the Cubs, four games to two, to take the World Series, with Bridges (two), Alvin "General" Crowder, and Rowe picking up the four winning games. In the final game, in Detroit, Cochrane scored the Series-winning run on Goose Goslin's ninth-inning single, and the crowd went whoopee.

After Navin's death, Walter Briggs became the sole owner of the ball club, and he immediately set about taking care of something that he and Navin had discussed. With new decks added in right and center field, the ballpark's capacity was increased to 36,000. Before the 1938 season, double-deck stands were erected in left and left-center field, and the seating capacity went up to 53,000. This change was made possible when the city of Detroit agreed to move Cherry Street, running behind left field. The name of the park was changed to Briggs Stadium, with the new owner commenting that he expected the facility to remain in his family for some time.

Another development in 1938 was the addition of the football Lions as tenants in the fall; the Lions would stay there until after the 1974 season, when they moved to the new Pontiac Silverdome, in nearby Pontiac, Michigan. The Lions had limited success in the Tigers' park. In the '40s, they won but 35 games in the decade, and in 1943 played a 0–0 tie with the Giants, the last time that has happened in the National Football League. Led by quarterbacks Bobby Layne and Tobin Rote, the Lions won three NFL championships in the '50s, in 1952, 1953, and 1957 (Rote's year), beating the Cleveland Browns in the title game each time. After the 1958 season, however, the Lions traded Layne to Pittsburgh and, as he was leaving town, the unhappy quarterback said the Lions "would not win for fifty years," a prediction which turned out to be all too accurate. On Thanksgiving Day in 1974, a throng of 51,157 saw the final Lions' football game in the ballpark, with the home team losing to the Denver Broncos, 31–27.

Briggs Stadium had several unique features. Its flagpole, 125 feet high, was in play in center field, near the 440-feet mark, and it was the highest obstacle in fair play ever in big league baseball. Often noted was the sign over one of the clubhouses: "VISITORS' CLUBHOUSE — NO VISITORS ALLOWED." In right field, the upper deck overhung the field by ten feet, often frustrating right fielders preparing to catch a long fly which suddenly landed in the upper stands for a home run. In addition, to deal

Briggs Stadium, Detroit, formerly known as Navin Field (National Baseball Hall of Fame Library, Cooperstown).

with this anomaly, lights were installed beneath the overhang, so the right fielder did not suddenly disappear into the darkness.

Babe Ruth hit some historic home runs in Detroit's ballpark. On July 18, 1921, he blasted what is considered one of the very longest homers in history — thought by some to be the longest — a shot to straightaway center that landed on the far side of the intersection outside the stadium, probably 600 feet on the fly. Years later, after many intervening home runs, the Bambino hit number 700 of his career in Navin Field — or, rather, out of Navin Field — on July 13, 1934, a boomer which carried more than 500 feet.

On May 2, 1939, another historic event took place when Yankee first baseman Lou Gehrig benched himself at Briggs Stadium, ending his consecutive-game streak at 2,130 games.

There were more than 30 home runs hit onto or over the right-field roof during the park's history. But left field was a different matter. In left it was some 15 feet farther down the foul line than in right, and the roof over the upper deck was set back even more. Only four right-handed sluggers ever hit a ball over the left-field roof—Harmon Killebrew, Frank Howard, Cecil Fielder, and Mark McGwire.

In 1940, the Tigers put together another pennant-winner, beating Cleveland—the "Cry-baby Indians," who had revolted against manager Ossie Vitt—on the last day of the season, as rookie Floyd Giebell outpitched the Indians' ace, Bob Feller. It was one of only three games that Giebell would ever win, but it stands huge in Tiger history. Manager Del Baker held his team together, with Greenberg's league-leading 41 homers and 150 runs batted in leading the way. Gehringer, first sacker Rudy York, catcher Birdie Tebbetts, and outfielder Barney McCosky were mainstays on the club, and the pitching was led by Bridges, Rowe, garrulous righthander Bobo Newsom, who had a 21–5 record, and a 19-year-old lefthander who was born and raised in Detroit, Hal Newhouser, who won nine games. Greenberg won another MVP award, and McCosky, with his .340 average, led the league in triples. The club had its highest single-season attendance, as it prepared for the World Series against the Cincinnati Reds.

For the opener in Cincinnati, Newsom was strong and won, 7–2. The next day Rowe faltered and Bucky Walters pitched the Reds to a 5–3 win. In Briggs Stadium for Game Three, Tommy Bridges won, but the next game went to the Reds to tie things up. Just before Game Five, Newsom learned of his father's death, but he pulled himself together and threw a three-hit shutout. For the sixth game, the Reds' Walters was superb, pitching a shutout and even hitting a home run. The deciding game came down to a duel between Newsom and Paul Derringer, and both hurlers were excellent. Detroit got a run in the third, but the Reds got two in the seventh against Newsom and Derringer held on for the 2–1 victory. It was a dramatic Series, but the drama had a sad ending for the Tigers.

Over the next couple of years, the Tigers declined, and Baker left after the '42 season, with an old catcher named Steve O'Neill taking over as manager. In 1941, the All-Star game came to Detroit for the first time, with Del Baker managing the American League team. Rudy York was the only Tiger to play in the game (Greenberg was in the armed services by this time), but the game was so exciting the fans barely noticed the lack of hometown players. Arky Vaughan of the Pirates looked like the day's hero, as his two home runs gave the Nationals a 5–3 lead going into the ninth. The Americans had one run in but two outs when Ted Williams smashed a dramatic three-run homer into the upper right-field stands to give Baker and his team an emotional 7–5 victory. The usually non-demonstrative Baker hugged and kissed the young Red Sox outfielder.

The economy of the city of Detroit was and has been based primarily on the automobile industry, starting with Henry Ford's Model T and Model A and growing ever stronger with the advent of General Motors, Chrysler and Packard. The United Auto Workers, under the inspired leadership in the '40s of Walter Reuther, became one of the strongest unions in the nation, and the high wages and lush benefits it secured for its members contributed to Detroit's prosperity.

The dark side, however, of the city's urban life was racial hatred, which became more pronounced as blacks from the south came to Detroit during the war seeking to share in the economic bonanza of manufacturing to fill ever-increasing military demands. White workingmen were not disposed to share and resented the newcomers. In June 1943, a racial disturbance at Belle Isle, one of the city's prime recreation centers, exploded into a riot in which 34 people were killed, 1800 were arrested, and millions of dollars of property damage occurred before President Franklin Roosevelt ordered the U.S. Army in to restore order. The 1943 race riot was a shadow which hung over Detroit for years.

In that same year, with the wartime manpower demands thinning major-league rosters, Detroit picked up a 34-year-old catcher named Paul Richards, who had not been in the majors since 1935. Richards was never much of an offensive threat, but he was a savvy operator behind the plate, and he soon saw an opportunity to make a major contribution with the young lefthander, Newhouser. Richards quickly spotted the great potential in the young pitcher, but he observed that Newhouser's nearly-uncontrollable temper was constantly getting him into difficulty. In '43, for example, Newhouser pitched well enough early in the season to make the All-Star team for the second year in a row (and to pitch three scoreless innings in the game at Shibe Park), and to be "recognized as the best lefthander in the league."[2]

But after the All-Star Game, everything went wrong for Newhouser. "The second half of the season was a nightmare of errors, bases on balls, bad pitching, temperamental outbursts, and losses." The young southpaw's lack of self-control, which often led to a lack of pitching control, resulted in an overall 8–17 record for the season, leading the league in walks (although he also finished second in strikeouts). H.G. Salsinger, the veteran Detroit baseball writer, said, "It is inconceivable that a pitcher who started out as brilliantly as Newhouser could become such a failure."[3]

In spring training in 1944, after Walter Briggs refused to agree to a trade of Newhouser to Cleveland for righthander Jim Bagby, Richards took him in hand. He made some technical adjustments in the pitcher's delivery, helped him develop a fine change-up and a slider, the newly-popular breaking pitch, and worked on his disposition. Newhouser recognized his problem and made a very conscious effort to curb his temper. It worked. Hal Newhouser of the Tigers swiftly became the best pitcher in baseball, winning 29 games in 1944, which, along with staffmate Dizzy Trout's 27 wins, almost won Detroit the pennant. The team finished one game behind the Browns, when Trout lost the last game of the season. Newhouser led the league in wins and strikeouts, finished just behind Trout in earned run average (2.22), innings, complete games, and shutouts, and was named the league's Most Valuable Player.

The following season, the Tigers won the pennant and Newhouser again won the MVP award, leading the league in wins (25), ERA (1.81), strikeouts, innings, shutouts, and complete games. The Tigers, bolstered by the return of Hank Greenberg from the army and the solid play of second-baseman Eddie Mayo, Rudy York at first, and outfielders Roy Cullenbine and Doc Cramer, went on to win the World Series from the Chicago Cubs in seven games. Newhouser, knocked out early in the first game, came back to win Games Five and Seven, after fireballer Virgil Trucks, just out of the service, and Trout won two earlier games.

The following year the Tigers finished a distant second to the Red Sox. To all those doubters who said of Newhouser, "Just wait until the big boys come back from the war," the southpaw, now known as "Prince Hal," responded by winning 26 games with a 1.94 earned run average, finishing second to Ted Williams in the MVP voting.

Over the ensuing years, the Tigers were often in contention, under O'Neill, Red Rolfe, Fred Hutchinson, and Bucky Harris again, and they were well supported by the Detroit fans, but they were never quite able to put it all together. Walter Briggs, the clubowner, was no fan of night baseball, so lights were not installed in the park until 1948, the last park in the American League to do so, with the first night game there being played on June 15, 1948, as Newhouser pitched a two-hitter and the Tigers beat the A's, 4–1, before 54,480. A second All-Star game took place in Briggs Stadium in 1951, in conjunction with the city's 250th anniversary. The National League won it, 8–3, with four home runs. The American Leaguers had only two home runs, but both were hit by Tigers, Vic Wertz and George Kell.

In 1950, with Rolfe at the helm, the Tigers came close, finishing second to New York, but then they slipped back and finished last a couple of years later. Through the late '50s and into the '60s, Jack Tighe, Bill Norman, Jimmy Dykes, Joe Gordon, Bob Scheffing, and Chuck Dressen took turns as skipper (they even, in 1960, traded Dykes to the Indians for Gordon in mid-season, in the first-ever trade of managers), but nothing seemed to work. In 1966, there was a dreadful progression of managers, with Dressen suffering his second heart attack in two years, giving way after 26 games to interim manager Bob Swift, who was hospitalized in July for what turned out to be lung cancer, forcing the designation of coach Frank Skaff as the club's third manager of the season. Dressen died on August 10 and Swift on October 17, and Skaff, who was let go at the end of the year, figured he was lucky to get out of Detroit alive.

In July 1967, another series of race riots exploded in Detroit, brought about this time principally by black residents who were angered by school and housing segregation and "the casual brutality of a police force that was too white and too loosely supervised." Thousands of white residents fled to the city's white suburbs after these riots and Detroit became a majority-black city, while the auto industry started to experience a decline, brought on by foreign competition against its gas-guzzling products. The decline has accelerated in the years since, with the city of Detroit paying a stiff price as a result.[4]

But Detroit still had its Tigers, and better days were looked for. In 1956, a syndicate led by broadcasting millionaire John Fetzer purchased the Tigers franchise from the Briggs heirs (Walter died in 1952 and his son Spike ran the club after that), and Fetzer got complete control in 1961. He changed the name of the ballpark to Tiger Stadium for the '61 season, and it was the name the stadium would bear for the balance of its existence. Although the park was aging, Detroit fans were happy with it; some of its seats put spectators as close to the game as in any ballpark in the majors. In the mid-'60s, writer George Plimpton brought readers right out onto the field with him in his book *Paper Lion*, about his true-life adventures with the football Lions.[5]

For 1967, the Tigers hired as their manager Mayo Smith, a man who, after a brief big-league playing career with the 1945 Philadelphia Athletics, had put together a mediocre record as a manager with the Phillies and Reds. In Smith's first season in Detroit, the Tigers were in an exciting four-way fight for the pennant, which Boston won. Detroit finished tied for second with the Minnesota Twins, a game behind the Red Sox and two ahead of the White Sox. The Tigers were led by Al Kaline, who had come to them in 1954 as a 19-year-old from Baltimore, led the league in hitting as a 20-year-old the following season, batting .340, and gone on to a solid Hall-of-Fame career. First-baseman Norm Cash, catcher Bill Freehan, and outfielders Jim Northrup and Willie Horton provided offensive power, while Earl Wilson, Denny McLain, Mickey Lolich, and Joe Sparma led the pitching staff.

The following year, Smith's Tigers won the pennant with a record of 103–59, 12 games ahead of runner-up Baltimore, and their attendance in Tiger Stadium soared over the two million mark for the first time. Horton banged 36 home runs, while Freehan and Cash each added 25. The big story for the '68 Tigers, though, was righthanded pitcher Denny McLain, who posted a record of 31–6, the first 30-game winner in the majors since Dizzy Dean in 1934. McLain did it with an ERA of 1.96, 280 strikeouts, 28 complete games, and only 63 walks. He won both the Cy Young and Most Valuable Player awards for the American League. Oddly enough, the pitching hero of the '68 World Series, in which the Tigers defeated the Cardinals in seven games, was not McLain but lefthander Mickey Lolich, who threw three complete-game victories and outpitched the Cards' Bob Gibson, 4–1, in the finale. The hitting of Cash and Kaline led the way for the Tigers, who were able to celebrate their first world championship in 23 years.

In the following year, with the league now split into two divisions, Detroit won 90 games but was easily outpaced by the Orioles, who finished nineteen games ahead of them. McLain led the league in victories once more, with 24, garnering another Cy Young, and Lolich added 19, but the offense sputtered. When the club slipped to fourth the next year, with a losing record, Mayo Smith was let go, and the fiery Billy Martin replaced him. McLain spent most of 1970 on suspension after his gambling obsession and bookmaking activities came to light, and his won-lost record for the year was 3–5. After the season, Denny McLain was traded to Washington.[6]

Under Martin, the club did better. It climbed to second in 1971, with both Lolich and Joe Coleman (obtained in the McLain trade) winning 20 games. The Tigers again hosted the All-Star game in 1971, the Americans winning, 6–4, with Cash, Kaline, and Lolich all playing prominent roles, although the headlines went to Reggie Jackson's home run to the light tower in right field. In '72, the Tigers nosed out Boston by half a game to win the AL East, with Lolich and Coleman again leading the way. The red-hot Oakland A's won the league championship series, three games to two, when the Tigers could score only three runs in Lolich's 19 innings of work in which he yielded only three runs himself. A mediocre 1973 saw Martin's firing, and in '74, now under the old Yankee catcher Ralph Houk, the Tigers slid into the cellar, where they stayed the following year.

In 1974, a committee from the Pontiac Silverdome approached the

Tigers, with a proposition to move the club's home games to that site, approximately 25 miles northwest of Detroit, which would have meant the end of Tiger Stadium. John Fetzer rebuffed the overture, saying, "This franchise belongs to the inner city of Detroit; I'm just the caretaker." The fans in Detroit applauded.[7]

In 1976, a rookie pitcher named Mark Fidrych came out of nowhere to win 19 games for the Tigers, start the All-Star game, and lead the league in earned run average. Fidrych, who soon picked up the nickname "The Bird," for his resemblance to the "Sesame Street" television character, with his frizzy blond curls, was a delight for the fans, talking to himself on the mound, talking to the baseball, manicuring the mound, aiming the ball like a dart, and strutting around the mound after every out. "The Bird" quickly became the favorite of Tiger fans, who packed the ballpark when he was scheduled to pitch, and he filled stadiums all around the American League. Unfortunately for Fidrych, Detroit, and the game of baseball, he tore his rotator cuff the next season and only won ten more games before his career ended in 1980, "a magical footnote in Tiger Stadium history."[8]

Those sad seasons for Mark Fidrych were three more mediocre seasons for Ralph Houk which resulted in his discharge, but late in the 1979 season, after Les Moss had been tried in the manager's chair and found wanting, the club hired the former manager of Cincinnati's "Big Red Machine," George "Sparky" Anderson.

In the meantime, ownership of Tiger Stadium was transferred in 1977 to the city of Detroit, though this switch was not supposed to mean much in the operation of the ball club. The stadium had been cited for 32 building code violations, so Fetzer sold it for one dollar, with the Tigers signing a 30-year lease and the city agreeing to make $15 million worth of renovations. This was Fetzer's effort to preserve the old ballpark. Several years earlier, however, Tigers general manager Jim Campbell had said, "Tiger Stadium is getting tired underneath. I mean the wiring and plumbing. We never stop painting or checking the concrete and structural steel. But the costs go up, up, up." And in 1972, the Tigers' yearbook displayed a full-scale model of a domed stadium supposedly to be ready for occupancy in 1975. Nothing came of that, but the vibrations that threatened the old ballpark were beginning to be felt. The city replaced the green wooden seats in the park with plastic ones in blue and orange — the ball club's colors — and the green interior of the ballpark was painted blue to match the seating.[9]

One more problem surfaced on February 1, 1977, when a fire destroyed the ballpark's press box. But the club went to work quickly and constructed a new enclosed press box in time for the opening of the season. Late in the '78 season, though, another malfunction arose and some 10,000 bleacher seats were closed to the public as unsafe; a city spokesman said the problem was "rusting in some secondary supports."[10]

Sparky Anderson as manager did not work immediate magic; his '79 club was fifth when he took over and it finished fifth. But in 1980 it moved up to fourth and in 1983 to second. Kirk Gibson, a young outfielder from nearby Pontiac, was asserting himself in the club's offense, and second-baseman Lou Whitaker and shortstop Alan Trammell were establishing themselves as the best keystone duo in the business. Lance Parrish took over the club's catching, and righthander Jack Morris became one of the league's top pitchers, with Dan Petry and Milt Wilcox just behind him.

In 1984, it all came together for the Motor City and for new owner Tom Monaghan, the founder of Domino's pizza chain. The stadium was given a facelift in 1983 when the sale of $3.6 million worth of bonds allowed the sheathing of the park in blue tile and white aluminum. Not everyone liked the new look, as it was compared to the inside of a public bathroom and the shower room at the YMCA. But things went just fine for the baseball team playing in it. Just before the season, the Tigers traded with the Phillies to get a tall, lefthanded Puerto Rican relief pitcher named Willie Hernandez, and Hernandez seemed to make everything click. With Trammell, Gibson, Parrish, Whitaker and outfielder Chet Lemon supplying much of the offensive fireworks, the Tigers ran up a record of 104–58, leaving Toronto far behind in the East, then swept Kansas City three straight in the league championship series, before routing San Diego in five games in the World Series. Morris, Petry and Wilcox led Anderson's starting rotation with fine seasons, but it was the unexpected Willie Hernandez who showed the way. He appeared in eighty games, all in relief, had a 9–3 won-lost record, a 1.92 earned run average, and 32 saves. Whenever the Tigers needed him, Willie was there. As a result, he was voted both the Cy Young and the MVP awards. The Tigers, Sparky Anderson, and Willie Hernandez were the toast of Detroit, and when the Series was won the fans stormed the field and tore the outfield to shreds.

Of course, a championship season is always followed by "next year," and 1985 was for the Tigers a third-place finish, although still with a winning record. First baseman Darrell Evans led the league with 40 home runs, but that was about it. Trammell and Whitaker continued their wizardry around second, as they would do for years, but the next pennant came after the club had left Tiger Stadium. In 1987, the Tigers won the American League East on the last day of the season, with Anderson's boys

The home team taking batting practice, Tiger Stadium, 1985 (photograph by the author).

edging Toronto by two games, when southpaw Frank Tanana shut out the Blue Jays, 1–0. The Tigers were surprised by the Minnesota Twins in the league championship series, four games to one, in the last playoff games ever played in Tiger Stadium.

After 1987, there were few highlights for Tigers fans, except possibly for the 51 home runs that portly first-baseman Cecil Fielder hit in 1990. In 1992, the club was sold to Mike Ilitch, who also owned the Detroit Red Wings hockey club and, more importantly, Little Caesar's Pizza, the source of his financial wherewithal. In 1993, the ballpark underwent a renovation estimated at $8 million, with Tiger Plaza, complete with a food court, souvenir shops, and patio, opening on " the Corner," Michigan and Trumbull, and a video scoreboard being installed in the stadium. The Tiger Den was an area on the lower deck with padded seats and waiters to take the fans' orders. But it was still an aging ballpark.

After the players' strike of 1994, which cancelled half the season and the World Series, serious planning for a new ballpark got underway. That it did was not a surprise; in 1990 the Tigers' management sent out an eight-page questionnaire to the club's season ticket holders, asking for suggestions of features they would like to see in a projected new ballpark. And in April 1988, Tiger fans who were opposed to any abandonment of Tiger Stadium got together to give the old place a group hug on its 76th birthday, surrounding the ballpark arm-to-arm, in an effort to convince management not to think about a change. Management paid little attention, and Mayor Coleman Young, who hoped for a domed stadium, sneered, "It's obvious the damn thing's falling down," though there were not any major structural issues with the old park.[11]

In January 1990, the Tiger Stadium Fan Club unveiled a well-thought-out plan for saving and renovating the old ballpark, "leaving intact what is good about Tiger Stadium, and just adding what's required to make it a competitive, modern ballpark," as one of the authors of the plan said. The fan club's project, called the "Cochrane Plan" in honor of the team's old catcher-manager, drew praise from many of the top architects in Michigan, but it was dismissed out of hand by club management. Bill Haase, vice president of operations, said, "We have made the decision that there won't be renovation," and Jim Campbell snorted, "We've been through all of that. It's tired and worn out. We need a new facility."[12]

On June 10, 1990, the fan club gave Tiger Stadium another group hug, surrounding the old park with their bodies, their memories, and their hopes, but it was apparent even then that their efforts were in vain.

Finally, on October 29, 1997, ground was broken for a new ballpark, in the downtown part of the city, about a mile from the old ballpark. Hal Newhouser was there and threw out a symbolic "first pitch," to Brandon Glenn, an eleven-year-old second baseman for the Detroit Cobras youth team. So the countdown was on.

As the 1999 season passed by, it became apparent that Comerica Park, as the new facility was to be called, would be ready for the opening of the 2000 campaign, so the final game in Tiger Stadium would be on September 27, 1999, when the club's home schedule ended. Tickets for the final game went on sale in May and sold out in 33 minutes. Soon scalpers on the Internet were selling tickets for the best seats for prices like $600, with even $5 bleacher seats bringing $255. A club spokesman commented, piously, "In a perfect world, the most loyal fans would be sitting in the seats for the last game and paying face value for tickets."[13]

As the season went on, pieces of the old ballpark were departing — oak armrests from the seats, even a trough-style urinal — as fans looked for some sort of memento of their favorite place and brought tools with them to help in securing it. Detroit officials wondered what would be left of the old ballpark when the last game was played.

12. Used to Be Briggs Stadium

The day arrived at last, Monday afternoon, September 27, with a 4:00 P.M. start time. Weather forecasts had said rain was possible, but the day dawned bright and clear and temperatures reached 85 degrees. Five hours before game time there were already ten thousand people "milling around the park, buying souvenirs, taking photos, and sharing stories of Tiger Stadium." The mood seemed "festive and celebratory, though certainly bittersweet," but there were no protests or disruptive behavior. One spectator said, "This is more like an Irish wake. It's a celebration of life instead of a death."[14]

The park's gates opened at 1:30, and all who arrived before 3:30 had their tickets embossed with a commemorative seal. K-Mart provided each person entering with a souvenir ticket holder on a neck chain. The Tigers starters wore the uniform numbers of the All-Time Tigers Team, announced the day before, and reserves wore the numbers of the other All-Time nominees. (There were few surprises in the All-Time team: Greenberg, Gehringer, Trammell and Kell in the infield; Gibson, Cobb,

Tiger Stadium, as its final days neared (National Baseball Hall of Fame Library, Cooperstown).

and Kaline across the outfield; Bill Freehan, the catcher — that one *was* a surprise, with Mickey Cochrane ignored; Jack Morris, Newhouser, Lolich and reliever John Hiller on the mound; and Sparky Anderson the manager.) The bases were to be changed after each inning, to provide souvenir prizes.

The saloons along Michigan Avenue had set up beer tents for the expected throng, and folks in the neighborhood held backyard cookouts. Current Tigers players greeted the incoming fans at the park gates, shaking hands and signing autographs. Media credentials had been issued to more than 800 journalists, from Detroit as well as from all around the world, and in the hours before the game these men and women mostly interviewed and photographed each other. Periodically a Tiger player or personality would come out onto the field for interviews.

Not everyone was cheerful at the day's activities. One neighbor jacked up the price of parking in her vacant lot from $10 to $20 for the game, complaining that the neighbors were being left high and dry and this was the last chance to make any money. A souvenir store proprietor on Michigan Avenue lamented that the closure of the ballpark "finishes me." But most people were taking it in stride, finally accepting the closure as inevitable.

Alan Trammell, the longtime Tiger shortstop and now a coach, said, "You look around and realize you spent more than half your life in this place. So much of my life went on here, so many good times, many powerful memories. If I break down when it's over, don't blame me."[15]

Willie Hernandez was there; his comment was that the home team's small locker room was "worse than high school." Dennis Archer, the city's mayor and a longtime fan, recalled the antiquated restrooms, with long lines for women and prehistoric plumbing for men, and said they would not be missed.

Doug Brocail, a Detroit relief pitcher, flew his father in from Colorado. "I just want to play catch with my father on this field before they close the place," Brocail said. "Without his help, I wouldn't be here." Kimera Bartee, a Tiger outfielder, squatted down around third base with a bunch of film canisters, which he filled with dirt from the playing field. Once they were all filled, he carried them over to the rail and tossed them to fans as souvenirs of the day. Then he signed autographs for a while.

Bud Selig, the commissioner, was there. He looked around and said, "I love this place. It was a ballpark, all you can expect from a ballpark. When you look at all the players who played here — Hal Newhouser, Ty Cobb — I understand all the emotion."[16]

There were spectators there that last day who had been there on their first date, years before, and others who had returned from far away just to recall their childhood visits to Briggs Stadium. "It's such a good party, it's too bad the stadium's got to close to make it all come together," commented one elderly lady, and Dick McAuliffe, who had played in the Tigers infield for 14 years, said, "You're sorry to see it go, but time moves on."

There was a pregame ceremony, with speeches by Mayor Archer, Governor John Engler, who drew great applause for his comment that Tiger Stadium would be an immediate entry if "there were a Hall of Fame for stadiums," and George Kell, who had played so well for the Tigers and served them as a broadcaster for many years after his playing career. The great Al Kaline, still a huge favorite in Detroit, spoke of his love for the ballpark and how the day's events left him feeling "humbled and overwhelmed."

Billy Rogell, the club's shortstop from 1930 to 1939, came out to throw out the first ball. Rogell, 95 years old, minced no words about his feelings: "I hate to see this place go. The first game I played in this park was in 1925. As far as I'm concerned, there's nothing wrong with this ballpark."

Lineup cards were brought to home plate by Kaline and by fellow Hall-of-Famer George Brett for the visiting Kansas City Royals, both in uniforms. The two men embraced to a tumultuous ovation, and then it was game time for the crowd of 43,356, which raised the season's attendance to more than two million, the first time the Tigers had reached that figure since 1988.

Righthander Brian Moehler started for the Tigers and, before throwing his first pitch, he kneeled down to write his late father's initials in the dirt. Kansas City threatened in the first inning but failed to score, and then Detroit's leadoff hitter, Luis Polonia, clubbed a long home run to left center field, driving the crowd wild. The Royals came back to tie it on rookie Mark Quinn's home run, and the score was 2–2 until Tiger rightfielder Karim Garcia homered with a man on in the sixth to put the home team up by two. In the seventh inning stretch the fans were feeling very good, and they sang "Take Me Out to the Ball Game" with vim and gusto.

In the bottom of the eighth, the Tigers loaded the bases with nobody out and the place was rocking. After Gabe Kapler forced a runner at the plate, rookie catcher Robert Fick came up, with a .194 average since his recent call-up from the minors, where he had spent an injury-filled season. Manager Larry Parrish thought about pinch-hitting for the lefthanded Fick, to enable more players to get into the historic game, but the young catcher convinced Parrish to let him bat. A good decision: Fick drilled a pitch far up onto the right-field roof for a mammoth grand slam, the last home run ever hit in Tiger Stadium. Fick admitted that he slowed down his home run trot, sensing that the fans might want a little time to reflect on his bomb. "I was soaking it in," he said. "I didn't mean to show anyone up, but I was happy."[17]

When Detroit closer Todd Jones retired the Royals in order in the ninth for the 8–2 win, it was all over, except for the closing ceremony, led by the Tigers' longtime and beloved broadcaster Ernie Harwell. The current Tigers sprawled out in front of the dugout to take in the show, while some 65 Tiger greats jogged (or walked) onto the field, taking their old positions. The first to show was "the Bird," Mark Fidrych, who scooped up some dirt from the mound as a souvenir. He was followed by Rogell, Cecil Fielder, Kell, Frank Tanana, Willie Horton, Jimmy Outlaw (from the 1945 champs), Reno Bertoia, U.S. Senator Jim Bunning, Steve Kemp, Morris, Lolich, Chet Lemon, Gates Brown, and more, with the final three coming out together, Kirk Gibson, Lou Whitaker and Alan Trammell, the latter two of whom were teammates longer than any other two players in major league history.

When they had all reached the field, they formed a line from the center field flagpole to home plate and, to the strains of Beethoven's "Moonlight Sonata," lowered the American flag and passed it down the line, until old Eldon Auker passed the folded flag to Brad Ausmus, the '99 team's catcher, asking him to raise it the next spring over Comerica Park. Then the groundskeepers dug up home plate for a motorcade to the new park, where the fans watched it being installed by three current players, a scene that they booed heartily. Today, they were saying, is about Tiger Stadium, not the new place.

Each of the old-time Tiger greats threw a baseball into the stands for another round of souvenirs, and then George Campbell, great-nephew of old Charlie Bennett, for whom Bennett Park was named, threw a pitch, the very final pitch, to Ausmus, with a ball that was to be used for the first pitch at Comerica. The whole ceremony was touching, nicely conceived, and well carried out, and the fans who then filed out were saying they would not forget it.

The Tigers got ready to leave on their final road trip, and Tiger Stadium was done. Unfortunately, there had been no decision made about the disposition of the old ballpark, which led to almost a decade of bickering over this plan and that, this proposal compared to some other, with money for development being pledged and then not delivered, with the Old Tiger Stadium Conservancy being involved and then left out, until finally, on June 30, 2008, demolition began. There had been plans to convert it into condominiums, a prison, a Wal-Mart, residential lofts, a minor-league baseball park, a museum, and a conference center, among others.

The Detroit Economic Growth Corporation was involved, as was the City Council, and the maneuverings were not pretty to watch. Longtime Detroit sportswriter Joe Falls had said that, whatever was to be done with the old ballpark, "Do it gently." It was not to be. On June 8, 2009, demolition of the remainder of the old park got underway and was completed on September 22, with no prospects for redevelopment at the site. Tiger Stadium was named a State of Michigan Historic Site in 1975 and listed on the National Register of Historic Places in 1989, but it exists no more.

Chapter 13
Ballpark in the Bronx

It opened in 1923, at East 161st Street and River Avenue in the Bronx, designed by the Osborn Engineering Corporation, and the Yankees built it because Charles Stoneham of the Giants tired of having the American League team as tenants in his Polo Grounds. When the Yankees acquired Babe Ruth from Boston in 1920 and drew 1.3 million customers (outstripping the Giants by about 300,000 fans), and then played the Giants in the World Series in 1921, Stoneham's resentment of their success led to his insistence that the Yankees play somewhere else.

New York had fielded a team in the American League since 1903. The club was originally called the Hilltoppers, but it had limited success under managers like Clark Griffith, Frank Chance, and even the notorious Hal Chase. In 1918, Jacob Ruppert, who had owned the franchise with Tillinghast L'Hommedieu Huston since 1915, named Miller Huggins, a diminutive infielder who had been player-manager of the Cardinals for five years, as the Yankees' new skipper, although Huston, the co-owner, overseas with the army at the time, objected to the hiring of Huggins. The team's performance improved under the new manager, even before the acquisition of Ruth, but when the Bambino arrived, hitting home runs and showing a personality like few in baseball had displayed, things moved quickly upward. A third-place finish in 1920 was followed by pennants the next three years, and the Yanks had no further need to remain under the Giants' shadow.

A hire by the Yankees late in 1920 turned out to be of major significance in the team's history. Edward Barrow was taken on as business manager, and he took control of the team's personnel, with all the machinations that represented. Ed Barrow had considerable experience in the American League, as manager of the Detroit club in 1903-04 and as manager of the Red Sox in 1918, when his team won the World Series, and a couple of years after. Barrow, in his career with the New York Yankees that lasted until 1945, simply created the greatest dynasty in sports history, trading for players, developing a farm system, signing youngsters, and filling in whatever holes needed to be filled. Working with Miller Huggins and Joe McCarthy, his field managers, and George Weiss, who ran the farm system for him, and winning pennants in fourteen of his twenty-five seasons, Barrow brought the club unprecedented success. In 1953, shortly before his death, Ed Barrow was elected to the Baseball Hall of Fame.

All of this was still ahead of the Yankees when Ruppert and Huston decided to build their own ballpark, eventually settling on a ten-acre site, formerly a lumberyard, in the lower Bronx, right across the Harlem River from Coogan's Bluff and the Polo Grounds. With the game of baseball just recovering from the Black Sox scandal, the Yankee owners were ridiculed for building a ballpark with a seating capacity of nearly 60,000. To this ridicule they had a two-word answer: "Babe Ruth."

The ballpark that Ruppert and Huston built had three tiers, although the triple deck, as originally constructed, stretched only to the right and left field corners. The concrete lower deck was pushed well out into left field. It was short down the lines, 285 feet to left and 295 to right, but the dimensions quickly bulged out to 395 feet in short left-center, 425 in right-center, 457 feet in the area of left center long known as Death Valley, and on back to 490 feet in dead center field. There was a large foul territory behind the plate but not much down the foul lines. The concrete used to build the park was an extremely hard and durable variety developed by Thomas Alva Edison. A distinguishing characteristic of the new stadium was a frieze made of copper running along the grandstand's upper deck, an addition to the park that Osborn Engineering constructed when Ruppert asked for something to give the ballpark "an air of dignity." The frieze became known over the years as "the façade," and it was one of the memorable features of Yankee Stadium.[1]

Jake Ruppert, known as "Colonel" because of a commission he had held in the National Guard, had served as a Democratic congressman with the blessings of Tammany Hall from 1899 to 1907 and had inherited the Ruppert Brewery, the source of his wealth, from his father in 1915. On May 21, 1923, a month after the new stadium opened, Ruppert bought out his partner, Huston, to take over sole control of the Yankees, except for the small interest he permitted Ed Barrow to purchase. Ruppert and Huston had disagreed often on matters of Yankee business, and from then on Ruppert was in charge.

Yankee Stadium opened for live action on April 18, 1923, with John

Yankee Stadium at its grand 1923 opening (National Baseball Hall of Fame Library, Cooperstown).

Philip Sousa leading the band, Governor Al Smith tossing out the first ball, and Ruth spurring his team to a 4–1 victory over Boston with a three-run homer. The announced attendance for the huge crowd was 74,217, although this may have been inflated somewhat. Whatever it was, it was the highest attendance for a baseball game ever, to that time. The new ballpark was a success, and sportswriter Fred Lieb of the *Evening Telegram* gave it a name it never lost, "The House That Ruth Built."

About a week after Yankee Stadium's opening, President Warren G. Harding showed up for a game. Babe Ruth met with the chief executive beforehand and then hit a home run in the game itself. The appearance of the president helped the stadium to become a place of significance, a place where important people came to be seen.

The 1923 Yankees, who went on to win the pennant by 16 games over Detroit, had in their lineup along with Ruth, names like Wally Pipp, Joe Dugan, Bob Meusel, and Wally Schang, with Sam Jones, Herb Pennock, Joe Bush, Waite Hoyt and Bob Shawkey on the mound. They beat the Giants, four games to two, in the World Series, led by Ruth's three home runs. In the next two years, Washington led the league, with the Yankees dropping to seventh place in 1925; Ruth didn't even lead the league in home runs (although Meusel did). It was during that season, on June 2, that Wally Pipp showed up one day with a headache and was replaced in the lineup by a young fellow out of Columbia named Lou Gehrig; Pipp never did get his job back. Ironically, Pipp had spotted Gehrig playing at Columbia and urged that he be signed.

In 1926, the Yankees were back on top, finishing three ahead of Tris Speaker's Indians, with Ruth's 47 home runs leading the league. The Yanks had by now added Tony Lazzeri, Earle Combs, and Mark Koenig to their lineup, and Urban Shocker won 19 games to go along with Pennock's 23. They lost the Series to the Cardinals, four games to three, despite Ruth's four long balls, but they were just getting warmed up. Over the off-season, the upper deck was extended over the lower deck in left field.

The 1927 Yankees, called by some the best of all time, put together a record of 110–44 and finished 19 games ahead of the Athletics. Ruth hit his high of 60 homers that year, and Gehrig led the league in runs batted in with 175. Hoyt, Wilcy Moore, Pennock, Shocker, Dutch Reuther, and George Pipgras led Huggins's pitching staff, and they kept it up in the World Series, routing the Pirates in four games. Hoyt, Pipgras, Pennock and Moore each won one, and Ruth hit the only two homers of the Series.

In 1928, the Yankees won again, though they were given a run for it by Connie Mack's A's. Ruth hit 54 home runs, he and Gehrig tied for the RBI leadership, and Pipgras (with 24 wins) and Hoyt (with 23) led the pitchers. Again, New York swept their National League opponents, this time the Cardinals, in the World Series, as Gehrig hit four homers and Ruth three, his three all coming in Game Four.

The Yankees didn't know it at the time, but they were about to be displaced at the top of the American League, even though they would shortly display in their lineup one of the best catchers ever, a tall young man from Louisiana named Bill Dickey. Philadelphia won pennants over the next three years, with the Yanks finishing 18, 16, and 13½ games back. Huggins left after 1929, replaced for one season by Bob Shawkey, and in 1931 the club had a new manager, the former Chicago Cubs skipper, Joe McCarthy.

In 1932, the club under McCarthy won another pennant, although by this time Philadelphia's Jimmy Foxx had replaced Ruth as the league's premier power hitter. The Yankees swept the Cubs in four games in the World Series. It was in Game Three, at Wrigley Field, that Ruth supposedly "called his shot," pointing to center field before a pitch and telling the Cubs, who were riding him hard from their bench, that he was hitting the next pitch out of the ballpark in that direction. Ruth did hit a long home run to center on the next pitch, but the story about calling his shot was apparently dreamed up by *New York World Telegram* writer Joe Williams the next day, and it took off from there. Charlie Root, the Cubs pitcher, always flatly denied that Ruth had pointed to center field; if he had, Root said, "I would have knocked him on his ass with the next pitch." In any event, the "called-shot" home run was the last World Series hit ever for Babe Ruth.

The Yankees finished second over the next three years, as names like Red Rolfe, George Selkirk, Ben Chapman and Frank Crosetti appeared in the box scores, and Lefty Gomez, Red Ruffing, and Johnny Murphy took over the pitching chores for McCarthy. In 1936, a rookie outfielder from San Francisco came on the scene, and with the arrival of Joe DiMaggio the Yankees were ready for another long run of success.

To help with this anticipated run, there were substantial changes made in the ballpark. The wooden bleachers became concrete and moved a bit into the extremely deep outfield, which was still called "Death Valley." The left-field foul line was pushed back to about 300 feet. Second and third decks were built over the stands in short right-center field. Runways between the ends of the triple-deck stands and the bleachers were put into use as bullpens. By 1938, Yankee Stadium had taken on the shape that it would retain until the renovation of 1973.

The club won pennants in 1936–37–38–39, with young DiMaggio and the veteran Gehrig leading the way for the first three seasons. The Yankees won the World Series each of those seasons, whipping the Giants in 1936 and 1937 and sweeping the Cubs the next year. In January 1939, Jake Ruppert died, but his death made little difference in the operation of the ball club. Ed Barrow continued to run it, now for the benefit of Ruppert's heirs.

In 1939, Gehrig stepped down, his body wracked with amyotrophic lateral sclerosis, now usually called simply "Lou Gehrig's disease," replaced after playing a record 2,130 consecutive games by a smooth fielder named Babe Dahlgren. The Yankees barely looked back. DiMaggio led the league with a .381 average, and up-and-coming stars like outfielder Charlie Keller and second-baseman Joe Gordon made themselves felt. Young pitchers like Atley Donald, Monte Pearson, Marius Russo and Steve Sundra bolstered the efforts of Ruffing and Gomez, and the club again won the World Series in four games, this time over Cincinnati, with Keller hitting three homers.

The All-Star game visited Yankee Stadium for the first time in 1939. Manager Joe McCarthy put six Yankees in his starting lineup, and the American League won, 3–1, with DiMaggio hitting the only home run.

Over the years Yankee Stadium hosted many events besides baseball games. Thirty championship boxing matches were held there, featuring such headliners as Gene Tunney, Jack Dempsey, Carmen Basilio, Tony Zale, Sugar Ray Robinson, even Muhammed Ali in 1976, and, most prominently, Joe Louis, who defended his heavyweight title eight times at the ballpark in the Bronx. The most famous of these was his 1938 fight with Max Schmeling, the German who was publicly supported by Adolf Hitler; Louis knocked out his challenger in the first round.

College football was a big favorite at Yankee Stadium, with Army and Notre Dame meeting there every year from 1925 to 1946, except 1930. New York University played 96 home games at the Stadium, while nearby Fordham played 19 there. The Whitney Young Urban League Classic, featuring top black colleges, started in Yankee Stadium and finished there in 1987, the last football game played in the park. Professional football started in Yankee Stadium in 1926, with Red Grange and the first American Football League, and continued sporadically through the demise of the Yankees of the All-America Football Conference in 1949. From 1956 to 1973, the New York Giants of the NFL played in Yankee Stadium, until the "renovation" moved them to Yale Bowl, later to Shea Stadium, and then to their stadium in New Jersey. While they were in Yankee Stadium, though, they played what is often called "the greatest game ever," the 1958 NFL championship game won dramatically in overtime by Johnny Unitas and the Baltimore Colts, 23–17.

Soccer was an attraction in Yankee Stadium over the years, starting in 1931 and continuing with many international matches, winding up in 1976 with the New York Cosmos of the North American Soccer League, featuring their star, Pele.

The Jehovah's Witnesses held religious conventions attracting huge crowds, from 1950 into the late '80s, and Billy Graham drew a turnout of 100,000 in 1957. Three different popes, Paul VI, John Paul II, and Benedict XVI, celebrated Mass at Yankee Stadium, and a memorial service was held there in 2001 for the victims of the September 11 terrorist attacks. Finally, the Isley Brothers, Billy Joel, U2, Bono, and Pink Floyd held concerts in the ballpark at various times from 1969 to 1994.

Returning to baseball and the Yankees: the Tigers won the 1940 pennant, but the Yanks came back to win pennants in 1941, '42, and '43. Nineteen forty-one was the year of Joe DiMaggio's 56-game hitting streak and his second Most Valuable Player award (he would win another in 1947) and a five-game victory over the cross-town Dodgers in the World Series. The Series was marked by Mickey Owen's famous passed ball in Game

Yankee Stadium, with the Polo Grounds across the Harlem River (National Baseball Hall of Fame Library, Cooperstown).

Four, which permitted the Yanks to come from behind with four runs to win. In 1942, when second baseman Joe Gordon was the league MVP, the Yankees were upset in the Series by the Cardinals, four games to one, with Cards' rookie right-hander Johnny Beazley winning two games, including Game Five on Whitey Kurowski's game-winning home run. In 1943, the

Yankees, despite the loss to the military of DiMaggio, Phil Rizzuto, Red Rolfe, and Red Ruffing, turned the tables on the Cardinals, defeating them in the World Series in five games. Yankee righthander Spud Chandler was the league's MVP that season, on the basis of his 20–4 won-lost record and a league-leading ERA of 1.64, and he pitched two beauties in the Series, winning Game One, 4–2, and the closing Game Five with a 2–0 shutout. In that final game, the only runs scored on Bill Dickey's sixth-inning homer with a man on against the St. Louis ace, Mort Cooper.

For the next couple of years, the Yankees were not much of a factor; more top players went off to war, although of course other teams suffered the same losses. In January 1945, for $2,800,000 the Ruppert heirs sold the ball club and Yankee Stadium to an unlikely trio, Daniel R. Topping, Delbert E. Webb, and Larry MacPhail. Dan Topping, who was married at the time to ice-skating queen Sonja Henie (his third marriage, it would last only until 1946, after which he was married to three additional women), inherited great wealth from his grandfather Daniel Reid, known as the "Tinplate King" for the fortune he made in tin. Del Webb was a real estate developer from Arizona who received many military contracts during World War II, including the construction of a huge "relocation center" near Parker, Arizona, for Japanese-American internees; Webb would in future years be involved with some questionable characters when he built Las Vegas casinos. Larry MacPhail, of course, was a baseball lifer we have met before, one of the great imaginative innovators of the game, but a man plagued by his unstable personality, on for his third big league adventure after the Reds and Brooklyn. With MacPhail running the show, Ed Barrow left the Yankees.

In 1946, with all the stars back from the military, the Yankees could do no better than third, behind Boston and Detroit, although their attendance for the year soared above two million for the first time. Joe McCarthy stepped down as manager early in the year, unhappy with MacPhail as his boss, to be succeeded by Dickey for most of the season and then Coach Johnny Neun for the final fourteen games.

The club hired veteran Bucky Harris to manage the 1947 team, and with DiMaggio back close to his former self, batting .315 with 20 home runs, the Yankees won the pennant by 12 games. The club got fine pitching from Allie Reynolds (picked up from Cleveland in a trade for Gordon), Frank "Spec" Shea, Spud Chandler, and southpaw relief pitcher Joe Page. A homely young rookie catcher named Larry Berra, who was quickly given the nickname "Yogi," began to establish himself with the club. Outfielder Tommy Henrich led the league in triples and was third in doubles, and

George McQuinn, picked up for nothing when the A's released him, hit .304 at first base. The Yankees beat Brooklyn, four games to three, in the World Series, a set of games marked by two especially memorable plays. In Game Four, Dodger Cookie Lavagetto hit a double with two out in the ninth against Yankee pitcher Floyd Bevens, which not only ended Bevens's bid for a no-hitter but also won the game for the Dodgers. In Game Six, Al Gionfriddo made a great catch of DiMaggio's 415-foot near-homer, which saved three runs and helped the Dodgers extend the Series another day. Nevertheless, Joe Page throttled the Dodgers with five innings of one-hit relief pitching to win Game Seven at Yankee Stadium.

As the Yankees were celebrating in their clubhouse after the seventh game victory, Larry MacPhail came in, stirred up by a nasty confrontation with his old nemesis Branch Rickey on the field, and, full of alcohol, soon turned the celebration on its head, punching a sportswriter, spewing insults right and left, and dramatically announcing his resignation as president and general manager of the club. Later on, there was a more formal victory party at the Biltmore Hotel, but MacPhail, very drunk, continued his bad behavior and again announced his retirement. Webb and Topping lost no time in buying out MacPhail's interest in the ball club the next morning, for two million dollars.

The 1948 Yankees finished third, and Bucky Harris was let go as manager. As his replacement, the club brought in an old-timer named Casey Stengel, fresh off a successful stint managing in the Pacific Coast League. Stengel, though, was regarded as something of a clown by writers in the big leagues, based on his earlier nine years managing in the National League, with Boston and Brooklyn, with only one winning season and no finish above fifth place. Some clown: in his first five years with the Yankees, Stengel's teams won five pennants and five World Series crowns. After a second place finish in 1954 (despite winning 103 games), Stengel's Yankees went on to win the next four pennants and two more World Series. He was notorious for his platooning of players and for long sessions of "Stengelese," his own brand of talk with which he beguiled the New York baseball writers, but his players performed for him, and mostly they won.

In the midst of all this success, there were some interesting developments regarding the Yankees' famous ballpark. In December 1953, Dan Topping and Del Webb sold Yankee Stadium and the land it sat on to a Chicago businessman named Arnold Johnson, who enjoyed financial ties with both of them. Johnson also purchased Blues Stadium in Kansas City, where the Yankees' top farm team played. Johnson then sold the land under Yankee Stadium to the Knights of Columbus, the Catholic fraternal organization, for $2.5 million, and promptly leased the land back for 28 years, with buy-back and renewal options, and sub-leased the stadium and the ground it sat on back to Topping, Webb, and the Yankees, along with a 20-year second mortgage on the stadium and the lease rights to the land.

"The net financial effect of these deals," wrote one commentator, "was that Johnson raised the money to buy Yankee Stadium and related properties through an elaborate series of paper transactions that risked none of his own money."[2]

After the 1954 baseball season, however, Johnson bought the Philadelphia Athletics franchise from the Mack family and then moved it to Kansas City. There were efforts at the time by Philadelphia interests to purchase the team in order to keep it in the Quaker City, but these efforts were frustrated by the heavy-handed opposition of the Yankee owners, very influential in American League affairs and doing their best to help their friend Johnson. Under baseball's conflict-of-interest rules, Johnson, as a club owner, could not continue to own Yankee Stadium, so he sold all of the stock in his stadium holding company in January 1955 to an old business associate, John William Cox, a sale that was, incredibly, completed without a written contract — and Commissioner Ford Frick never asked to see one. Seven years later, Cox donated title to the stadium plus primary leasing rights to his alma mater, Rice University (in Houston, Texas). Cox, who was president of both General Package Corporation and the Automatic Canteen Company of America, said, "I will always be grateful to Rice for the educational opportunities it afforded me," in explaining his gift, which made Rice the only college in Texas owning a ballpark in New York City.[3]

The Yankees in Casey Stengel's early years were still led by DiMaggio, Henrich, Rizzuto, Page, and Reynolds, but soon they were the Yankees of Mickey Mantle, Yogi Berra, Vic Raschi, Hank Bauer, Whitey Ford, Andy Carey, Bill Skowron, Gil McDougald and Jerry Coleman. The names changed, but the outcome seemed to be about the same, year after year. In 1948, George Weiss, formerly the farm director, took over as general manager, and he seemed to have a magic touch, picking up just the right player late in the season to fill in a hole where he was needed. For the legions of Yankee-haters across the country, it was a stretch that seemed to go on forever, with the team's needs supplied from time to time by trades with Arnold Johnson's Kansas City Athletics, which functioned almost as a farm club for the Yankees. Roger Maris, Hector Lopez, Bobby Shantz, Clete Boyer, Art Ditmar, and Ralph Terry were among the top players the A's traded to New York during Johnson's tenure in KC. Again, the commissioner never seemed to think there were any questions to be

Whitey Ford on the mound, Yankee Stadium, June 7, 1958 (photograph by the author).

raised about the multiple Kansas City–Yankees trades, no matter how one-sided they seemed to be.

In 1959, though, the White Sox won the pennant, and Stengel's Yankees could do no better than third. The next year the Yanks came storming back and won the flag by eight games over Baltimore. They lost the Series to Pittsburgh, on the home run by Bill Mazeroski in Game Seven, and afterwards let Stengel go, telling the press that he was getting too old. ("I'll never make the mistake of being seventy years old again," Casey rejoined.) Shortly thereafter, the Yankees also got rid of George Weiss as their general manager. Weiss was not always the most pleasant character around — he often treated his players with disdain — but he surely knew how to put a team together. Now he, with Stengel, was gone.[4]

The All-Star game came back to Yankee Stadium in 1960, the second of two played that summer, and only 38,362 fans turned out for it, as the National League won, 6–0.

Ralph Houk, the Yankees' longtime backup catcher and coach, was named manager, and he led the team to the pennant in 1961, as the home run duel between teammates Mickey Mantle and Roger Maris captivated the nation, climaxing with Maris's historic 61st long one which broke Babe

Ruth's record set in 1927. Houk's team defeated the Reds in the World Series, and won the pennant and Series again in 1962, beating the San Francisco Giants in the Series. The Yankees won another league title the next year but were swept by the L.A. Dodgers in October, as Sandy Koufax, Don Drysdale, and Johnny Podres stifled the Yankee bats. After the '63 season, Houk gave up the manager's job and moved up to become New York's general manager. His successor was the Yankees' great catcher, Yogi Berra, who had reached the end of his storied playing career.

As the 1964 season moved along, however, Houk and the front office staff made up their minds that Berra was not the kind of manager they wanted and it was decided to get rid of him after the season. In spite of this, Berra and the Yankees won the pennant, finishing a game ahead of the White Sox. When they lost the World Series to the Cardinals, four games to three, though, Berra was fired, and Johnny Keane, the winning manager in the Series, was hired away from the Cardinals to take the Yankee job.

A major change took place during the 1964 season, when Topping and Webb sold almost all of their shares in the Yankees to the Columbia Broadcasting System, ending an ownership tenure of almost 20 years. Topping retained a small interest and stayed on as club president for a couple more years, until September 1966, when CBS bought the rest of his shares and named Michael Burke to run the baseball club. Burke had no background in baseball, but he had served with the Central Intelligence Agency (CIA) and in a stint as executive director of Ringling Brothers Barnum & Bailey Circus.

There were feelings of anxiety, some expressed, some left unsaid, about a broadcasting giant buying a baseball team, particularly the Yankees, the biggest headliner in the media capital. A couple of American League owners, Arthur Allyn of the White Sox and Charlie Finley of Kansas City, opposed the deal, but they were the only ones to do so. Arthur Daley wrote in the *Times*, "It's the possible ramifications of this deal that produce such feelings of anxiety.... If this deal is a portent of the future, it is an ominous one. The dollar sign is beginning to obscure the standings of the teams." The Department of Justice checked to see if there were any antitrust violations in the sale. (It found none.) Still, the sale to CBS went through with little overt opposition. Unfortunately for Burke and CBS, after 1964 the Yankees endured a lengthy stretch, ending in 1976, in which they failed to win any titles.[5]

In 1965, Keane's Yankees fell to sixth place, with a record of 77–85. When they began the '66 season with only four wins in their first 20 games,

Keane was fired and Houk came down from the front office to take over as manager again. It did little good: the Yankees won 66 and lost 73 under Houk for a combined record of 70 wins and 89 losses for the year and finished tenth and last in the American League. Mel Stottlemyre had the distinction of leading the league in games lost with 20, Maris and Tom Tresh each hit a lowly .233, while third-baseman Clete Boyer was barely ahead of them at .240. It was the team's first last-place finish since 1912, and back then there had been only eight teams in the league. In 1966, nine teams finished ahead of New York. Yankee-haters around the country sat back and smiled contentedly.

The next year was just about as bad, with the Yankees winding up with a won-lost mark of 72–90, although Kansas City managed to finish tenth behind them. Whitey Ford won just two games apiece in 1966 and 1967, as his fine career came to an end. Ralph Houk continued as manager through 1973 but the team was unsuccessful, finishing as high as second in the East only once, in 1970, as Mickey Mantle phased out a great career with several sub-par seasons. After the 1973 season, Houk resigned and left the Yankees, going on to manage Detroit and Boston in future years.

While these less-than-exciting events were taking place on the field, there were more meaningful developments away from the playing field. Michael Burke's major accomplishment as Yankee president was to convince Mayor John Lindsay (who seemed quite willing) and the city of New York to spring for major renovation of a Yankee Stadium that was showing its age, after CBS hinted that it might build a ballpark in the New Jersey Meadowlands and move the Yankees there. This subtle threat seemed to force the city's hand. In March 1971, Lindsay announced the city's commitment to spend $24 million to acquire Yankee Stadium and the ground it stood on, upgrade the place, and lease it back to the ball club for 30 years. The sum in question was the same amount the city had spent to build Shea Stadium for the Mets, although it ultimately fell far short of what was required in the end for redoing Yankee Stadium. The city exercised its right of eminent domain to acquire the ballpark before starting the renovation; Rice University received $2.5 million in the condemnation process (bringing, with the lease payments over the years, the total to $3.7 million the school received as a result of John Cox's gift). Why the city of New York, which was in considerable fiscal trouble at the time, should have taken such huge financial steps for the benefit of the wealthiest baseball team in the universe was a question no one bothered to answer or even ask.

In 1973, CBS sold the Yankees franchise to a shipbuilder from Cleveland named George Steinbrenner, opening up a whole new chapter in the club's history. Steinbrenner modestly told the press, "We plan absentee ownership as far as running the Yankees is concerned.... I won't be active in the day-to-day operations of the club at all," a disclaimer that came to seem odder and odder as the years of his ownership passed.[6]

The facelift of the ballpark got underway after the 1973 season. For 1974 and 1975, the Yankees played in Queens, sharing Shea Stadium with the Mets.

The "renovation" resulted in what many considered a much different Yankee Stadium. The columns reinforcing the tiers of the grandstand were taken out, the roof was replaced, and new lights were installed. The original wooden seats were replaced with plastic ones, a bit wider in order to accommodate the average New Yorker's added girth. The upper deck grew upwards by nine rows, a new upper concourse was added, and a new middle tier, featuring a larger press box and 16 luxury boxes, was installed. A blacked-out batter's eye went into center field, with about a third of the bleacher seats being taken out as a result. A wall was built behind the bleachers, and the park's overall seating capacity was reduced to 57,545. The distinctive copper facade around the stadium's roof was removed, although a white painted replica of it was added to the top of the wall over the outfield. The playing field was lowered by some seven feet and reduced in size in order to create a "Monument Park" in the outfield, where Yankee greats of the past were memorialized. The cost of the changes came to $160 million, and many admirers of the old Yankee Stadium felt that the "new park" was definitely inferior to what it had been. After playing the 1974 and 1975 seasons at Shea, the Yankees returned to the much-altered Yankee Stadium in April 1976.

Sadly, one of the issues which Michael Burke had raised with Lindsay was the possible rehabilitation of the declining and even dangerous area of the South Bronx around the ballpark. Unfortunately, all of the funds expended went into Yankee Stadium itself, with none allocated to any neighborhood upgrade. There would be none later, as it became clear as the year 1976 passed that New York City was broke. The renovation of Yankee Stadium was one of many factors that pushed the city over the edge.

In 1974, the displaced ball club, now under the direction of Bill Virdon, finished second in the East to Baltimore, and the next year it slipped to third, with Virdon being dismissed partway through the season in favor of the Yankees' former second baseman, Billy Martin. The fiery Martin had already served as manager of the Twins, Tigers, and Rangers for parts of six seasons (with a couple of first-place finishes) when he came back to New York, but it would be just the first of five different terms of Martin as the Yankee skipper. He and George Steinbrenner had a tangled relationship.

Billy Martin was a strange man. He was aggressive, opinionated, and alcoholic. As a player, while his numbers were nothing outstanding, he was known for coming through in the clutch. He made a game-saving catch in the last game of the 1952 World Series, and he was the MVP of the '53 Series. In May 1957, his birthday party at the Copacabana nightclub, attended by Mantle, Bauer, and Berra, turned into a highly-publicized drunken brawl, and Martin was traded to Kansas City a month later. Proud of his facility with his fists, Martin frequently got into fights with other players and, sometimes, outsiders. As a manager, he showed that he could push a team to the top, but the ease with which he got into trouble usually made his managerial stays brief.

Jim Northrup played for Martin as a Detroit outfielder. He described what it was like: "He put us in a frame of mind that took all the fun out of the game. When it's no fun, it's not worth playing."[7]

The Yankees finished third under Martin in 1975 and won the pennant in 1976, their first since 1964. Still, they were swept by Cincinnati's Big Red Machine in the World Series, with Johnny Bench, George Foster and Joe Morgan leading the way. In 1977, though, the Yankees under Martin won both the pennant and the World Series, defeating the Los Angeles Dodgers in six games. Reggie Jackson hit .450, with five home runs, three of them in the final game, each on the first pitch.

Martin had difficulties with both owner Steinbrenner and outfielder Jackson, and in 1978, after pulling Jackson from a game for not hustling, Martin told the press, "They deserve each other. One's a born liar, and the other's convicted," referring to the conviction Steinbrenner received for making illegal contributions to Richard Nixon's 1972 campaign. Martin was forced to resign a few days after that, in favor of Bob Lemon. Not long afterward, though, Steinbrenner responded to the outpouring of fan support for Martin by having it announced at the annual Old-Timer's Day game that Billy would be rehired as manager for 1980. The team won another World Series, under Lemon, in 1978, again in six games over the Dodgers, but when it faltered in 1979 Lemon was discharged and Martin reinstated as manager, even sooner than planned. The club finished fourth, and when Martin got into a fight after the season in a Minneapolis hotel, Steinbrenner fired him again.

Billy Martin went to Oakland, where he managed the A's for four years, but Steinbrenner brought him back to New York for the 1983 season. The Yankees finished third, and Martin was let go, only to be rehired partway through 1985, after the team had played just 16 games under Yogi Berra. When he got into a fight with one of his pitchers late in the season, Martin was dismissed again. Lou Piniella led the club in 1986 and 1987. Then, Steinbrenner made Martin the manager one more time at the start of the '88 campaign, before he was fired after 68 games in favor of Piniella again. How long the Martin managerial merry-go-round might have lasted cannot be known, since Martin died in an alcohol-fueled vehicular death on Christmas Day in 1989.

Another beloved Yankee icon was catcher Thurman Munson, 32 years old and the team captain when he died in the crash of his private plane, which he was piloting, on August 2, 1979. He was memorialized at the Stadium the next day, and an empty locker with his number 15 painted on it was maintained in the Yankee clubhouse until the park closed.

Meanwhile, the Yankees, managed by Gene Michael, won the 1981 pennant, after winning the first half of the strike-divided season, but lost to the Dodgers in the World Series. Another drought followed, marked by the various comings and goings of Billy Martin, before the club, now under the leadership of Joe Torre, won a World Series over the Atlanta Braves in 1996. In 1998 and 1999, the Yankees had World Series sweeps over San Diego and Atlanta, and in 2000 Torre's boys won a third straight Series, this time a cross-town affair over the Mets in five games. The following year, the Yankees won the American League pennant but were beaten in seven games by the Arizona Diamondbacks. They won division titles from 2001 through 2006 but failed to win the league championship except in 2003, when they lost the World Series to the Florida Marlins in six games.

The Yankees were led on the field in the Torre years by players like shortstop Derek Jeter, first baseman Jason Giambi, outfielder Bernie Williams, and pitchers Roger Clemens, Andy Pettite, and Mike Mussina, as well as a superb relief pitcher named Mariano Rivera. In 2004, they picked up the highest-paid player in baseball history, shortstop Alex Rodriguez, from Texas, and moved him to third base, because Jeter already had the shortstop position covered. The Yankees annually had the highest payroll in the game, but the results did not always reflect that fact. When the club invited Torre to take a pay cut after the 2007 season, he said "no, thanks" and left.

In the meantime, the end loomed for historic Yankee Stadium. In June 1993, word had gotten out that Steinbrenner was considering several sites for a new ballpark for the Yankees, in different parts of New York

City, including 32nd Street and 11th Avenue in Manhattan, as well as the Meadowlands in New Jersey. Nothing came of this gambit, but it alerted the city to the coming need for a new facility. In April 1998, a 500-pound piece of concrete cracked off under the upper tier of Yankee Stadium near leftfield (luckily, not during a game), and the park was closed for two weeks of inspection, while the engineers concluded that the park was slowly coming apart. George Steinbrenner wanted the city to replace the ballpark with a brand-new facility by then — no more renovations — so this gave him leverage. In the twenty-first century, a baseball park is supposed to increase a team's revenue stream considerably, with luxury boxes, restaurants, memorabilia shops, bookstores, and so forth, and if there was one thing important to Steinbrenner it was increasing his team's revenue stream. The old Yankee Stadium was derelict in some of these areas, so a new ballpark was a necessity, and the city was willing to build it for him.

In December 2001, three days before he was to leave office, Mayor Rudolph Giuliani, a rabid Yankees fan, announced plans for new stadiums for both the Yankees and Mets that projected to $1.6 billion. Little more than a week later the new mayor, Michael Bloomberg, shot down Giuliani's plan, "given the deficit in the operating budget" and other fiscal restraints.[8]

But it was only a delay. In August 2006, ground was broken for a new facility in nearby Macombs Dam Park, across East 161st Street, with Bloomberg taking part in the ceremony along with George Steinbrenner and other celebrities. New York City would indeed build the Yankees a new ballpark. The team played in 2007 and 2008 with the new park rising outside. The All-Star game was played in the old park in 2008 as a celebration of its years and history, and as the end of the season approached, it was clearly to be the final days of the ballpark.

The last game was scheduled for September 21, 2008, which became a huge day in New York City. In honor of the closing, a vintage 1917 train made the journey from Grand Central Terminal to the Bronx. Beer was flowing freely outside, and the ballpark was opened to the fans seven hours before game time. Thousands who had been in line since early that Sunday morning took full advantage of the early opening to walk around the dirt warning track and into Monument Park. Of course, only those with tickets were allowed in (scalpers outside were selling few tickets, and those few for prices like $500), and ushers closed the doors sooner than had been announced earlier because of the crowds. Many fans filled plastic bags with handfuls of dirt from the field as mementos, some scraped paint off the walls, while others simply rubbed their hands sadly against walls and railings.[9]

There was not much chance to get more tangible souvenirs. The Yankees hired an additional 1,600 security guards for the final weekend to prevent spectators from removing any part of the Stadium, particularly the seats, and numerous wrenches and other tools had been confiscated from fans during the season. The city and the Yankees had not yet reached agreement on exactly how the proceeds from the pieces of the ballpark would be divided, but the prices would be high and fans were not to get any of those pieces for free. New York city policemen arrested twelve persons for trying to steal pieces of the Stadium at the final game.

But the fans took the day seriously. "If an icon like this can go away," one man commented, "then it makes you question your own significance." Another looked around forlornly and said, "You can't move that history across the street; it's like a wake." A man from Union City, across the Hudson, said, "The new stadium is beautiful, but I don't know if the ghosts are going to be there. You can feel that, standing here — Babe Ruth, DiMaggio. It's not going to be the same."[10]

One fan said, "This is like paying your last respects to a dying, old relative." Then he brightened and went on, "The only difference is that you know in six months, she'll come back to life across the street." But Tina Lewis, part of the Bleacher Creatures who sat in the outfield and chanted the Yankee lineup before each game, said, "This is one of the saddest days of my life. It'll never be the same — for me, at least. All week, there's been a big hole in my heart."[11]

It was time for the ballplayers, both present Yankees like Derek Jeter, manager Joe Girardi, Mike Mussina, and Joba Chamberlain, who walked along the roped line of fans and signed autographs or posed for photos, and the legends of the Yankee past. Yogi Berra was there; he said, choking up, "It's going to break my heart; I played with a helluva lot of nice guys in here." Bernie Williams, the old center fielder, said, "You talk about the magic, the aura, but what really made the stadium was the fans. Concrete doesn't talk back to you. Chairs don't talk back to you. It's the people who were there, day in, day out, that makes this place magic."[12]

The old-time players came out onto the field, to great rounds of applause: Willie Randolph, Bobby Richardson, Goose Gossage, Ron Guidry, David Cone, David Wells, Reggie Jackson, Whitey Ford, Don Larsen, Wade Boggs, Paul O'Neill, Tino Martinez, each one taking his old position on the field, joined by the current Yankee at that position. Also coming out were the children of Mickey Mantle, Elston Howard, Roger Maris, Billy Martin, Thurman Munson, and others. (Conspicuously missing were Joe Torre and Roger Clemens, who had not been invited.)

Jeter of the current Yankees was given a crystal bat for having broken Lou Gehrig's record for most hits in Yankee Stadium.

Onto the field came a 92-year-old lady, Julia Ruth Stevens, the daughter of Babe Ruth, to throw out the first pitch. Ironically, Julia, who had lived for many years in Conway, New Hampshire, had become a dedicated Red Sox fan, but she said, "I've always had a lot of respect for the Yankees because New York was where Daddy had his greatest success." She threw her pitch, and the last game at Yankee Stadium got underway.[13]

Visiting for the final game were the Baltimore Orioles, fitting perhaps because it was an earlier Baltimore Orioles team that moved to New York in 1903, eventually to become the Yankees. The 2008 Yankees, well back in third place in the American League East, were on the verge of elimination from the playoff picture as they went out to play their final home game, and they managed to avoid that fate that night. (It came soon enough afterwards.) They beat the Orioles, 7–3, with Andy Pettite throwing five innings to pick up the win, evening his record at 14–14. A 27-year-old southpaw named Chris Waters started for Baltimore, but he didn't make it through the sixth inning, giving up five runs along the way. The Orioles took a 2–0 lead in the top of the third, but the Yankees scored three in the bottom of the inning and two more in the fourth. Backup catcher Jose Molina, batting ninth, had three hits, including the last home run ever hit in the ballpark, but the team's two biggest stars, Jeter and Alex Rodriguez, were 0-for-7 between them. The paid attendance was announced at 54,610, and the victory closed the book on Yankee Stadium, with a record of 4,133 Yankee wins, 2,430 losses, and 17 tie games.

The game ended, and the fans filed quietly out. They had been there for their small part of history, and it was time to close it up. The ghosts, as well as so many living memories, were out that night in the Bronx, and the Yankees put on perhaps the biggest and most elaborate show ever for a closing game. The Babe would have loved it.

A Few Final Words

So there they are, the classic ballparks. One of those we have closed was built before the classic period, Baker Bowl in Philadelphia, and one came about eight years after the last of the classics, Yankee Stadium in 1923. But the others came in quick succession over a relatively short period of time: Shibe Park, Forbes Field, and Sportsman's Park in 1909; Comiskey Park and League Park in 1910; the Polo Grounds in 1911; Navin Field, Fenway Park, Crosley Field and Griffith Stadium in 1912; Ebbets Field in 1913; Weeghman Park, later called Wrigley Field, in 1914; and Braves Field in 1915.

Fenway and Wrigley, of course, are still functional ballparks, serving as home bases for the Red Sox and Cubs. Weeghman Park was originally a Federal League facility, but after that outlaw league folded following the 1915 season, Charles H. Weeghman was allowed to purchase the Cubs and move them into his nice new ballpark. In 1920, when the Wrigley family of chewing gum notoriety bought the team from Weeghman, the park's name was changed to Cubs Park, eventually becoming Wrigley Field in 1926. It was the last park in the major leagues to install lights, the Cubs refusing to play night games in Chicago until 1988. Since the Cubs moved into the park, they have won six pennants (the last in 1945) and no World Series. There has been talk of "the curse of the billy goat" as an explanation for the Cubs' lack of success, but that curse only arose in 1945 and can hardly explain the total absence of a championship in Wrigley Field. Even with great players over the years like Rogers Hornsby, Stan Hack, Phil Cavaretta, Billy Williams, Ernie Banks, and Ryne Sandberg, they have been unable to fly a World Series flag over Wrigley Field.

The Red Sox park in Boston has always been called Fenway Park, named after the Fenway section of the city in which it sits. Over the years the only significant changes to the ballpark have been brought about by fires in 1926 and 1934. The first World Series played in the park was in 1914, when the Braves borrowed it as they defeated the Athletics. In 1918, the Red Sox defeated the Cubs in Fenway, but the 1920 sale of Babe Ruth to the Yankees brought upon the Sox "the Curse of the Bambino," and the team never won another world championship until 2004. Just to prove that the curse was indeed lifted, the Red Sox won another World Series in 2007. Top stars who have worn Red Sox uniforms over the years have included Ted Williams, Jimmy Foxx, Carl Yastrzemski, Bobby Doerr, Dom DiMaggio, Lefty Grove and Tex Hughson, but none of them were able to overturn the Bambino's curse, which was handled by the likes of David Ortiz, Manny Ramirez, Curt Schilling, Jason Varitek, and Pedro Martinez.

Baseball fans pay a good bit of attention to the places where their teams play, and in time they are likely to become quite attached to the ballpark to which they have become accustomed. They become comfortable with the surroundings, the concession stands, the scoreboard, the view of the playing field, even the seating. (With some of these parks — Comiskey, for instance — the players were more anxious to move than the fans, because of inadequate facilities.) For most of the parks we have considered, though, the team's fans recognized that the ballpark's time had come, it was outmoded or worse, and a replacement was due, sad as they were to leave the old place. For some, there was anger: anger at the team leaving town, for Ebbets Field and the Polo Grounds, or anger at the closing of the ballpark, for Tiger Stadium, or at least dismay, as there was at Comiskey. Should there be attempts to close Wrigley or Fenway, there would be angry fans in the north side of Chicago and in Boston. Indeed, several years ago there was an outburst of buttons reading "Save Fenway Park." For now, the buttons seem to have accomplished their aim.

Some of the old parks witnessed riotous behavior and extensive vandalism at their closings — Forbes Field, Shibe Park, the Giants' Polo Grounds — but most of the finales were concluded with sadness and respect. Of course, when Braves Field closed, no one knew it was the last game, not even the club's owner, and few took notice of the finality of the last game at League Park, although it was not hard to figure out that the Indians would be coming there no more.

Quite a few ballparks built after the classics we have discussed have closed down, and few fans have shown much emotion about the disappearance of Riverfront, or Veterans Stadium, or Busch Stadium (not everyone in St. Louis can keep up with which Busch Stadium it is, or was). Municipal Stadium in Cleveland became known as "the mistake by the lake," and few grieved over its replacement. Memorial Stadium in Baltimore was a fine facility and it was missed, but Baltimore replaced it with Camden Yards, with its evocation of the past.

No, there have not been many baseball parks with the history, the character, the appeal, of those that appeared on the scene in the years between Shibe Park in 1909 and Yankee Stadium in 1923. They are gone, all but two of them, and they are missed.

Chapter Notes

Introduction

1. Paul Goldberger, "Home," *New Yorker*, March 23, 2009.

Chapter 1

1. *Philadelphia Inquirer*, Aug. 9, 1903, and *Public Ledger*, Aug. 9, 1903.
2. Dick Bartell with Norman Macht, *Rowdy Richard: A Firsthand Account of the National League Baseball Wars of the 1930s and the Men Who Fought Them* (Berkeley, CA: North Atlantic Books, 1987), 111–112.
3. *Evening Bulletin* (Philadelphia), March 20, 1923.
4. Prendergast won thirteen games over two seasons for the Phillies; Pickles Dillhoefer was 1-for-11 in eight Phillies games. Alexander won 183 games for the Cubs and Cardinals.
5. Murphy's will left a half-interest in the ballpark to his widow, with the other half passing to four nephews.
6. *Philadelphia Record*, June 14, 1938.
7. *Ibid.*, June 25, 1938.
8. *Ibid.*, June 26, 27, 1938.
9. *Evening Bulletin* (Philadelphia), June 28, 1938.
10. *Ibid.*, June 30, 1938. The final detail was taken care of on August 30, 1938, when the probate court in Chicago finally approved the Phillies' move out of Baker Bowl. The court's approval was necessary because one of the Murphy heirs at that time was a minor.
11. *Philadelphia Record*, July 1, 1938.
12. *Ibid.*, July 2, 1938.

Chapter 2

1. Peter Jedick, *League Park* (Cleveland: Peter Jedick Enterprises, 1978).
2. Both Lajoie and Flick were later voted into the Hall of Fame.
3. The good news is that Somers, after disposing of the Indians, was able to rebuild his investments, and when he passed away in 1934 his estate was worth $3 million, despite the Great Depression.
4. Sewell, whose record of only 114 strikeouts in 7,132 at bats is the best in baseball history, was elected to the Hall of Fame in 1977.

5. *Cleveland Plain Dealer*, March 16, 1945.
6. Chuck Heaton, *Cleveland Plain Dealer*, Feb. 8, 1974; Robert Dolgan, *Cleveland Plain Dealer*, Sept. 5, 1976.
7. Author's interview, Oct. 18, 2009.
8. *Cleveland Plain Dealer*, Sept. 22, 1946.
9. *Ibid.*

Chapter 3

1. George Sullivan, "Braves Field," *Bostonia*, Summer 2003.
2. *New York Times*, Sept. 22, 1952.
3. *Boston Globe*, Sept. 22, 1952.

Chapter 4

1. Terry made the remark to sportswriters on January 25, 1934, then saw his Giants lose the last two games of the season to Casey Stengel's sixth-place Dodgers and finish two games behind St. Louis for the National League pennant.
2. Philip J. Lowry, *Green Cathedrals* (Reading, MA: Addison-Wesley, 1992), 118.
3. Lawrence S. Ritter, *Lost Ballparks: A Celebration of Baseball's Legendary Fields*, (New York: Viking Penguin, 1992), 53–55. Eddie Taylor was the Braves third sacker.
4. Much of the information on Larry MacPhail came from Ralph Berger's work in SABR's Baseball Biography Project.
5. Magerkurth had given an indication of what was to come when, in his very first National League game in 1929, he ejected Giants manager John McGraw.
6. There was some speculation that Casey had crossed up Owen with a spitball, but Owen later confirmed that the pitch was Casey's big-breaking curve ball.
7. Roger Kahn, *The Boys of Summer* (New York: Harper & Row, 1972).
8. The Flushing site was the future location of Shea Stadium. For all the despair he created for Dodger fans, the major biography of Moses gives only a portion of one paragraph to his dispute with O'Malley. Robert A. Caro, *The Power Broker: Robert Moses and the Fall of New York* (New York: Alfred A. Knopf, 1974), 1018.
9. The Price cartoon was in the *New Yorker* of October 8, 1938.
10. *New York Times*, Sept. 25, 1957.
11. *New York Herald-Tribune*, Sept. 25, 1957.

Chapter 5

1. The A's finished last 18 times in their 54 seasons, while the Brownies were in the cellar eleven times in 53 years. The Red Sox had ten last-place finishes before 1960. Of course, the Senators were often in last place during the season but did not finish there.
2. *Sporting News*, March 30, 1911, 4; *Sporting Life*, March 25, 1911.
3. Francis Stann, "Griffith Stadium," *SPORT*, December 1952, 54.
4. *New York Times*, January 29, 1956.
5. Ritter, *Lost Ballparks*, 86.
6. *Sporting News*, Nov. 7, 1964, 23.

7. Stories that Cambria tried but failed to sign a Cuban pitcher named Fidel Castro are apparently not accurate.

8. Calvin Griffith, originally named Robertson, was actually Clark Griffith's nephew, but in 1923 the old man adopted Calvin and his sister Thelma to help the Robertsons (his sister and her husband) through some difficult times.

9. *Washington Post*, Sept. 22, 1961.

10. *Ibid.*

Chapter 6

1. Ritter, *Lost Ballparks*, xi.
2. *New York Times*, May 28, 1957.
3. *New York Herald-Tribune*, Sept. 28, 1957.
4. *Ibid.*, Sept. 30, 1957.
5. *New York Times*, Sept. 30, 1957.
6. Joseph M. Sheehan, "Adieus Prove Difficult for Men Behind Scenes at Polo Grounds," *New York Times*, Sept. 30, 1957.
7. *New York Herald-Tribune*, Sept. 30, 1957.
8. *Ibid.*
9. Howard M. Tuckner, "Two Trumpets and a Trombone Sound Dirge in Empty Ballpark," *New York Times*, Sept. 30, 1957.
10. *New York Times*, Sept. 19, 1963.
11. *Philadelphia Inquirer*, Sept. 19, 1963.
12. *New York Times*, Sept. 19, 1963.
13. *Philadelphia Inquirer*, Sept. 19, 1963.

Chapter 7

1. *Sporting Life*, September 6, 1902.
2. Steve Steinberg, "Matty and the Browns: A Window onto the AL-NL War," *NINE*, Spring 2006, 106.
3. *St. Louis Star-Times*, April 25, 1932.
4. Edward Woolley, "The Business of Baseball," *McClure's Magazine,* July 1912.
5. *New York Times*, Jan. 5, 1916. A fine biographic study of Robert Hedges by Steve Steinberg can be found in the SABR Baseball Biography Project.
6. Dan O'Neill, "The Grand Old Lady," *St. Louis Post-Dispatch*, May 27, 1990.
7. E.G. Brands, *The Sporting News*, May 30, 1941.
8. For more on Gray, see William C. Kashatus, *One-Armed Wonder: Pete Gray, Wartime Baseball, and the American Dream* (Jefferson, NC: McFarland, 1995).
9. Berardino, who played for the Indians in their championship year of 1948, is the only person to have won a World Series and have a star on the Hollywood Walk of Fame, which he got in 1993.
10. Bill Veeck with Ed Linn, *Veeck—As in Wreck* (New York: G.P. Putnam's Sons, 1962), 14.
11. *Ibid.*, 219–221. Eighty-nine-year-old Connie Mack, now retired as the A's manager, was in the stands and even held up a voting placard.
12. *Ibid.*, 222.
13. *St. Louis Post-Dispatch*, May 8, 1966.
14. Veeck and Linn, *Veeck—As in Wreck*, 297.

15. *St. Louis Post-Dispatch*, May 27, 1990.
16. *Ibid.*, May 6, 1966.
17. *Chicago Daily News*, May 9, 1966.
18. *St. Louis Post-Dispatch*, May 9, 1966.
19. *Ibid.*
20. *Ibid.*

Chapter 8

1. Susan Dellinger, *Red Legs and Black Sox: Edd Roush and the Untold Story of the 1919 World Series* (Cincinnati: Emmis Books, 2006), 340, 342. The author is Roush's granddaughter.
2. *New York Times*, April 13, 1907. Cox, though only once elected to public office, ran Cincinnati for 27 years.
3. Ritter, *Lost Ballparks*, 46.
4. "The Great Flood of 1937," *Ohio Valley History*, Winter 2006, 60. Grissom, who had been back and forth between the minors and the Reds the previous three seasons, had his best year in 1937, going 12–17 for the last-place Reds and appearing in the All-Star game. In 1952, after his pitching career was over, Grissom was acquitted of manslaughter after a death occurring in a barroom fight.
5. It seems curious to note that both Giles and his predecessor MacPhail are in the Hall of Fame.
6. William Nack, "The Razor's Edge," *Sports Illustrated*, May 6, 1991, 52.
7. *New York Times*, Oct. 31, 1996.
8. Jim Brosnan, *The Long Season* (New York: Harper & Bros., 1960).
9. Jim Brosnan, *Pennant Race* (New York: Harper & Bros., 1962).
10. *Cincinnati Enquirer*, June 25, 1970, and *Cincinnati Post*, June 25, 1970.
11. *Cincinnati Enquirer*, June 25, 1970.
12. Earl Lawson, "Tears and Toasts Spell Crosley Field Farewell," *Sporting News*, July 11, 1970.

Chapter 9

1. "Most Magnificent Ball Park In World," *Pittsburgh Dispatch*, March 7, 1909.
2. Zivic was called "unquestionably the dirtiest fighter ever to scrape his laces across another fighter's cut eye." Randy Roberts, "Between the Whale and Death," in *Pittsburgh Sports: Stories from the Steel City*, ed. Randy Roberts (Pittsburgh: University of Pittsburgh Press, 2000), 19.
3. Ritter, *Lost Ballparks*, 67.
4. What most listeners did not know was that Rowswell's aunt *did* live beyond the left field wall, although it was some fifteen miles beyond. The author was advised of this little-known fact by Cornell professor Scott McMillin, a distant relative of Rowswell.
5. Joe Garagiola, *Just Play Ball* (Flagstaff: Northland, 2007), 152.
6. Jimmy Cannon, "End of Forbes Field New Era for Bucs," *King Features Syndicate*, July 7, 1970; Bill James, *The Bill James Historical Baseball Abstract* (New York: Villard Books, 1986), 70.
7. "June 28, 1970: A Play-By-Play Account of the Final Pirate Game at Forbes Field," in *Forbes Field: Essays and Memories of the Pirates' Historic Ballpark, 1909–1971*, ed. David Cicotello and Angelo J. Louisa (Jefferson, NC: McFarland, 2007), 95.
8. *Pittsburgh Press*, June 29, 1970.

9. "June 28, 1970: A Play-by-Play Account," 110.
10. *Pittsburgh Press*, June 29, 1970.
11. *Sporting News*, July 11, 1970.

Chapter 10

1. In 1909, Ben Shibe invented the cork-center baseball for the Reach Company. Spalding soon followed suit. Another connection was that Shibe's daughter married Al Reach's son.
2. David M. Jordan, *The Athletics of Philadelphia: Connie Mack's White Elephants, 1901–1954* (Jefferson, NC: McFarland, 1999), 43.
3. Charles C. Alexander, *Ty Cobb* (New York and Oxford: Oxford University Press, 1985), 106. Travers's bio notes one game, eight innings pitched, 26 hits, seven walks, one strikeout, and an ERA of 15.75. He later became a Roman Catholic priest.
4. Bruce Kuklick, *To Every Thing a Season: Shibe Park and Urban Philadelphia 1909–1976* (Princeton, NJ: Princeton University Press, 1991), 56.
5. *Bradenton Herald*, July 26, 2005.
6. Bob Ford, "Path to the Vet Led Through N.J.," *Philadelphia Inquirer*, July 26, 1989.
7. Kuklick, *To Every Thing a Season*, 4.
8. *Philadelphia Inquirer*, Sept. 28, 2003.
9. *Ibid*.
10. *Ibid*.
11. John F. Morrison, "Souvenir Hunt Rips Old Ball Park Apart," *Evening Bulletin* (Philadelphia), Oct. 2, 1970.
12. Allen Lewis, "Phils Bid Old Park Adieu — Fans Ransack the Place," *Sporting News*, Oct. 17, 1970.

Chapter 11

1. Rich Lindberg, *Total White Sox* (Chicago: Triumph Books, 2006), 400.
2. Ritter, *Lost Ballparks*, 30.
3. *St. Louis Post-Dispatch*, May 12, 1983.
4. Lowry, *Green Cathedrals*, 135.
5. *USA Today*, July 12, 1990.
6. *Chicago Tribune*, April 17, 1991.
7. *Ibid.*, Oct. 1, 1990.
8. *Chicago Sun-Times*, Oct. 1, 1990.
9. *Ibid*.
10. *Utica Sunday Observer-Dispatch*, Sept. 30, 1990.
11. *Chicago Tribune*, Oct. 1, 1990.

Chapter 12

1. The triple crown for hitters consisted of leading the league in batting, home runs, and runs batted in; for pitchers it was wins, earned run average, and strikeouts.
2. *Detroit Free Press*, June 25, 1943.
3. David M. Jordan, *A Tiger in His Time: Hal Newhouser and the Burden of Wartime Ball* (South Bend, IN: Diamond, 1990), 87, 90.

4. Daniel Okrent, "Notown," *Time*, Oct. 5, 2009, 32.

5. George Plimpton, *Paper Lion: Confessions of a Last-String Quarterback* (New York: Harper & Row, 1966).

6. McLain's post–Tigers career was tempestuous. In Washington, he was part of a cabal trying to get manager Ted Williams fired. His arm went bad and his big-league career ended after 1972. His weight shot up to 330 pounds, and he served two separate prison terms after convictions for drug trafficking, embezzlement, and mail fraud (the first conviction was reversed).

7. Lowry, *Green Cathedrals*, 42.

8. Tom Haudricourt, "Tales of Tiger Stadium Abound," *Milwaukee Journal Sentinel*, July 11, 1999.

9. *Sporting News*, Feb. 6, 1971, Aug. 6, 1977.

10. *Ibid.*, Sept. 30, 1978. A couple of years later, the bleacher area was closed again, for a different reason: a brawl among the spectators and bottles and stones hurled at visiting outfielders

11. Tom Hundley, "While Officials Push for New Stadium, Fans Hope," *Chicago Tribune*, May 10, 1990.

12. *Detroit Free Press*, April 2, 1990.

13. *Detroit News*, May 7, 1999.

14. Tim Wiles, "Magic Happens: The Final Game at the Corner," *Cooperstown Freemans Journal*, October 22, 1999. Much of the description of the last game activities is based on the recollections of Tim Wiles, an historian at the National Baseball Library in Cooperstown.

15. Richard Willing, "Tiger Stadium's Last Hurrah," *USA TODAY*, Sept. 28, 1999.

16. Kevin Allen, "Tiger Stadium Bows Out," *USA TODAY*, Sept. 28, 1999.

17. Kevin Allen, "Final Home Run Also Comes in an Unforgettable Package," *USA TODAY*, Sept. 28, 1999.

Chapter 13

1. In the 1973 "renovation," the copper frieze "was sold for $75,000 to a guy in Albany, N.Y., who promptly melted it to sell for piping and other pedestrian uses." Tom Verducci, "It's Gone! Goodbye!" *Sports Illustrated*, Sept. 22, 2008, 55.

2. Neil J. Sullivan, *The Diamond in the Bronx: Yankee Stadium and the Politics of New York* (2001; rpt. New York: Oxford University Press, 2002), 85.

3. Kathleen Corr, "The House That Ruth Built, the House That Rice Owned," *The Rice Thresher*, Oct. 16, 1998.

4. Anthony J. Connor, *Voices from Cooperstown: Baseball's Hall of Famers Tell It Like It Was* (New York: Galahad Books, 1982), 256.

5. *New York Times*, Aug. 16, 1964.

6. *Ibid.*, Jan. 4, 1973.

7. George Cantor, *The Good, the Bad, and the Ugly Detroit Tigers* (Chicago: Triumph Books, 2008), 44.

8. Sullivan, *The Diamond in the Bronx*, 202–203.

9. The schedule released by the Yankees said Monument Park and the track would be open to fans from 1 to 4 P.M., but they were closed off by 2:30.

10. *New York Daily News, New York Times*, both Sept. 22, 2008.

11. *New York Post*, Sept. 22, 2008, and *New York Daily News*, Sept. 22, 2008.

12. Sam Donnellon, "Players, Not Ghosts, Tell the Story," *Philadelphia Daily News*, Sept. 22, 2008.

13. Harvey Araton, "A Daughter's Last Time at Her Father's House," *New York Times*, Sept. 22, 2008.

Bibliography

In addition to the works and publications listed below, much use was made of annual publications like the *Sporting News Baseball Register*, the *Sporting News Dope Book*, and *Who's Who in Baseball*, as well as the Baseball Biography Project of the Society for American Baseball Research (SABR), available online at http://bioproj.sabr.org/bioproj.cfm?a=cms, c,219,58.

Books

Alexander, Charles C. *Ty Cobb*. New York & Oxford: Oxford University Press, 1985.
Bartell, Dick, with Norman Macht. *Rowdy Richard: A Firsthand Account of the National League Baseball Wars of the 1930s and the Men Who Fought Them*. Berkeley: North Atlantic Books, 1987.
Brosnan, Jim. *The Long Season*. New York: Harper & Bros., 1960.
_____. *Pennant Race*. New York: Harper & Bros., 1962.
Cantor, George. *The Good, the Bad and the Ugly Detroit Tigers*. Chicago: Triumph Books, 2008.
Caro, Robert A. *The Power Broker: Robert Moses and the Fall of New York*. New York: Alfred A. Knopf, 1974.
Cicotello, David, and Angelo J. Louisa, eds. *Forbes Field: Essays and Memories of the Pirates' Historic Ballpark*. Jefferson, NC: McFarland, 2007.
Connor, Anthony J. *Voices from Cooperstown: Baseball's Hall of Famers Tell It Like It Was*. New York: Galahad Books, 1982.
Dellinger, Susan, *Red Legs and Black Sox: Edd Roush and the Untold Story of the 1919 World Series*. Cincinnati: Emmis Books, 2006.
Garagiola, Joe. *Just Play Ball*. Flagstaff: Northland, 2007.
James, Bill. *The Bill James Historical Baseball Abstract*. New York: Villard Books, 1986.
Jedick, Peter. *League Park*. Cleveland: Peter Jedick Enterprises, 1978.
Jordan, David M. *The Athletics of Philadelphia: Connie Mack's White Elephants, 1901–1954*. Jefferson, NC: McFarland, 1999.
_____. *A Tiger in His Time: Hal Newhouser and the Burden of Wartime Ball*. South Bend, IN: Diamond, 1990.
Kahn, Roger. *The Boys of Summer*. New York: Harper & Row, 1972.
Kashatus, William C. *One-Armed Wonder: Pete Gray, Wartime Baseball and the American Dream*. Jefferson, NC: McFarland, 1995.

Kuklick, Bruce. *To Every Thing a Season: Shibe Park and Urban Philadelphia*. Princeton: Princeton University Press, 1991.
Lindberg, Rich. *Total White Sox*. Chicago: Triumph Books, 2006.
Lowry, Philip J. *Green Cathedrals*. Reading, MA: Addison-Wesley, 1992.
Plimpton, George: *Paper Lion: Confessions of a Last-String Quarterback*. New York: Harper & Row, 1966.
Ritter, Lawrence S. *Lost Ballparks: A Celebration of Baseball's Legendary Fields*. New York: Viking Penguin, 1992.
Roberts, Randy, ed. *Pittsburgh Sports: Stories from the Steel City*. Pittsburgh: University of Pittsburgh Press, 2000.
Sullivan, Neil J. *The Diamond in the Bronx: Yankee Stadium and the Politics of New York*. New York: Oxford University Press, 2002.
Veeck, Bill, with Ed Linn. *Veeck—As in Wreck*. New York: G.P. Putnam's Sons, 1962.

Articles

Corr, Kathleen. "The House That Ruth Built, the House That Rice Owned." *The Rice Thresher*, October 16, 1998.
Goldberger, Paul. "Home." *New Yorker*, March 23, 2009.
"The Great Flood of 1937." *Ohio Valley History*, Winter 2006.
Nack, William. "The Razor's Edge." *Sports Illustrated*, May 6, 1991.
Okrent, Daniel. "Notown." *Time*, October 5, 2009.
Stann, Francis. "Griffith Stadium." *SPORT*, December 1952.
Steinberg, Steve. "Matty and the Browns: A Window onto the AL-NL War." *NINE: A Journal of Baseball History and Culture*, Spring 2006.
Sullivan, George. "Braves Field." *Bostonia*, Summer 2003.
Verducci, Tom. "It's Gone! Goodbye!" *Sports Illustrated*, September 22, 2008.
Warrington, Bob. "The Phillies Leave Baker Bowl." *Along the Elephant Trail*, Issue #58, 2005.
Wiles, Tim. "Magic Happens: The Final Game at the Corner." *Cooperstown Freemans Journal*, October 22, 1999.
Woolley, Edward. "The Business of Baseball." *McClure's Magazine*, July 1912.

Newspapers

Boston Globe
Bradenton (FL) *Herald*
Chicago Daily News
Chicago Sun-Times
Chicago Tribune
Cincinnati Enquirer
Cincinnati Post
Cleveland Plain Dealer
Detroit Free Press
Detroit News
Milwaukee Journal Sentinel
New York Daily News
New York Herald-Tribune
New York Post
New York Times
Philadelphia Daily News
Philadelphia *Evening Bulletin*
Philadelphia Inquirer
Philadelphia Public Ledger
Philadelphia Record
Pittsburgh Dispatch
Pittsburgh Press
St. Louis Post-Dispatch
St. Louis Star-Times
Sporting Life
The Sporting News
USA Today
Utica (NY) *Sunday Observer-Dispatch*
Washington Post

Index

Aalco Wrecking Co. 89
Aaron, Henry 62, 86, 116
Abrams, Cal 42
Adams, Babe 109
Adcock, Joe 62, 116
Addie, Bob 58
Adelis, Pete 132
Aldridge, Vic 111
Alexander, Grover Cleveland 8, 10–11, 195
Ali, Muhammed 177
All-American Football Conference 177
All-Star game 30, 56, 79, 82, 86, 97, 101, 105, 113, 116, 131, 133, 142–144, 148–149, 158–160, 162, 176, 182, 198
Allen, Richie 135, 147
Allie, Gair 114
Allison, Bob 56
Allyn, Arthur C., Jr. 147, 183
Alou, Matty 118–119
Alpine Musical Bar 15
Alston, Walter 42, 44
Altrock, Nick 54, 58
Amberg, Richard 89
American Association (major) 60, 72–73, 108, 122, 140
American Association (minor) 22, 33, 38, 94
American Football League 28, 35, 103, 177
American League 18, 22, 24–25, 31, 33, 39, 48, 52, 56, 73, 75, 77, 82–83, 86, 92, 122, 131, 140, 145, 162–163, 172, 181
Amoros, Sandy 43
Anderson, Craig 70
Anderson, George "Sparky" 104–105, 163–164, 168
Andy the Clown 146–148, 150, 153
Anheuser-Busch 84, 86–87, 90
Antonelli, Johnny 67
Aparicio, Luis 145
Appling, Luke 79, 142, 144, 153

Archer, Dennis 168–169
Arizona Diamondbacks 187
Armed Forces Radio 64
Army football 177
Army-Navy game 64
Arnovich, Maury 130
Ashburn, Richie 42, 133, 139
Atlanta Braves 187
Auker, Eldon 155–156, 170
Aurelio, Thomas 65
Ausmus, Brad 170
Avenue Grounds 91
Averill, Earl 56

Bagby, Jim 20
Bagby, Jim, Jr. 159
Bailey, Ed 101–102
Baines, Harold 149
Baker, Del 158
Baker, Frank 124–126
Baker, William F. 8–11
Baker Bowl 4–6, 8–16, 129, 191, 195
Baldschun, Jack 103, 135
Ball, Philip 75–78, 81
Baltimore Colts 177
Baltimore Orioles 149, 162, 182, 185, 190
Bancroft, Dave 10–11, 62
Bank Street Grounds 91
Banks, Ernie 191
Barber, Red 37
Barnes, Donald 78–81
Barrow, Edward 172–173, 176, 179
Barry, Jack 124
Barry, Maggie 6
Bartee, Kimera 168
Bartirome, Tony 114
Basilio, Carmen 177
Batts, Matt 83
Bauer, Hank 181, 186
Baugh, Sammy 58

203

Index

Baumholtz, Frank 101
Bearden, Gene 31
Beatles 106, 144
Beazley, Johnny 178
Beck, Walter "Boom Boom" 9
Becquer, Julio 55
Bee Hive 30
Beggs, Joe 98
Belinsky, Bo 135
Bell, Cool Papa 111
Bell, Gus 86, 101–102, 114
Beloit College 38
Bench, Johnny 103–105, 186
Bender, Chief 123–125, 139
Benedict XVI, Pope 177
Bennett, Charley 154
Bennett Park 154
Benswanger, Bill 112–113
Berardino, Johnny 82, 197
Berg, Moe 59
Berger, Wally 28, 33, 97
Bernheim, Bernard 108
Bernheim, Isaac W. 108
Berra, Lawrence "Yogi" 43, 117, 179, 181, 183, 186–187, 189
Berry, "Jittery Joe" 24
Bertoia, Reno 170
Bevens, Floyd 41, 180
Bickford, Vern 31
Bidwell, Charles 87
Bidwell, Violet 87
Bidwell, William 87
"Big Red Machine" 104–105, 163, 186
Bingham, Dennis 4, 151
Bishop, Max 125–126, 129
Black, Joe 32
Black Sox 92, 141–142, 145, 173
Blackwell, Ewell 100–101, 104
Blass, Steve 118
Bleacher Creatures 189
Bloomberg, Michael 188
Bluege, Ossie 55, 59
Blues Stadium 180
Boggs, Wade 189
Boley, Joe 126
Bonds, Bobby 105
Bonham, Ernie 39
Bono 177
Bonura, Zeke 50
Bossard, Gene 153
Bossard, Roger 153
Boston Bees 15, 30, 79
Boston Braves 6, 10, 20, 25–33, 36–37, 41, 65, 84, 92, 97, 100, 112, 125, 134, 180, 192
Boston Bulldogs 28
Boston Redskins 28

Boston Red Sox 10, 21, 23, 27, 30–31, 35, 48–49, 55, 81, 124–125, 129, 147, 154, 161–162, 172, 174, 179, 184, 190–192, 196
Boston Shamrocks 28
Boston University 33
Boston Yanks 35
Boudreau, Lou 22, 24
Bowerman, Frank 74
Boyer, Clete 181, 184
Boyer, Ken 56, 87, 90
Braddock, Jimmy 143
Bragan, Bobby 115, 130
Branca, Ralph 41–42, 63, 69
Brannick, Eddie 67
Braves Field 2–3, 25–33, 191–192
Breadon, Sam 76
Brecheen, Harry 80–81, 116
Brett, George 1, 169
Bridges, Tommy 100, 155–156, 158
Briggs, Spike 161
Briggs, Walter O. 155–156, 159–161
Briggs Stadium 3, 156–158, 160, 169
Bristol, Dave 103
Brocail, Doug 168
Brock, Lou 1, 62, 90
Brooklyn Dodgers 9, 13, 27, 29, 31–32, 34–35, 37–47, 63–65, 70, 81–82, 97–98, 100, 102, 115, 133, 177, 179–180, 196
Brooklyn Robins 20, 35
Brooklyn Superbas 34
Brooklyn Tigers 35
Brosnan, Jim 102
Brotherhood Park 60
Brown, Gates 170
Brown, Paul 103
Brown, Willard 81–82
Brudnak, John 153
Brush, John T. 61, 93
Brush Stadium 61
Buchek, Jerry 88
Budweiser Stadium 85
Buhl, Bob 135
Bunning, Jim 135, 170
Burdette, Lou 116
Burgess, Smoky 115
Burick, Si 104
Burke, Kitty 95
Burke, Michael 183–185
Burke, Thomas A. 22
Burns, George 66
Busch, August 84–85, 87–88
Busch Stadium 3, 85, 87–88, 192
Bush, Donie 111
Bush, Guy 112, 127
Bush, Joe 174
Byrne, Tommy 43

Caballero, Ralph "Putsy" 133
Cadore, Leon 27
Café Shibe 130
Cain, Bob 83
Callison, Johnny 135
Cambria, Joe 55, 197
Camden Yards 193
Camilli, Dolph 13, 39
Campanella, Roy 32, 34, 41–42, 45–46
Campbell, Jim 163. 166
Campbell, Teresa 104
Candy, John 150
Cannon, Jimmy 118
Caray, Harry 148
Carey, Andy 181
Carey, Max 111
Carnegie, Andrew 107
Carnegie Tech 4, 107, 109
Carnera, Primo 10
Carpenter, Robert R.M. 131
Carpenter, Robert R.M., Jr. 131, 134–135
Carrasquel, Alex 55
Carroll College 74
Case, George 54
Casey, Hugh 39, 196
Cash, Norm 161–162
Castleman, Slick 14
Castro, Fidel 197
Catlin, George 119
Cavaretta, Phil 113, 191
Central Intelligence Agency 183
Century of Progress Exposition 142
Cepeda, Orlando 88
Cervantes, Alfonso J. 89
Chamberlain, Joba 189
Chance, Frank 91, 172
Chandler, Albert B. 40
Chandler, Spud 179
Chapman, Ben 22, 54, 176
Chapman, Ray 20
Chapman, Sam 132
Charles, Ezzard 110, 143
Charleston, Oscar 111
Chase, Hal 172
Chateaugay 113
Chavez Ravine 45–47
Chester, Hilda 44
Chicago American Giants 143
Chicago Bears 10, 57–58
Chicago Cardinals 143–144
Chicago Cubs 7–8, 11–12, 28, 61, 81, 91, 97, 108–109, 112–113, 118–119, 124, 126–127, 135, 140–141, 151, 156, 160, 175–176, 191–192, 195
Chicago Orphans 140
Chicago White Sox 20, 79, 85, 92, 128–129, 140–142, 144–153, 161, 182–183

Christman, Mark 80
Christopher, Russ 130
Church, Bubba 133
Cicotte, Eddie 141
Cimoli, Gino 45, 117
Cincinnati Bengals 103
Cincinnati Clowns 106
Cincinnati Red Stockings 17, 91
Cincinnati Reds 37–38, 79, 86, 91–106, 121, 141–142, 158, 161, 163, 176, 179, 183, 198
Cincinnati Tigers 106
Clark, Joseph S. 134
Clarke, Fred 108
Clemens, Roger 187, 189
Clemente, Roberto 115–119
Cleveland Bears 22
Cleveland Blues 18, 24
Cleveland Browns 156
Cleveland Buckeyes 22, 24
Cleveland Indians 20–24, 31, 35, 55, 64, 79, 82, 134, 144, 146, 158, 161, 175, 179, 195
Cleveland Naps 19
Cleveland Spiders 17–18
Coates, Jim 117
Cobb, Ty 1, 51, 109, 124, 126, 154–155, 167–168
Cochems, Eddie 74
Cochrane, Mickey 126–127, 129, 155–156, 168
"Cochrane Plan" 166
Coleman, Gordie 102
Coleman, Jerry 181
Coleman, Joe 82, 131
Coleman, Joe, Jr. 162
Collins, Eddie 124–126, 141, 153
Collins, Joe 42
Collins, Ripper 79
Colored World Series 10
Columbia Broadcasting System 183–184
Columbia Park 7, 122–123
Columbia University 175
Combs, Earle 175
Comerica Park 166, 170
Comiskey, Charles 73, 140–142, 150
Comiskey, Chuck 150
Comiskey Park 2–4, 141–153, 191–192
Concepcion, Dave 104
Cone, David 189
Conn, Billy 110
Connecticut General Life Insurance Co. 132
Connie Mack Stadium 3–4, 134–135, 139
Cooke, Bob 66
Coombs, Jack 124–125
Cooper, Mort 79–80, 179

Index

Cooper, Walker 32, 63, 79–80, 113
Copacabana 186
County Stadium 116
Coveleski, Harry 7–8
Coveleski, Stanley 7, 20
Covington, Wes 70, 116, 135
Cox, Billy 32, 41–42
Cox, George B. 93, 198
Cox, John William 181, 184
Cox, William 131
Cramer, Doc 130, 160
Cravath, Clifford "Gavvy" 8, 10
Crawford, Sam 51, 154
Creamer, Robert 62
Cronin, Joe 54–55
Crosby, Bing 113
Crosetti, Frank 176
Crosley, Powel, Jr. 38, 94, 96, 102, 105–106
Crosley Field 38, 94–106, 191
Crow, John David 87
Crowder, Alvin "General" 54, 156
Crowther, Bosley 4, 45
"Cry Babies" 22, 158
Cubs Park 191
Cullenbine, Roy 160
Cuyler, Kiki 111

Dahl, Steve 147
Dahlgren, Babe 131, 176
Dale, Francis L. 104–105
Dale, Ronnie 105
Daley, Arthur 183
Daley, Richard M. 150
Dalrymple, Clay 70
Daniels, Bennie 45, 58–59
Danning, Harry 62
Darby Dan Farm 113
Dark, Alvin 31, 63
Davenport, Jim 88
Davis, Curt 39
Davis, Spud 79
Davis, Zachary Taylor 140
Day, John 60–61
D.C. Stadium 57, 59
Dean, Dizzy 56, 79, 87–88, 155, 162
Dean, Paul 79, 95, 155
Delahanty, Ed 5
Del Greco, Bobby 114–115
Deliverance Evangelistic Church 139
DeLucia, Rich 151
Dempsey, Jack 64, 177
Denver Broncos 156
Derringer, Paul 79, 97–98, 100, 158
Detroit Cobras 166
Detroit Lions 156, 161
Detroit Red Wings 165
Detroit Tigers 8, 19, 23–24, 51, 55–56,
 79–83, 99–100, 102, 109, 113, 124–125,
 129, 142, 148, 154–156, 158–170, 172,
 174, 177, 179, 184–186
DeWitt, Bill, Jr. 82–83, 102–104
DeWitt, Bill, Sr. 78–79
DeWitt, Charles 82
Dickey, Bill 175, 179
Dickson, Murry 101, 114
Dietz, Dick 105
Dihigo, Martin 111
Dillhoefer, Pickles 11, 195
Dillinger, Bob 82, 90, 132
Dilworth, Richardson 129
DiMaggio, Dominic 192
DiMaggio, Joe 22, 30, 41, 50, 55, 82, 98,
 176–177, 179–181, 189
DiMaggio, Vince 112
Dinneen, Bill 75
"Disco Demolition Night" 147, 150
Ditmar, Art 181
Doby, Larry 144
Dodgers Sym-pho-ny Band 44
Doerr, Bobby 131, 192
Domino's Pizza 164
Donald, Atley 176
Donnelly, Blix 80
Donovan, Dick 145
Dooly, Bill 13
Dotson, Richard 149
Doyle, Jack 66
Doyle, Larry 62, 66
Dressen, Chuck 42, 63, 96, 160–161
Dreyfuss, Barney 107–108, 110–113, 121
Dropo, Walt 150
Drysdale, Don 183
Dudley, Bill 110
Dugan, Joe 174
Duncan, Pat 92
Dunn, Jack 125
Dunn, James C. 20
Dunn Field 18, 20
Durham, Israel 8
Durocher, Leo 34, 38–42, 47, 63–64, 66,
 79
Dyer, Eddie 81
Dykes, Jimmy 101, 125–126, 128, 132, 142,
 144, 160–161

Eagleton, Thomas F. 89
Earnshaw, George 126–127, 129
Easter, Luke 62
Ebbets, Charles H. 34–35
Ebbets Field 2, 4, 34–39, 41–47, 59, 63,
 88, 97, 191–192
Edison, Thomas Alva 173
Edwards, Bruce 40
Ehlers, Arthur 83

Ehmke, Howard 127
Einhorn, Eddie 148
Eisenhower, Dwight D. 31
Eller, Hod 92
Elliott, Bob 31, 112
Engler, John 169
Ennis, Del 133
Erskine, Carl 31, 42
Estalella, Roberto 55
Evans, Darrell 164
Evers, Hoot 24
Evers, Johnny 27, 91
Ewing, Buck 104
Exposition Park 107

Faber, Red 141
Face, Elroy 115–117, 121
Fain, Ferris 131–133, 139
Falahee, Debbie 153
Falls, Joe 171
Falstaff beer 82
Farley, Bill 137
Faust, Nancy 148, 152
Federal League 19, 75, 125
Feller, Bob 22–24, 31, 144, 158
Fenway Park 2–3, 25, 27–28, 152, 154, 191–192
Ferrell, Rick 54, 56
Ferrell, Wes 54
Fetzer, John 161, 163
Fewster, Chick 36–37
Fick, Robert 169–170
Fidrych, Mark 163, 170
Fielder, Cecil 158, 165, 170
Finley, Charles O. 183
Firpo, Luis 10, 64
Fisk, Carlton 4, 149, 151–153
Fleischmann, Julius 93
Fletcher, Elbie 112
Fletcher, Scott 151
Flick, Elmer 19, 195
Florida Marlins 187
Fogel, Horace 8
Fondy, Dee 115
Forbes, John 108
Forbes Field 2, 4, 26, 52, 108–114, 116–121, 123, 191–192
Ford, Henry 10, 159
Ford, Whitey 43, 102, 117, 181, 184, 189
Fordham University 177
Fort Duquesne 108
Foster, George 186
Foster, Rube 10
Four Horsemen 109
Fowler, Dick 131
Fox, Nelson 145, 153
Fox, Pete 155–156

Foxx, Jimmy 21, 54, 77–78, 126–129, 139, 175, 192
Frankford Yellowjackets 10
Franklin Field 130
Freehan, Bill 161–162, 168
Freese, Gene 102
French, Larry 79
Frey, Lonny 97
Frick, Ford 86, 181
Friend, Bob 67, 114–117
Friestedt, Fred 150
Frisch, Frankie 62, 66, 79, 112
Fuchs, Emil 28–29
Fuentes, Tito 88
Fuller Construction Co. 48
Furillo, Carl 32, 40–42

Gaedel, Eddie 83
Gaffney, James 26–27
Galan, Augie 40
Galbreath, John W. 113
Galehouse, Denny 80
Gamble, Oscar 138, 147
Garagiola, Joe 115
Garcia, Karim 169
Garver, Ned 83
"Gashouse Gang" 79
Gehrig, Lou 155, 157, 175–176, 190
Gehringer, Charlie 155–156, 158, 167
"General Hospital" 82
George Washington University 38, 58
Georgetown University 58
Germano, Frank 38
Giambi, Jason 187
"Giants Victory March" 69
Gibson, Bob 162
Gibson, Josh 57, 111
Gibson, Kirk 164, 167, 170
Giebell, Floyd 158
Giles, Bill 136
Giles, Warren C. 96–97, 104, 198
Gillenwater, Carden 30
Gilliam, Jim "Junior" 42
Gionfriddo, Al 41, 180
Girardi, Joe 189
Giuliani, Rudolph 188
Giusti, Dave 119
Glavine, Tom 1
Gleason, Kid 141
Glenn, Brandon 166
"Go-Go-Sox" 145
Goliat, Mike 133
Gomez, Lefty 142, 155, 176
Gomez, Ruben 66
Gonzalez, Tony 135
Gooding, Gladys 44–46
Goodman, Ival 97–98

Gordon, Joe 160–161, 176, 178–179
Gordon, Sid 66
Goslin, Goose 52, 54, 111, 155–156
Gossage, Goose 189
Gowdy, Hank 52
Graham, Billy 177
"Grandstand Manager's Day" 83
Grange, Red 10, 177
Granger, Wayne 105
Grant, Eddie 62, 69
Gray, Pete 81
Gray, Sid 45–46
Great Depression 21, 94, 127, 195
Greb, Harry 110
Green, Lenny 59
"Green Weenie" 114
Greenberg, Hank 113, 155, 158, 160, 167
"Greenberg Gardens" 113
Griffey, Ken 151
Griffith, Calvin 56, 197
Griffith, Clark 50, 52, 55–56, 58–59, 172, 197
Griffith Stadium 48–49, 51–59, 191
Grimes, Burleigh 38, 127
Grimm, Charley 32
Grissom, Lee 95–96, 198
Grissom, Marv 64
Groat, Dick 68, 114–117, 135
Groh, Heinie 92
Grove, Robert "Lefty" 54, 126–127, 129, 139, 192
Guerra, Mike 55
Guidry, Ron 189
Guillen, Ozzie 149–150, 153
Gustine, Frank 112, 121
Gutteridge, Don 80

Haas, Mule 126–128
Haase, Bill 166
Hack, Stan 191
Haddix, Harvey 115–117
Haefner, Mickey 55
Hale, Sammy 126
Hall, Irv 131
Hall of Fame 38, 53, 55–56, 82, 88–89, 96, 104, 112, 130, 133, 135, 161, 169, 173, 195, 198
Hamilton, Billy 5
Hamner, Granny 133
Haney, Fred 115
Hanley, Hugh 104
Harder, Mel 22
Harder, Pat 144
Harding, Warren G. 174
Haring, Claude 130
Harris, Bucky 52–53, 59, 155, 160, 179–180

Hart, Jim 88
Hartnett, Gabby 112
Hartung, Clint 63
Harwell, Ernie 170
Hatten, Joe 40
Hatton, Grady 101
Hauser, Joe 125
Hawn, Goldie 150
Hearn, Jim 63
Hearns, Warren E. 89
Heath, Jeff 31
Hedges, Robert Lee 73–76
Heffner, Don 103
Heilmann, Harry 155
Heintzelman, Ken 133
Helms, Tommy 103
Henie, Sonja 179
Henrich, Tommy 39, 41, 50, 179, 181
Herbert Hoover Boys Club 89–90
Herman, Babe 36–37, 95
Herman, Billy 30, 39
Hermanski, Gene 42
Hernandez, Willie 164, 168
Herrmann, August A. "Garry" 92–94, 106
Hershberger, Willard 98–99
Hickman, Jim 70, 119
Higbe, Kirby 39, 130
Higgins, Pinky 130
Hilldales 10
Hiller, John 168
Hitler, Adolf 177
Hoak, Don 115–116
Hodges, Gil 32, 41–42, 45
Holbrook, Bob 32–33
Holloman, Alva "Bobo" 85
Holmes, Tommy (player) 30–31, 33
Holmes, Tommy (writer) 66
Homestead Grays 22, 57, 110–111
Hoover, Herbert 127
Hope, Bob 22
Hopp, Johnny 80
Hornsby, Rogers 28, 83–84, 101, 191
Horton, Willie 161–162, 170
Hough, Frank 122, 125
Houk, Ralph 162–163, 182–184
House of David 22
Howard, Elston 189
Howard, Frank 158
Howard, Ron 150
Howsam, Bob 104
Hoyt, LaMarr 149
Hoyt, Waite 174–175
Hriniak, Walt 153
Hubbell, Carl 62, 66, 79, 133
"The Huckster" 125–126, 132
Hudson, Sid 54
Huggins, Miller 61, 172–173, 175

Hughson, Cecil "Tex" 192
Hunt, Ron 70
Huntingdon Street Grounds 8
Hurley, Ed 83
Huston, Tillinghast L. 172–173
Hutchinson, Fred 101–103, 160

Ilitch, Mike 165
Indiana University 101
Irvin, Monte 63, 66
Isley Brothers 177
I.W. Harper bourbon 108

Jackson, Joe 141–142
Jackson, Larry 135
Jackson, Michael 144
Jackson, Reggie 162, 186, 189
Jackson, Travis 52, 62
Jacobsen, Baby Doll 77
Jakucki, Sig 80
James, Bill 118
Jansen, Larry 63
Javery, Alva 30
Jay, Joey 102
Jedick, Peter 17
Jehovah's Witnesses 177
Jenkins, Ferguson 135
Jennings, Hughie 154
Jester, Virgil 32
Jeter, Derek 187, 189–190
Jethroe, Sam 32
Joel, Billy 177
John Paul II, Pope 177
Johnson, Alex 88
Johnson, Arnold 134, 180–181
Johnson, Ban 18–19, 48, 73, 122, 124, 140, 154
Johnson, Bob 50, 130
Johnson, Charley 87
Johnson, Deron 103
Johnson, Lance 151
Johnson, Walter 1, 51–53, 59, 111
Jones, Butch 122, 125
Jones, Sam 174
Jones, Sheldon 32
Jones, Todd 170
Jones, Willie "Puddinhead" 133
Joost, Eddie 131–132, 134
Joss, Addie 19
Judge, Joe 59
Jurges, Billy 66
"Jury Box" 27, 29–30, 33

Kahn, Roger 41
Kaline, Al 161–162, 168–169
Kampouris, Alex 97
Kansas City Athletics 181–184

Kansas City Monarchs 10, 22, 40, 81
Kansas City Royals 149, 164, 169–170
Kapler, Gabe 169
Keane, Johnny 86, 183–184
Keeler, Willie 1
Kell, George 23, 82, 160, 167, 169–170
Keller, Charlie 98, 176
Kelly, Gene 130
Kelly, George 62
Keltner, Ken 22, 24
Kemp, Steve 170
Kennedy, John F. 51
Kerr, Buddy 66
Kerr, Dickie 142
Kessinger, Don 120
Kessler brothers 126, 132
Kiesling, Walt 110
Kilfoyl, Jack 18, 20
Killebrew, Harmon 50, 56, 59, 158
Killefer, Bill 10–11
Kiner, Ralph 70–71, 113, 144
"Kiner's Corner" 113–114
King, Nelson 119
Kittle, Ron 149
Klein, Chuck 9, 12, 15
Kluszewski, Ted 101–102, 104, 145
Knights of Columbus 180
Koenig, Mark 175
Konstanty, Jim 133
Koshorek, Clem 114
Koufax, Sandy 45, 183
Kralick, Jack 58–59
Kramer, Jack 80
Kreevich, Mike 80
Kubek, Tony 117
Kucks, Johnny 43
Kuhel, Joe 54, 56
Kurowski, Whitey 80, 113, 178
Kuzava, Bob 24

Laabs, Chet 80
Labine, Clem 42–43, 63
Lajoie, Napoleon 19–20, 122, 195
Landis, Jim 145
Landis, Kenesaw Mountain 92, 131, 141–142, 155
Lane, Frank 144
Langdon, Dot 132
Lanier, Max 80–81
Lapp, Jack 124
Larsen, Don 43, 189
LaRussa, Tony 149
Lavagetto, Cookie 40–41, 44, 180
Law, Vernon 115–118
Layne, Bobby 110, 156
Lazzeri, Tony 175
Leach, Tommy 108

210   Index

League Park (Cincinnati) 91
League Park (Cleveland) 2, 17–24, 191–192
Leavitt, Charles W., Jr. 107
Lee, Don 59
LeFlore, Ron 148
Lehigh University 4
Leiber, Hank 15
Lemon, Bob 31, 64, 186
Lemon, Chet 164, 170
Lemon, Jim 50, 56
Leonard, Benny 10
Leonard, Emil "Dutch" 54–55
Lersch, Barry 137
Leslie, Sam 15
Lewis, Allen 132, 139
Lewis, Buddy 54
Lewis, Tina 189
Lewis & Clark Expedition 89
Leyendecker, Edward 104
Liddle, Don 64
Lieb, Fred 174
Lindberg, Rich 142
Lindbergh, Charles 89
Lindsay, John 184–185
Lindstrom, Freddie 52
Liston, Sonny 143
Little Caesar's Pizza 165
Littlefield, Dick 115
Litwhiler, Danny 80, 130, 139
Lobert, Hans 66
Lockman, Whitey 63, 133
Loes, Billy 42
Logan, Eddie 67
Logan, Johnny 32
Lolich, Mickey 162, 168, 170
Lollar, Sherm 145
Lombardi, Ernie 97–99
Long, Dale 117
Lopata, Stan 133
Lopez, Al 112, 145, 147
Lopez, Hector 181
Lopresti, Mike 152
Lord, Bris 124
Los Angeles Dodgers 102, 145, 183, 186–187
Lou, Bonnie 105
Loughran, Tommy 10
Louis, Joe 143, 177
Louisville Colonels 108
Lowry, Phil 148
Lucchesi, Frank 136
Luderus, Fred 10
Luzinski, Greg 149–150
Lynn, Fred 148
Lyons, Steve 151
Lyons, Ted 142, 144, 153

Mack, Connie 7–8, 12–13, 15, 18–19, 27, 122–132, 134, 142, 155, 175, 197
Mack, Connie, Jr. 135
Mack, Earle 132, 134
Mack, Roy 132, 134
MacPhail, Larry 37–40, 94–96, 179–180, 198
Magee, Sherry 7–8, 27
Magerkurth, George 38, 196
Maglie, Sal 63–64, 66
Mahaffey, Art 135
Malone, Pat 127
Maney, Joe 30
Manhattan College 35
Manhattan Polo Association 60
Mantilla, Felix 116
Mantle, Mickey 1, 42, 56–57, 102, 117, 181–182, 184, 186, 189
Manush, Heinie 54, 155
Maranville, Rabbit 27, 29, 33
Marberry, Firpo 59
Marchildon, Phil 131
Marichal, Juan 104–105
Marion, Marty 80, 84–85, 145
Maris, Roger 102, 117, 181–182, 184, 189
Marquard, Rube 62, 66, 124
Marshall, George Preston 57–58
Marshall, Willard 63, 66
Martin, Billy 162, 185–187, 189
Martin, Pepper 79, 128
Martinez, Pedro 192
Martinez, Tino 189
Martin's Mud-Cat Band 79
Masi, Phil 31
Masterson, Walt 59
Mathews, Eddie 32, 116
Mathewson, Christy 7, 28, 62, 71, 74, 123–124
Mauch, Gene 103, 135–137
May, Lee 104–105
Mayo, Eddie 130–131, 160
Mays, Carl 20
Mays, Willie 56, 62–64, 67–69, 86, 88, 102, 105, 116
Mazeroski, Bill 115–117, 119–121, 182
McAleer, Jimmy 75
McAuliffe, Dick 169
McCahan, Bill 131
McCarthy, Joe 131, 173, 175–176, 179
McCarver, Tim 137–138
McCormick, Frank 97–98, 100
McCosky, Barney 132, 158
McCuddy's Bar 149
McDaniel, Lindy 88
McDevitt, Danny 45
McDiarmid, C.J. 94
McDonald, Arch 55

McDonald, John 95–96
McDougald, Gil 117, 181
McDowell, Jack 151
McGlothlin, Jim 104
McGowen, Roscoe 45
McGraw, John 7, 61–62, 66, 71, 93, 122, 124, 141–142, 196
McGraw, Mrs. John 66–67, 69
McGwire, Mark 158
McInnis, Stuffy 124
McKechnie, Bill 27–28, 79, 96–100, 104, 111
McKinney, Frank E. 113
McLain, Denny 162, 200
McMillan, Roy 101
McNeely, Earl 52
McQuinn, George 80, 180
Medwick, Joe 39, 79, 88, 155
Memorial Stadium 193
Memphis Chicks 81
Merkle, Fred 61
Merritt, Jim 104
Meusel, Bob 174–175
Meyer, Billy 114
Meyer, Dick 86
Meyer, Russ 133
Michael, Gene 187
Miller, Bing 126–127
Miller, Bob 133
Miller, Eddie 101
Milwaukee Braves 42–43, 65, 102, 116
Milwaukee Brewers 73
Minnesota Twins 55, 58–59, 161, 165, 185
Minor, Benjamin 50
Minoso, Orestes "Minnie" 145–146, 151
Mize, Johnny 63, 87, 113
Mizell, Vinegar Bend 116
Moehler, Brian 169
Molina, Jose 190
Monaghan, Tom 164
Monroe, Lucy 47
Monteagudo, Rene 55
Montreal Expos 136–137
Montreal Royals 40
"Monument Park" 185, 188, 200
Moore, Terry 79, 88
Moore, Whitey 98
Moore, Wilcy 175
Moran, Pat 10, 92–93, 104
Morgan, Cy 124
Morgan, Joe 186
Moriarty, George 155
Morris, Jack 164, 168, 170
Moses, Robert 43–44, 67, 70, 196
Moses, Wally 130
Moss, Les 163
Muckerman, Richard C. 81–82

Mueller, Don 63, 67–68
Mulcahy, Hugh 15, 130
Muncrief, Bob 80
Municipal Stadium 21–24, 192
Munson, Thurman 187, 189
Murphy, Bob 70–71
Murphy, Charles 8, 10, 12, 195
Murphy, Johnny 176
Murphy Estate 12–13, 15
Murray, Red 66
Murtaugh, Danny 115–118
Musial, Stan 56, 79–80, 82, 86, 88–90, 133, 137
Musick, Phil 121
Mussina, Mike 187, 189
Mustangs 144
Myer, Buddy 54
Myers, Billy 98, 100

Nagurski, Bronko 10
National Association 72
National Bohemian beer 50
National Commission 92–93
National Conference of Christians and Jews 45
National Football League 10, 28, 35, 57, 64, 87, 92, 109, 130, 143
National League 5, 10, 12, 18–19, 27, 31–32, 40–42, 44, 48, 60–61, 65, 70, 73, 77, 79–80, 84–85, 92, 96, 101–102, 108, 111, 116, 122, 140–141, 144, 160, 180
National Mine Safety & Health Administration 110
National Park 48
Navin, Frank J. 154–156
Navin Field 3, 154–155, 157, 191
Neale, Greasy 92
Necciai, Ron 114
Negro American League 22
Negro League 10, 24, 41, 63, 81, 106, 116, 130, 143
Negro National League 40
Nelson, Jimmy 119
Nelson, Lindsay 70–71
Nelson, Rocky 117
Neun, Johnny 100, 179
New Sportsman's Park 73
New York Cosmos 177
New York Giants (baseball) 3, 7–9, 11, 13–15, 34, 41–44, 52, 54–55, 60–70, 74, 82, 86, 93, 123–124, 141, 172, 174, 176, 196
New York Giants (football) 64, 156, 177
New York Gothams 60
New York Hilltoppers 172
New York Metropolitans 60
New York Mets 3, 62, 70, 119, 135, 188

New York University 177
New York Yankees 20–22, 35, 37–43, 52, 54–55, 61, 64, 77, 79–80, 82–83, 86, 98, 102, 111, 116–117, 126, 128, 131, 142, 144, 155, 157, 160, 162, 172–190, 192
Newcombe, Don 34, 41–43, 63
Newhouser, Hal 24, 49, 80, 82, 131, 158–160, 166, 168
Newsom, Bobo 54, 59, 79, 100, 158
Nicholson, Bill 133
Nickerson Field 33
Nicola Building Co. 108
Nieman, Butch 30
Niggeling, Johnny 55
Nixon, Richard 31–32, 116, 186
Nolan, Gary 104
Nolan, Joan 89
Nordman, Eddie 104
Norman, Bill 160
North American Soccer League 177
Northrup, Jim 161, 186
Notre Dame University 74, 109, 177
November, Julius 65
Noyes, Thomas 48, 50
Nugent, Gerald P. 11–15, 129, 135
Nuxhall, Joe 100

Oakland A's 162, 186
O'Brien twins 114
O'Connell, Danny 59
O'Connor, Jack 75
O'Doul, Lefty 21
Oeschger, Joe 27
Ogden, Curly 52
Old Tiger Stadium Conservancy 170
Oldring, Rube 124
Oliva, Tony 55
Oliver, Al 119
Olympic Games 21
O'Malley, Walter 43–44, 47, 65, 196
"$100,000 Infield" 124, 139
O'Neill, Paul 189
O'Neill, Steve 158, 160
Onslow, Jack 144
Ortiz, David 192
Osborn, Gene 119
Osborn Engineering Corp. 172–173
O'Toole, Frank 105
O'Toole, Jim 102
Ott, Mary 79
Ott, Mel 9, 15, 41, 62–63, 66, 71
Outlaw, Jimmy 170
Owen, Marv 155
Owen, Mickey 39, 177, 196

Pacific Coast League 180
Packard Building 15

Pafko, Andy 32, 42, 64
Page, Joe 179–181
Paige, Satchel 83, 101
Palace of the Fans 91
Pall, Donn 149
Pappas, Milt 103, 119
Parrish, Lance 164
Parrish, Larry 169
Pascual, Camilo 55–56
Paskert, Dode 10
Pasqua, Dan 151
Passeau, Claude 14–15, 130, 135
Patterson, Floyd 143
Patterson, Red 57
Paul, Gabe 104
Paul VI, Pope 177
Pearson, Monte 98, 176
Peckinpaugh, Roger 52, 111
Pele 177
Pennock, Herb 133, 174–175
Pennsylvania Supreme Court 19
Perez, Tony 103–104
Perini, Lou 25, 30, 32–33, 84
Perkins, Cy 125
Petry, Dan 164
Pettite, Andy 187, 190
Philadelphia Athletics 7–8, 10, 12–13, 18, 21, 27, 48, 58, 61, 74, 77, 79, 82–83, 85, 98, 122–134, 137, 139, 142, 155, 160–161, 175, 180–181, 192, 196–197
Philadelphia Base Ball Park 5
Philadelphia Eagles 10, 58, 92, 130, 134–135, 144
Philadelphia Phillies 5–15, 18, 25, 27, 35, 40, 42, 70, 86, 97, 103–104, 122, 129, 131–135, 137, 139, 161, 164, 195
Philadelphia Stars 130
Philippe, Deacon 108
Pierce, Billy 145
Pierce, Jack 44
Pieretti, Marino 55
Piersall, Jimmy 146
Piniella, Lou 187
Pink Floyd 177
Pinson, Vada 102–103
Pipgras, George 175
Pipp, Wally 174–175
Pitt Stadium 109
Pittsburgh Athletic Club 107
Pittsburgh Pirates 4, 45, 52, 59, 66–67, 88, 103, 107–119, 121, 132, 158, 175, 182
Pittsburgh Steelers 109
Pizer, Howard 151
Plank, Eddie 124–125
Players League 60, 73
Plimpton, George 161
Podres, Johnny 42–43, 183

Polo Grounds 2–3, 60–70, 82, 88, 172–173, 191–192
Polonia, Luis 169
Pontiac Silverdome 156, 162
Posey, Cumberland 110
Post, Wally 86, 101–102
Postal, Frederick 48
Posvar, Wesley 121
Potter, James 7
Potter, Nelson 80
Povich, Shirley 55, 58–59
Powers, Johnny 67
Powers, Michael "Doc" 124
Prendergast, Mike 11, 195
Price, George 44, 196
Prince, Bob 114, 119–120
Proud Clarion 113
Purkey, Bob 102

Quesada, Elwood "Pete" 58
Quinn, Bob 30
Quinn, Jack 126
Quinn, Mark 169

Ramirez, Manny 192
Ramos, Pedro 55–56
Randle, Sonny 87
Randolph, Willie 189
Raschi, Vic 41, 82, 145, 181
R.C. Ballinger & Co. 7
Reach, A.J. 5, 7, 122, 199
Reading Railroad 5
Redland Field 91–92
Reed, Howie 138
Reese, Peewee 34, 39–42, 45, 47
Reid, Daniel 179
Reinsdorf, Jerry 148–149
Reiser, Pete 34, 39–40
Reuther, Dutch 175
Reuther, Walter 159
Reyburn, John E. 124
Reynolds, Allie 23, 41, 50, 179, 181
Reynolds, Harold 151
Rhodes, Dusty 64, 67–68
Rice, Sam 52–53, 59, 111
Rice University 181, 184
Richards, Paul 50, 144–145, 159
Richardson, Bobby 117, 189
Richardson, William 50
Rickards, Tex 46
Rickey, Branch 38, 40, 75–78, 114–115, 180
Rigney, Bill 63–64, 66–68
Ringling Brothers Barnum & Bailey Circus 183
Ripple, Jimmy 100
Rivera, Mariano 187
Riverfront Stadium 3, 105, 192

Rizzuto, Phil 83, 179, 181
Robert F. Kennedy Stadium 3, 59
Roberts, Curt 114
Roberts, Robin 42, 101, 133, 139
Robinson, Bradbury 74
Robinson, Frank 101–103
Robinson, Jackie 32, 34, 40–43, 47, 55, 100, 133, 137
Robinson, Sugar Ray 177
Robinson, Wilbert 35–36, 47
Robison, Frank 17
Robison Field 73, 77
Rockne, Knute 74
Rodriguez, Alex 187, 190
Rodzilsky, Andrew 146
Roe, Preacher 41–42
Rogell, Billy 155, 169–170
Rogers, Col. John 5, 7, 122
Rogers, Roy 106
Rojas, Cookie 70
Rolfe, Red 83, 160, 176, 179
Roman Catholic H.S. 130
Rommel, Eddie 125–126
Rooney, Art 109
Roosevelt, Franklin D. 56, 94
Roosevelt Stadium 44
Root, Charlie 176
Rose, Pete 103–105
Rote, Tobin 156
Rothstein, Arnold 61
Roush, Edd 92, 104, 106, 198
Rowe, Lynwood "Schoolboy" 155–156, 158
Rowland, Clarence "Pants" 141
Rowswell, Rosey 112, 114, 198
Rudolph, Dick 27
Ruehlmann, Gene 105
Ruel, Muddy 52
Ruffing, Red 79, 98, 176, 179
Rugo, Guido 30
Ruppert, Jacob 172–173, 176
Ruppert Brewery 173
Ruppert heirs 176, 179
Russell, Kurt 150
Russo, Marius 176
Ruth, Babe 1, 9, 21, 29, 56, 61–62, 77, 92, 111–112, 125, 142, 149, 157, 172–176, 183, 189–190, 192
Ryan, Blondy 66
Ryan, Connie 30, 113
Ryan, Nolan 51

Saam, Byrum 130
Saigh, Fred 84
Sain, Johnny 31, 33
St. Louis Brown Stockings 72
St. Louis Browns 25, 33, 48, 58, 73–85, 87–88, 101, 132, 134, 141, 196

St. Louis Cardinals 27, 30–31, 38–41, 56, 73–74, 76–82, 84–90, 98, 100, 102, 115, 127, 155, 162, 172, 175, 178–179, 183, 195, 196
St. Louis Terriers 75
St. Louis University 74
Sallee, Slim 92
Salsinger, H.G. 159
Sandberg, Ryne 191
Sanders, Ray 80
San Diego Padres 104, 164, 187
San Francisco Giants 88, 104, 183
Saucier, Frank 83
Sauer, Hank 113
Sawyer, Eddie 133
Scarborough, Ray 144
Schacht, Al 54
Schaefer, Germany 154
Schaffer, Rudie 84
Schalk, Ray 141
Schang, Wally 124, 174
Scheffing, Bob 160
Scheib, Carl 131
Schenley, Mary 107
Schilling, Curt 192
Schmeling, Max 177
Schmidt, Mike 119
Schoendienst, Red 89–90, 144
Schreiber, Ted 70
Schroeder, Bob 130
Schumacher, Hal 66
Schwab, Matty 67
Seattle Mariners 150–151
Selig, Bud 168
Selkirk, George 176
Selma, Dick 138
Seminick, Andy 133
Sensenderfer, Robert 13
Sewell, Joe 20, 195
Sewell, Luke 80, 101
Sewell, Truett "Rip" 113, 121
Shannon, Mike 88
Shantz, Bobby 117, 133, 181
Shaw, Bob 145
Shawkey, Bob 174–175
Shea, Frank "Spec" 179
Shea Stadium 70, 177, 184–185, 196
Shepard, Larry 118
Shettsline, Billy 10
Shibe, Benjamin 122–123, 125, 129, 199
Shibe, John 129
Shibe, Tom 129
Shibe Park 2, 4, 10, 12, 15, 26, 75, 108, 123–125, 127–135, 137, 139, 144, 159, 191–193
Shocker, Urban 77, 175
Short, Chris 70, 135
Shotton, Burt 9, 40–41

Siebert, Dick 130–131
Sievers, Roy 50, 56, 70, 82
Simmons, Al 50, 125, 127–128, 142
Simmons, Curt 101, 133
Simpson, Dick 103
Simpson, Wayne 104
Sisler, Dick 42, 103, 133
Sisler, George 77, 88
Skaff, Frank 161
Skinner, Bob 88, 115, 135
Skowron, Bill 181
Slaughter, Enos 79, 81, 90
Smith, Al 174
Smith, Earl 53
Smith, Elmer 20
Smith, Gene 104
Smith, Hal 117
Smith, Mayo 101–102, 161–162
Smith, Red 13, 67, 70
Smith, Willie 119
Snider, Duke 32, 41–42
Sockalexis, Louis 20
Soderholm, Eric 147
Solari, Gus 72
Somers, Charles 18–20, 195
Sousa, John Philip 174
South End Grounds 27
"South Side Hit Men" 147
South Side Park 140
Southern Association 81
Southworth, Billy 30–31, 79–80
Spahn, Warren 31, 101
Sparma, Joe 162
Speaker, Tris 20, 24, 175
Spink, Alfred 72
Sportsman's Park 2, 3, 72–82, 84–85, 88–89, 191
Stanky, Eddie 31, 40–41, 63, 86, 100, 147
Stargell, Wilver 117–118
Stark, Abe 44, 46
Stautner, Ernie 110
Steinbrenner, George 185–188
Stengel, Casey 9, 30, 38, 71, 116–117, 180–182, 196
Stephens, Vern 80, 90
Stevens, Julia Ruth 190
The Sting 144
Stobbs, Chuck 57
Stocksick, Bill 88, 90
Stockton, J. Roy 87
Stone, Ron 137
Stoneham, Charles 61, 172
Stoneham, Horace 41, 61, 64–66, 68–69
Stottlemyre, Mel 184
Stoviak, Stan 15
Strunk, Amos 124, 136
Stuart, Dick 115, 117, 135

Suder, Pete 132
Sundra, Steve 176
Swarthmore College 107, 126
Swift, Bob 83, 161
Szala, Walt 119

Taft, William Howard 50, 110
Taft family 8
Tammany Hall 173
Tanana, Frank 165, 170
Tanner, Chuck 147
Taylor, Eddie 196
Taylor, Tony 70, 137
Taylor, Zach 83
Tebbetts, Birdie 101, 158
Temple, Johnny 101
Terry, Bill 34, 62, 66, 71, 196
Terry, Ralph 117, 181
Texas Rangers 185, 187
Thigpen, Bobby 151
Thobe, Harry 101
Thomas, Frank E. 151
Thomas, Frank J. 45, 66–68, 114
Thomas, Ira 124
Thompson, Gene 98
Thompson, Henry 81–82
Thompson, Jim 149
Thompson, Sam 5
Thomson, Bobby 42, 63–64, 67, 69
Three Rivers Stadium 3, 114, 118
Tiger Den 165
Tiger Stadium 3, 4, 161–167, 169–171, 192
Tiger Stadium Fan Club 166
Tighe, Jack 160
Tinker, Joe 91
Tobin, Jim 30
Tolan, Bobby 104–105
Toledo Mud Hens 19
Toomey, Jim 90
Topping, Daniel R. 179–181, 183
Torborg, Jeff 151
Toronto Blue Jays 164–165
Torre, Joe 187, 189
Torres, Gilberto 55
Tracy, David 82
Trammell, Alan 164, 167–168, 170
Travers, Aloysius 125, 199
Travis, Cecil 54, 59
Traynor, Pie 111–112, 119, 121
Tresh, Tom 184
Trippi, Charley 144
Trosky, Hal 22
Trout, Paul "Dizzy" 24, 80, 160
Troy Trojans 60
Trucks, Virgil 160
Tucker, Raymond R. 89
Tunney, Gene 177

U-2 177
Unitas, Johnny 177
United Auto Workers 159
University of Maryland 58
University of Michigan 38
University of Pennsylvania 5, 107
University of Pittsburgh 109, 118, 121

Valdisseri, Kenneth 148
Valo, Elmer 45, 132
Vance, Dazzy 36–37
Vander Meer, Johnny 37, 97, 100–101, 104
Varitek, Jason 192
Vaughan, Arky 112, 158
Veale, Bob 118
Veeck, Bill 22–24, 33, 82–85, 145, 147–149
Veeck, Mike 147
Ventura, Robin 149
Verban, Emil 80
Vernon, Mickey 54, 59
Versalles, Zoilo 59
Veterans Stadium 3, 135, 139, 192
Virdon, Bill 115, 117, 185
Vitt, Ossie 22, 158
Voiselle, Bill 31
Von der Ahe, Chris 72–73

Waddell, Rube 75
Wagner, Hal 131
Wagner, Honus 1, 108–109, 121
Wagner, Robert 65
Waitkus, Eddie 133
Wakefield, Dick 24
Walberg, Rube 126–127, 129
Walcott, Jersey Joe 110-, 143
Walk, Bob 10
Walker, Dixie 34, 39–41
Walker, Greg 149
Walker, Harry 118
Walker, Mickey 10
Wallace, Bobby 96
Walsh, Dave 13
Walsh, Ed 140–141
Walters, Bucky 13, 79, 97–98, 100, 104, 158
Wambsganss, Bill 20
Waner, Lloyd 111–112
Waner, Paul 111–112
Ward, Arch 142
Warner, Glenn "Pop" 109
Washington, Harold 149
Washington Black Senators 57
Washington Elite Giants 57
Washington Park 34
Washington Potomacs 57
Washington Redskins 56–58

Washington Senators 48–56, 58–59, 79–80, 83, 111, 127, 162, 174, 196
Waters, Chris 190
Weatherly, Roy 22
Weaver, Buck 141
Webb, Delbert E. 179–181, 183
Weeghman, Charles H. 191
Weeghman Park 2, 191
Weil, Sidney 94
Weinrig, Benny 46
Weintraub, Phil 14–15
Weiss, George 173, 181–182
Wells, David 189
Wells, Willie 111
Wendt, George 150
Werber, Bill 98
Wertz, Vic 64, 160
West, Max 79
West Catholic High School 130
Westchester Polo Association 60
Western League 18, 122, 140, 154
Westrum, Wes 67
Wheat, Zack 126
Whelan, Danny 114
Whitaker, Lou 164, 170
White, Bill 135
White, Byron "Whizzer" 110
White, Joyner "Jojo" 155
White Sox Park 3, 140, 147
Whitehill, Earl 54
Whitney, Pinky 130
Whitney Young Urban League Classic 177
Whitted, Possum 10
Whiz Kids 133
Wietelmann, Whitey 30
Wilcox, Milt 164
Wilhelm, Kaiser 38
Wilks, Ed 88–89
Wilks, Ted 80–81
Williams, Bernie 187, 189
Williams, Billy 191
Williams, Joe 176
Williams, Ken 77
Williams, Smoky Joe 111

Williams, Ted 23, 56, 82, 113, 137, 144, 158, 160, 192, 200
Willkie, Wendell 106
Wilson, Earl 162
Wilson, Hack 9, 127
Wilson, Jim 32
Wilson, Jimmie 13, 15, 99
Wilson, Jud 111
Wilson, Larry 87
Wilson, Owen 109
Wilson, Woodrow 10
Wiltse, George "Hooks" 67
Wine, Bobby 137
Wolff, Roger 55, 131
Wolman, Jerry 134
Wood, Wilbur 150
Woodeshick, Hal 88
World Series 10, 20, 27, 31, 35, 39, 41–43, 52, 54, 56, 61, 64, 77–78, 80–81, 86, 92–93, 98, 100–102, 109, 111, 116, 127, 133, 141, 145, 149, 158, 160, 164–165, 172, 174–180, 182–183, 186–187, 191–192, 197
Wright, Glenn 111
Wrigley Field 3, 127, 175, 191
Wyatt, Whitlow 39, 79
Wynn, Early 54, 145
Wyshner, Peter 81

Yale Bowl 177
Yankee Stadium 2, 3, 42–43, 61, 64, 134, 152, 173–174, 176–182, 184–185, 187–191, 193
Yastrzemski, Carl 192
York, Rudy 158, 160
Young, Bobby 83
Young, Coleman 166
Young, Denton "Cy" 17, 24, 51

Zachary, Tom 52
Zale, Tony 177
Zernial, Gus 133
Zientara, Benny 101
Zisk, Richie 147
Zivic, Fritzie 110, 198

www.ingramcontent.com/pod-product-compliance
Lightning Source LLC
Chambersburg PA
CBHW020814230426
43666CB00007B/1012